SCOTLAND FIRST

SCOTLAND FIRST

FIRST

Truth and Consequences

HENRY McLEISH

MAINSTREAM
PUBLISHING
EDINBURGH AND LONDON

First published in Great Britain in 2004 by
MAINSTREAM PUBLISHING COMPANY (EDINBURGH) LTD
7 Albany Street
Edinburgh EH1 3UG

ISBN 1 84018 867 7

A catalogue record for this book is available from the British Library

Typeset in Bembo

Printed in Great Britain by
Antony Rowe Ltd, Chippenham

Contents

Introduction

The night of 7 November 2001 was the longest, loneliest night of my life. Around me were all the trappings of power. I was in Bute House, the gracious Georgian official residence of Scotland's First Minister, the spacious rooms filled with classically elegant furniture and art treasures. It was a place in history. The place every Scot would want to be.

Hours before, I had been in royal company at a gala dinner for Scotland's sporting greats in the presence of the Princess Royal at the Palace of Holyroodhouse. It was the kind of occasion at which I was proud to represent Scotland, another memory to be treasured.

And I knew that, within a few hours, I would have to give it all up, along with everything I had worked for throughout my political career. Worst of all, I would have to surrender the position that I cherished most of all – leader of my nation.

In 30 years of elected office, from council to Westminster to Scottish Parliament, I had served my country and my own people: as local councillor, member of two parliaments, minister and First Minister. I had lived through political upheavals and played a leading part in the historic changes that restored our national Parliament after almost 300 years. I had represented my country on the world stage and I had a vision of how I could guide it towards an exciting future. For a passionate and patriotic Scot, there could be no higher achievement, no greater satisfaction.

All of that was now crumbling about me and my dreams were ending in a debacle. I could still take pride in my achievements, but my career was collapsing in a grisly mixture of farce and, for me, tragedy.

Sleepless and solitary, I moved through the private apartments that had been my second home for the most momentous year of my life. I sought no company or advice or support. I went over and over in my mind the tangled chain of events and malicious forces that had caused this comedown.

I was depressed, bewildered and bitterly angry with myself – because this ordeal was the result of muddle, mismanagement and mistakes which could have been avoided. I took full responsibility and I blamed no one but myself.

For months, I had been fighting for my political life, but I had come to the point where I could fight no longer. It was undeniably clear to me that nothing would clear up the mess; no matter how much I protested my moral innocence, the relentless attacks on myself and those closest to me would continue.

'Officegate', as it had inevitably come to be known in the media (perhaps one day someone in the media will cover a political predicament without adding 'gate' to it), had grown from a trivial matter into a full-blown political maelstrom. What had been an honest mistake had been magnified into a major political sensation and, with opposition politicians and a scandal-hungry press in full cry, even political 'allies' were feeding the campaign of smears and distortions.

My feeling of frustration was increased by the knowledge that I had not knowingly done anything wrong. Arrangements into which I had unwittingly and innocently entered 14 years earlier had come back to do all this unnecessary damage. Even my harshest critics acknowledged that I had made no personal gain – latterly confirmed after the most rigorous investigations by parliamentary authorities, Inland Revenue and the police. I had settled accounts and I knew that other MPs and ministers had found themselves embroiled in similar situations without a similar outcry.

Admittedly, I had handled the whole affair badly, but my mistakes bore no relationship to the scale and intensity of the campaign against me. There was no credit for 30 years of public service, no consideration that nothing like this had ever happened before in my life and no recognition of what I had tried to do for my constituency and my country. The press were in full cry and their coverage was disproportionate, merciless and at times grotesque. Others in the political community were happy to join in.

Worst of all was the intolerable strain and pressure being inflicted on my family. With gross unfairness, my wife was being implicated in matters for which she had no responsibility, and she would soon be forced out of her lifelong vocation as a social worker, helping others.

Politicians have to be tough individuals and my record shows I am resilient, but my family should not have been part of the ordeal. When my family were being affected, I decided enough was enough.

There was, too, my concern and respect for the office I held. I was only the second First Minister in a new parliament and a new form of government that had not had time to become established. I would not jeopardise those new foundations, for which I and many others had worked so long and so hard.

Long before dawn broke over Edinburgh's New Town, I had decided to resign.

As I waited for the last act in my career as a minister, I looked back on the life and calling that had taken me from lowly beginnings in a Fife coalfield family to the corridors of power, into the presence of some of the most significant figures of our time and, better than all of these, to the highest position in the land I love.

I also reflected on the lessons I had learned – and the lessons Scotland has still to learn.

PART I

A Coalfield Family

I

Pits and Pitches

Outsiders saw Methil in the 1940s and '50s as a grim, grimy and unattractive place, but those of us who were born and brought up there are proud of it. When I was born there in 1948, at 50 Morar Street, it seemed as if the town was stuck in the previous century.

Home births were still common and, true to Scottish working-class tradition, I spent my first night in a drawer as a makeshift crib because my parents, Harry and Mary, had not been able to buy a cot or pram. The young couple starting their own family had moved in with my mother's family, and at any time there were at least ten people living in a four-roomed house.

A once-prosperous coal-loading port on the Firth of Forth, Methil was dominated by the local pits and bings: a town of Victorian slums and miners' rows with seemingly endless trains of coal wagons running night and day down to the harbour and returning empty. In winter it was bleak, and in summer, when we played along the beaches, the tidemark was drawn in coal dust.

The Third Statistical Account of Scotland in 1951 said Methil was 'an overgrown mining village, unbalanced and with no "West End"'. A century before, it had been described as 'one of the most perfect pictures of decay to be met anywhere in Scotland'. Following the heyday of the coal trade in the early twentieth century, the decline began again. The rundown was accelerated in the 1950s and '60s with the closure of coalfields across the region, and locally that of Wellesley Colliery and the showpiece Michael Colliery after a disastrous fire which killed nine men. Miners and dockworkers were laid off, the pitheads and harbour were dismantled and the last working pit in the area, Lochhead Colliery at the well-named Coaltown of Wemyss, closed in 1970. The closure of the Frances and Seafield colleries in the '80s and '90s would seal the fate of coalmining in Fife. Later, as Fife council leader, I was proud to play my part in the rejuvenation and restoration of my hometown.

Despite the harshness and deterioration, it was, and still is, a warm, welcoming and very special place to me. I grew up there surrounded by hard-working, tolerant and community-minded people. I played in safety, developed at my own pace and was given every chance to better myself – a chance I almost threw away.

I had the classic Scottish coalfield upbringing – the son and grandson of miners, living in a street of mine workers. Fife was built on coal and, from the Industrial Revolution until the 1960s, coal was king. When I was born, there were 50 pits and 50,000 mineworkers in the county; now, there are just a couple of open-cast mines.

My family tree, stretching back to the early nineteenth century, shows a long line of colliers, railwaymen, weavers and quarriers. My maternal grandfather, Henry, after whom I was named, worked for the Wemyss Coal Company and spent 50 years underground. He often talked to me about working in a nine-inch seam, in which the men would lie on their bellies in a coffin-like situation, hewing coal with no supports. After experiencing the horrors of war in the trenches and his early life in the pits, he was looking for a better way of living and turned to the Bible, joining the Plymouth Brethren. A knowledgeable and tolerant man, he recited the gospel by heart and brought his own distinctive Christian influence to bear on those around him.

At his knee, I learned the Bible texts and, although I now have no formal religion, I absorbed his values. When I was elected to the Commons and said my work would be rooted in practical Christianity, I was thinking of the examples set by my parents and grandparents.

I must have taken my love of football from my grandfather. He played for East Fife and I played for the club 50 years after him, in the same position, at left-back.

He could quote the Bible word for word and his firm and sincerely held beliefs would not countenance playing any sport on a Sunday. I used to sneak away with my strip and boots in a bag to play on a pitch out of sight behind a block of shops so that he would not find me breaking the Fourth Commandment.

When he died, I was getting ready for an away game with East Fife at Queen of the South in Dumfries, and I had to choose between going to the funeral or going to the game. The family decided I should play for the club as a tribute to him.

When my father left school at 14 and went down the pit, it was his choice – but at the time he had no real option because he knew the family needed what money he could earn. Now, when we think of a boy of 14 going underground, we can see it was child labour, the worst form of exploitation. He was underground for 30 years and when he came up for the last time at the age of 44, he was on a stretcher with his legs shattered.

Long before that happened, my father declared that none of his sons would go down the mines. When I finally went down the Frances Colliery on an official visit as a councillor, I saw why. Even in what was supposed to be a 'modern' mine, I could not understand how people could work in such hellish conditions, like human moles amid darkness, dirt and danger, crawling about in narrow seams, doing gruelling physical work and literally dragging the coal out by brute force. When they went down for their shift, they knew their lives were in danger – yet they accepted that as the everyday risk.

When I was two or three, my mother and father moved to Institution Row, a line of miners' cottages with outside toilets known locally as 'Irish raw'. In 1952, we moved to a new housing estate for mineworkers which was being grafted on to the old village of Kennoway. To this day, my father still lives in our family home. It is the house in which I was brought up and in which my younger brother, Ronald, was born.

Deep mining was still seen as the future and Fife Council were building houses for the influx of workers from the worked-out coalfields in the west of Scotland. The street was still being built when we moved in, so the families bonded together in their brave new world. Now, my father has a picture of me with President George W. Bush in the White House on the mantelpiece of his council house in Kennoway: he points to it and says, 'Not bad for a working-class boy.' It's his way of reminding me that whatever setbacks I may have had, my achievements have made him proud of me.

My upbringing was modest, but a lot better than that of some of my childhood contemporaries. Even at our lower end of the social scale there was a pecking order, and among industrial workers my father was well paid. The first status symbol I ever knew was that we had the first ten-inch TV set in the village, so small that there was a special magnifying glass to see the picture.

People respected my father and said he was the hardest-working man they had ever known in their lives. He had the Scottish work ethic to an extreme, was completely committed and would never let his workmates down. He knew nothing else. His early life and hard times had made him a workaholic.

My father worked 'doublers' and 'treblers', which would be unthinkable in these days of industrial law. That meant he would leave home on Monday and return on Wednesday, having spent all that time underground. It was a Herculean routine, which in the former Soviet Union would have ranked as Stakhanovite.

To a much lesser extent, I followed his example in later years. When

I took a tumble to myself and realised I had to catch up and compensate for the years I wasted at school, I would get up at 5 a.m. like my father and would not go to bed until well after midnight. I was the same kind of workaholic and had to be doing things. My staff learned to expect a 7 a.m. call after I had been up and working for a couple of hours.

My father's underground career ended suddenly and terribly. Working as a beltman at the Wellesley Colliery, he was a victim of one of those accidents which shattered lives and which were everyday occurrences in any coalfield anywhere. A belt, which had broken on an earlier shift and had not been fixed properly, snapped with tremendous force and almost sheared both his legs off. He was in hospital for nearly a year.

It was that knock on the door in the early morning that is known and dreaded in every mining community in the world, with a policeman saying, 'We have some bad news for you.' It was not the worst news we could have heard, because we already knew people whose fathers and husbands had been killed underground. Families simply factored the fear out of their minds until something happened.

These days, there is a great deal of sentiment and romantic nostalgia about the miners' lives, but I have never believed it is work a man would do if he had a real choice. The men had to be rough and ready, and 'pit language' was the euphemism for the below-earth normal working parlance. But it bred a truly special breed with great solidarity and comradeship, not only of men but their womenfolk and families as well. They cared, they were involved in their community, they worked for the people of their class. They helped those who could not cope as well as they did or who were not as good at organising their lives or dealing with the authorities.

My grandparents helped run the local soup kitchens during the General Strike of 1926, and my grandmother, Mary Slaven Baird, who was 91 when she died, had been a member of the Co-operative Party and the Labour Party for as long as they had existed. She took on herself the responsibility for fighting for the interests of local people against unscrupulous landlords and did welfare work. She had a heart of gold but was also the kind of formidable woman, prepared to stand up for what is right, that you found so often in working-class communities in Scotland.

My mother, aged 59 when she died of cervical cancer, was a remarkable person and a real community servant. One of the first home-helpers in Fife, she carried on her own mother's devotion to the Labour Party. As the local party secretary, she was a tireless fundraiser and when she died, left the local branch with more funds than any other branch in Scotland. For her it was more social and welfare involvement than political, and hers was the practical form of socialism that meant helping the elderly and being a good neighbour.

The role of women like these has never been fully acknowledged. In my generation, I was to see the emergence of wives and mothers who sustained their communities during the hardships and persecution of the miners' strike and then went on to greater participation in politics. Such women were by no means 'the second sex' but were often the backbone – the unsung heroines – of the working class.

From the age of 2 or 3 until I was 15, when I left school and signed for Leeds United FC, all I did was play football. I wanted nothing to do with education. I didn't read as much as I should have done, although there was no shortage of books in both my parents' and grandparents' homes. I just wasn't interested in anything else.

When I was 12, my record for 'keepie uppies' was 1,760. It took me 20 minutes and, because I stood on my left foot throughout, I had it in plaster because of the strain. (My record with the much more difficult tennis ball, by the way, was 400.) So that was the sum total of my achievement by the age of 15: a pretty pointless 'keepie uppie' record.

While still attending school, I experienced the hardest work I have ever done in my life – and it was for my love of football – because I desperately wanted a Real Madrid strip. (I could never recite much Burns or Shakespeare but I could (and still can) recite the Real line-up of the day: Dominguez, Marquitos, Pachin, Vidal, Santamaria, Zarraga, Canario, del Sol, Di Stefano, Puskas, Gento.) In those days, older schoolchildren were released from school to help with the potato harvest. My mother, who was at the 'tattie-howking', said if I went for a day, I would earn enough for a Real strip. It was back-breaking work and the 14s 11½d for that one day was the hardest-earned money I ever made.

It was no surprise that when I left Buckhaven High School in 1963 I received a report card which summed up my life to that point and which was really a wake-up call for me to change my attitude. The rector's parting comment was: 'I am glad the boy is a good footballer, because he has no future in education.'

One of my main criticisms of my young self is that I didn't do enough reading. My father was an avid reader and a member of a book club, but I chose not to read the books young people should read and was not exposed to great literature, music and art. In the community in which I grew up, these were not regarded as important. They were wasted years and for the rest of my life I have been trying to fill that cultural black hole. That is why I have advocated free music tuition in every Scottish school, maximum access to the arts and encouraged children to read.

I missed out on an amazing amount of learning and education and it was largely through my own choice. My report cards were a bigger disappointment to my parents than to me because I regarded school as a necessary evil and during school holidays and at weekends played football all day long. I did nothing academically and was getting 20 per cent for French and 18 per cent for maths, but I was athletics and tennis champion and playing representative football, captaining Fife county. It was a football-daft schoolboy's dream come true when I was invited to Elland Road, Leeds United's ground, for a trial and was signed by the great Don Revie – but I was home and back at school eight weeks later.

My brief Leeds adventure began one Saturday. I was captain of Fife Schools in a game against Dundee Schools. We won 5–2 and I scored a hat-trick. Unknown to me, the Leeds United scout was on the touchline and on the Sunday morning on my way, as ever, to play football, an old man in a long coat and a white cap stopped me and said he was looking for 'the boy McLeish'. Mystified, I told him that was me and he said: 'I'll have to speak to your mum and dad.'

As a boy from a Scots working-class background, that was the start of my real education. Leeds United looked after boys from very different backgrounds and they taught me things I would not have otherwise learned – like taking us to a top-class hotel for the first time and showing us which cutlery to use. It was training for life, not just football, so that we would not embarrass ourselves or the club.

I just couldn't get used to being away from home, however, which is hardly surprising at that age, although some other talented youngsters I shared digs with went on to international stardom and are still idolised. They included Eddie Gray, who was destined to be one of Scotland's great players, as was Peter Lorimer, and Jackie Charlton was in the third team. For me, it was a privilege to clean the boots of the great Celtic and Scotland player Bobby Collins.

Back home, I signed for the local club East Fife when I was 16 – the youngest player ever to play for them – and my first game was in March 1964 against Queen's Park at Hampden. There were only 900 people in the stadium, which could hold 130,000 at that time, but it was still an enormous thrill to walk through the dressing-rooms and out onto that historic pitch.

When I was 18, I was picked for a trial for Scotland against a select side at Motherwell. We lost 5–2, but the *Daily Record* report of the game said: 'Only one young Scot impressed – Henry McLeish of East Fife, who scored a cracking opening goal.'

As a footballer, you became a bit of a local hero. You might not have made great academic achievements, but you were still highly regarded in your community. It was a big thing for my classmates when the team bus would come up to the school to pick me up before an away game.

I was then selected for the Scotland team for the Youth World Cup, hosted by Yugoslavia in Pristina, the now infamous capital of Kosovo. We drew all three of our games. However, my abiding memory of the game against Holland was that the organisers didn't have the Scottish national anthem, so they played 'Island of Dreams' by the Springfields!

I have always been infuriated when I have had lectures from so-called 'nationalists' who doubt the patriotism of other Scots, their support for their country and their flag. I never need reminding about what it means to be a Scot. I have a youth international cap; I have worn the blue jersey and the blazer with the Scottish badge; I have represented Scotland in my country's greatest sport.

I have always been more nationalist-minded (with a small 'n') than some of my Labour colleagues. It may have been the football, my upbringing and my background that made me raise issues of national identity. I would ask, 'Why shouldn't the Labour Party be identifiably the party of Scotland?' To other Scottish Labour colleagues, it had to be an identifiably United Kingdom party.

I still believe that sport at the highest level is an asset for any nation. Scotland has produced world-class sportsmen and women, so being a small nation is not a real excuse for failing to strive for the highest level of attainment. That is why sport was high on my political agenda: not just because of the benefits of participating in sport but also for the prestige that comes with staging events like the European football championship and the Ryder Cup.

Sport is a populist way of getting people to feel better about their own country. It does not mean you are a narrow nationalist. It does not mean you take a parish-pump view. It does not mean you then go on from football to blame the English for everything in life. It does mean that you promote the best of your country and are ambitious for your country. A small nation on the periphery of Europe becomes a nation with a leading place in the world. As I was later to discover, that kind of ambition for Scotland is singularly lacking in many of our politicians.

Football taught me the importance of self-worth and I still believe it is an important lesson for Scotland in the wider world. Even though we have world-class people and world-class resources, we are being held back by a lack of confidence in our own abilities.

But there was another, less glamorous, facet to football. Playing with East Fife and junior clubs like Glenrothes Juniors and St Andrews United, I visited every part of Scotland and played on nearly every club pitch in the country – in working-class areas, in towns and cities, and in mining and fishing communities. Football brought me closer to Scottish life and culture, and through football I saw the struggle for survival in some communities. I remember the shocking condition of Third Lanark just before the 'Hi-Hi's' disappeared, when we had to take our own soap and light bulbs to Cathkin Park.

The other thing football gave me from my early years and which lasted throughout my political life was a competitive urge. I used to berate people who asked, when my team had lost, 'Did you enjoy the game?' Even as a lad, any enjoyment I got depended on the result. I liked playing, but I loved winning and I would reply: 'We were beaten. How could I enjoy that?'

I never believed in that high-minded public-school sentiment: 'It isn't the winning that matters, but the taking part.' From what I have seen of public schoolboys, especially in politics, they are very bad losers. Like them, I was with the American coach who declared: 'Winning isn't everything. It's the *only* thing.'

I was in midfield and later left-back at a time when football was a tough business, but not as dirty as the modern professional game has become. When I see players on mega-salaries bringing the game into disrepute – spitting, jersey-pulling, diving, shielding the ball and getting opponents sent off – I do not recognise it as the same game. I played at a ferociously competitive level and am afraid I have to agree with the club historian who described me as an 'uncompromising' tackler. Challenges were bone-jarring and a 50–50 ball usually meant 2 hospital cases. Even in a friendly match with workmates, I went in so hard that I broke my leg. When I was taken into the Kirkcaldy Hospital, I was wheeled through to my father who was still a patient there, recovering from his horrendous leg injuries. It made my injury seem so trivial.

A teammate summed me up to a political profile writer: 'He took no prisoners, but perhaps was not the silkiest of footballers.' The same writer added: 'His managers, meanwhile, would complain that he too often came out of position' (something my MSP colleagues have noted I continued to do).

If my football and political careers have to be compared, I prefer the assessment of family friend and lifelong East Fife supporter, Lord Harry Ewing. He remembered me as 'a superb anticipator of opposition attacks'.

II

Into Politics

On my return from Leeds, I packed into three years at school all that I had missed in the previous years of squandered opportunity. I took my second chance and left with three Highers and ten O levels. I make no recriminations and I am not bitter, but I was only too aware of the gaps in my education. It is something I nearly missed out on completely because I was a stubborn boy who was obsessed by football.

The lesson I learned, and which I have tried to put into effect throughout my political career, is that most youngsters have something to offer but at a moment in time are either not interested or developed enough to exploit it. I was lucky to have the opportunity later to show what was there to be developed. My political purpose has always been to make sure every child does not make the mistakes I did – and, if they do, to ensure they have a second chance or as many chances as they need in life.

I also believe that Scottish education fails to make our young people confident or give them a sense of their own worth. I have always tried to appear assured, but I was never that confident anywhere other than on the football field. When Scottish boys and girls leave school they are expected to 'know their place', which leads to pigeon-holing and the stifling of both personal initiative and the enterprise our country needs so badly. They should leave school with a healthy regard for their own qualities and a knowledge of how they can improve themselves. Above all, they should have been taught that 'their place' is whatever they want to make it.

When I advanced in politics, and especially when I became First Minister, there was no shortage of people who wondered if I merited my advancement. After all, I was not middle or upper class; I had been a professional footballer; I wasn't from Glasgow or the west of Scotland; and did not belong to the cliquish university alumni who seemed to dominate Scottish politics. Whatever they thought, I believed that in our own ways Donald Dewar and I were equally fit and capable for the job.

I went to Heriot-Watt University at the age of 20 to study urban planning. Because of my new attitude, I was top in every year and won a scholarship annually. I don't say that to boast, but to show how a young person who had wasted his school years can catch up if given a second chance.

I am a passionate proponent of learning and education. As I matured and developed in that academic environment, I began to get a glimpse of Scotland as one of the world's leading centres of learning. Too many of our children are still wasted by our education system – every one of these is a mind thrown away and a valuable citizen lost, and all because that child did not fit in or perform to a set of expectations at a particular point in his or her life. To me, teachers are heroes and heroines because without them there would only be ignorance and intolerance. It takes something special to stand in front of a class of 30 and dominate, enthuse, inform and shape those young minds. In an ideal world, teachers would be paid the same as consultants. Sadly, far too many of our teachers are carrying out roles as substitute social workers, carers and parents, instead of being left free to teach. Apart from health, there is no greater profession than teaching. If you ask me, I admit that politicians are not in the same league.

The five-year urban planning course at Heriot-Watt covered everything, including engineering, the philosophy of modern art, site planning and architecture, and was a wide-ranging liberal-arts education. It even included special studies in the Grassmarket and the Old Town of Edinburgh, later to become the home of the new Scottish Parliament.

Many years later, at the time of the Holyrood Parliament building project, I reflected ruefully that my urban planning degree and training qualified me to take a hand in the difficult process of site selection and assessment, and all the architectural issues that became so controversial. However, Donald Dewar decided to exclude me. I confess at the time his attitude offended me. Now, in view of the controversy and the ongoing recriminations about Holyrood, I wonder whether I should have been grateful to him.

To some, politics is a chosen career and their creeds – such as they are – are carefully assembled to advance their ambitions. Others, like myself, are born into it and our beliefs are bred in us.

People have found it strange that, when asked what inspired me to go into politics, I have referred to a Tory Prime Minister and aristocrat. When Sir Alec Douglas-Home was asked the same question, he said 'public service' and I identify with that. It is an old-fashioned attitude but it is a Scottish tradition, irrespective of party.

I have never coveted any political position: I have had hopes, but never set myself any career targets nor plotted against colleagues. From student politics through local government to Westminster and my position as First Minister of Scotland, it has simply been a steady progression through working hard at things I saw needed to be done.

Despite my background and the example of my parents, a life in politics was not preordained for me. After Leeds United, although Aston Villa made an approach and I played 140 games as a professional for East Fife, it was obvious to me that football was not going to be my long-term future. My life from then on reflected the social change that was happening in Britain. The old industries were dying and with them the communities that depended on them. I was a direct beneficiary of both the huge expansion of higher education and the drive to create new housing and new communities.

At 19, I married my school girlfriend Margaret Drysdale and we moved into a brand-new home in Glenrothes, which was Scotland's second new town. Such was the dominance of football in my life that, to set the wedding day, I asked the manager of East Fife if there was a free Saturday in the league programme. He assured me 16 March was vacant and a clash of fixtures was avoided.

At that time, I was a trainee in the Fife County Council planning department, before going on to study at the new Heriot-Watt University. University gave me a chance for the first time to reflect on the compelling aspects of my life up to that point, especially my family influences, and it all pointed to a Christian, caring sense of community. As I have said, I have no formal faith but I understand and respect the values of those who do.

I joined the Labour Party in 1970 at the age of 22 and became chairman of the Young Socialists. Midway through university, I fought my first election against the sitting Conservative councillor in Glenwood ward in Glenrothes. It is hard now to think that in Fife you could be beaten by a Tory, even by only 15 votes.

After the reorganisation of local government in 1974, I was elected to Kirkcaldy District Council at the age of 26 – the start of nearly 30 years in elected office representing my own people – and became chairman of the planning committee in my first year. I lost out to a Scottish Nationalist in the SNP upsurge in 1977, the only time I have ever lost my seat. I felt as if the whole world had voted against me, not just a few hundred people, and the feeling of rejection was overwhelming.

However, I did not have to wait long to prove myself and only a year later I was nominated for the regional council seat of Kennoway,

Windygates and Leven, the area in which I had been born and brought up. I became council leader at the age of 34, although I was by far the youngest councillor and had to win respect by being like them, but also providing new ideas.

I was leader of the council for five years and was fortunate that my council chairman was Bert Gough, a miner who was a tremendous civic leader. Our relationship could not have been closer. Throughout our careers, Bert always regarded Gordon Brown and myself as 'his boys'. He was the progressive-minded civic head, I was the political catalyst, and between us we ran Fife Council with a firm hand.

During that time, we introduced free bus travel for older people, free nursery provision, a free home-help service and some of the most imaginative policies in education, not least in further education.

Twenty years later, after the establishment of the Scottish Parliament, the rest of Scotland caught up. Those policies which we developed in local government in Fife laid the foundations for more radical ideas, like free personal care for older people, introduced when I became First Minister. Free bus travel for 50,000 pensioners and nearly 5,000 handicapped and disabled people was introduced in 1982, so that one-sixth of the population of Fife have travelled free since then. The housebound, who cannot benefit from free bus passes, were compensated with free colour TV licences.

The ability to travel and have outings stimulates the older generation and in many cases actually appears to prolong their lives. It was so successful that there were complaints from commuters and travellers-to-work that they could not get on the buses because of old people. I told them to take it up with Age Concern!

With Gordon Brown, I fought tooth-and-nail to stop Stagecoach, under the direction of bus tycoon Brian Souter, from taking over the Fife buses. I freely admit we said some terrible things about Souter because we were appalled by his more ruthless practices. Yet eventually we found ourselves working with him and, because of our free bus passes, their Fife services are the most profitable. The knowledge that a multimillion-pound cheque would arrive every year without fail made the terms and conditions of the Fife operation better than any other part of his empire.

To me, these things are old-fashioned socialism in a modern guise. They make sense socially, economically and electorally. Lack of money is not a problem; the real problem is lack of will.

During the miners' strike, the *Daily Express* described me as 'the red claw in the velvet glove'. That was one of the most depressing periods I have ever worked through. Fife was hit so hard by what was, in effect, a government war against the miners and their families. As leader of the council, I could not stand back and watch the hardship that was inflicted on whole communities in an attempt to break their spirit.

We spent £1.2 million on sustaining people who were being deprived of the basic essentials of life: more money than was spent on the miners by any other region, and a lot of that expenditure was controversial. Doubts were raised about the legality of the financial support we were giving to a group of people who were defying the government. The miners' families, especially the womenfolk, were doing all they could to survive, with food and clothing appeals and soup kitchens and, in the mid-'80s, it seemed we were back in the '30s. My attitude was to help – and dare anyone in authority to challenge what we were doing.

Of course, it was the most misguided and most damaging of strikes there has ever been in Britain and it led to the destruction of the coal industry. In a human sense, it was an absolute disaster and caused untold misery. Despite that, the injustice being inflicted by the government on those families had to be opposed.

In the midst of this human hardship, I wrote personally to a number of Scottish entertainers and show-business personalities asking for their help. The only one who responded was Billy Connolly, who said he would do two events, one in the Carnegie Institute in Dunfermline and one in the Lochgelly Centre. He said he would appear for one or two hours. On both occasions he was on stage for 3½ hours, raising nearly £40,000 for the Fife miners and their families. He did not take a penny in appearance money or expenses and all he got for his trouble was tea and sausage rolls.

It was a heart-warming gesture of solidarity at a time when we were seeing family life crumble in the coalfields and hardship on an unimaginable scale because of the miners' loyalty to a misguided leader. Billy Connolly now has detractors who resent his worldwide success and his dismissal of the 'wee pretendy parliament', and there are other show-business figures who claim to be more patriotic Scots, but at that time he proved himself a real friend of the miners.

Politics must be rooted in your community, finding ways to help families living in poverty and people whose problems might seem trivial, but have become a blight in their lives. I would go on the phone for hours and give officials a hard, hard time. You would not win every time nor solve every problem, but you would win respect for trying. Politicians who forget those essentials should not be in politics.

Many of our councillors had been public sector workers and most of them did not have surgeries because they lived among the people, met them socially and bumped into them in the streets, pubs and social clubs every day. When the small burghs were replaced, much of that quality disappeared. A lot of mutual respect has gone out of local government and we politicians have to take responsibility for that. In recent times, the domination of party politics in local government is unhealthy.

I have been a partisan politician for most of my life and ideologies can have a powerful hold. Often, though, it is plain tribalism – and the worst politicians simply react to the jungle drums. If people are to be motivated and re-connected with local government, it has to be different. The public are now becoming disengaged because they feel politicians are not serving their interests. The party political process is very adversarial and intolerant. Surely there is agreement on wanting to see that our money is spent wisely, with value for money, efficient services and decent leadership? More scrutiny is needed in local government, but you cannot have real scrutiny by committees in which party whips operate.

I am a great advocate of proportional representation (PR) for local government. At that level, consensus achieves the best results and the parties should set local government free in many areas. For too many Labour councillors, everything has to be directly provided by the council. For too long, a feature of socialism has been the dependence on administration and bureaucracy.

We should move from ideologies to ideas. The two are not the same and government at every level would be improved if we recognised the difference.

Some services have to be delivered directly, but with other services it may be better to try non-profit or partnership arrangements, joint initiatives between public and private, imaginative ways of delivering services which are both good quality and cost-effective.

Everyone pays lip service to the importance of local government, but its potential is not being realised. The Labour Party has made an immense contribution to the welfare of our people at local level. Though the Tories tried to break it up through dismantling the regions and gerrymandering council boundaries, that did not work.

Of course, I would be the first to admit that there is too much posturing and too many empty gestures in local government. Much of it may be 'politically correct' but to their communities, the people who matter, it is meaningless and often downright ludicrous. I cannot see how the people of Glasgow benefited from their council opening a book for people to make statements against the Iraq war. Years ago, flying the Palestinian flag from Dundee City Chambers did nothing for the city's, or Scotland's, image abroad. And I have to admit that when I was a councillor it was a nonsense for Fife to declare itself a 'nuclear-free zone' – when there was enough nuclear power at Rosyth naval dockyard to destroy the world ten times over!

I love local government with a passion, not just because I spent so long as a councillor and council leader but also for its immediacy and relevance to people. Local authorities should be given more say in the cash they raise. Of all the money councils spend, 88 per cent is given to them by the central government. As a result, accountability is virtually non-existent. The council tax, over which there is so much agonising and which creates annual conflict in councils, accounts for only 12 per cent of their finances. Central government feels it cannot and will not trust councils and, in reality, it will not cede control to where it can do the most good. There is too much waste, too little modernisation, too many party politics and too much inefficiency.

Instead of waiting for the Scottish Parliament to pass acts, why can't local government take policy initiatives and do more themselves? Why does it need a First Minister or Minister for Local Government to tell them what they are going to do? Why should local authorities not be going to the Scottish Executive and telling them? After all, it is the councillors and local officials who know what is best for their own areas.

Issues like these should be part of a national debate. There is just not enough thinking going on – perhaps because we are afraid of the new ideas that might be thrown up. One of my favourite quotes is by Einstein: 'Imagination is more important than knowledge. Knowledge is limited. Imagination encircles the world.'

In politics and in the media, if someone comes up with a new idea, instead of being given credit for originality and effort, they are more likely to be castigated and ridiculed. That is a sad commentary on what was once a country of thinkers, the land of Burns, Adam Smith, Walter Scott, Napier, Hume and all the other great Scots who – as Arthur Herman's book title put it – 'invented the modern world'. Herman told 'the true story of how Western Europe's poorest nation created our world and everything it'. That is a huge claim, but well justified. Now, no other nation seems to be as hide-bound by our history as we are.

As a result of my age and the speed with which I had progressed in local government, it seemed to be taken for granted that I would be going to Westminster when the opportunity presented itself. Just such an opportunity arose – but I turned it down.

West Fife, which had been held for Labour by Willie Hamilton, was split in two under parliamentary boundary reorganisation in 1983 and I was approached for the half that became Dunfermline East.

West Fife was the last bastion of the Communist Party in Scotland and had been represented by the redoubtable Communist MP Willie Gallacher from 1935 until 1951, when Willie Hamilton wrested it from him.

In the reorganisation, Hamilton opted for what became Fife Central, leaving what remained of a Communist hinterland around Cowdenbeath and Lochgelly in the new Dunfermline East seat. Old habits and old loyalties die hard in Fife, and in recent years the Democratic Left (the new Communists) have made a strong showing, beating Labour in a local government by-election for Hill of Beath.

I had the backing of the big unions for the nomination in Dunfermline East but another contender was Gordon Brown. Even then, it was obvious that Gordon was a class act but because of his career as a broadcaster and his involvement at national level in Scottish politics, he did not have the same close local links as I did. However, I was happy to stand aside because it was obvious he should have a seat in Parliament and the Labour Party needed him there.

Just as important was my hankering to stay and represent the place of my birth and upbringing. I had always been well treated by my constituents in Fife Central and, if I went to Westminster, I still wanted to be their representative. Something was telling me to bide my time.

My first parliamentary election in 1979 was in the strongly Tory constutuency of Fife East, a 'no hope' seat that was used to blood Labour beginners. I was in good company – others who had cut their teeth in Fife East included John Smith, Harry Ewing and Helen Liddell.

I fought Willie Hamilton as a so-called left-winger in a re-selection battle in 1981, when the mechanism was being used in constituencies up and down the country to realign Labour. Willie castigated me as a 'carpetbagger', which was strange since the Fife Central constituency was my home ground and not his. The new seat took only 58 per cent of its voters from his old constituency and the rest came from Fife East and from Kirkcaldy.

Willie Hamilton was a nationally-known figure because of his anti-monarchy stance, which he worked up to get constant publicity as the rent-a-quote MP on anything royal. Of course, being well on the right wing of the Labour Party, it did him no harm in a constituency with a hard-left tradition. A controversial figure in many other ways, he was also criticised for living in London and was seen to be at odds with the rest of the Labour Party on Europe and defence.

At the selection meeting in Cowdenbeath Town Hall, we tied the first ballot at 19–19. On the night of the re-run a week later, *News At Ten* had a wonderful cartoon of the Queen at the ballot box, casting a vote marked 'McLeish'!

If by some weird and wonderful chance Her Majesty had had a vote, it might have made all the difference, for Willie won by a single vote. It was so close that he took no chances: one of his votes was a blind person who was brought into the poll in a wheelchair and another was an elderly lady, Mrs Tulloch, who had to be carried up the stairs by Hamilton's supporters.

In 1987, Willie Hamilton eventually retired, having held West Fife and Fife Central for 37 years and 11 elections. Some reports said he was 'forced out', but the majority view in the constituency was that it was time for a change.

There were 40 nominating bodies and I got every one of them because I had worked so hard that I was indelibly associated with the constituency. Fife Central was a safe Labour seat, with majorities of 10–15,000. In 1987, I increased Labour's vote from 43.1 per cent to 56.1 per cent and almost doubled Hamilton's majority to 15,709 over the Tories. The only real battle was for second place, with the Tories taking 17.5 per cent, the Liberals 15.9 per cent and the SNP 15.5 per cent, not that I cared who the runner-up was. What spoiled it for me was that I had to resign my Kennoway and Windygates council seat and in the by-election it fell to the Scottish National Party.

With the collapse of the Tory Party and the end of two-party politics, the SNP became the Opposition in Scotland. I had some respect for the old-style nationalists who were motivated by patriotism and concern for the future of Scotland; however, throughout my political career their hallmark has been a mean-spirited and nasty form of nationalism. Their campaigning was always the typical Scottish National Party propaganda, a virulent attack on Labour for 'selling out' Scotland and socialism. For a party that claims to be Scottish, they showed – and continue to show – a lamentable lack of understanding of the Scottish character. Scots take a mature view of politics and feel insulted when their politics are reduced to the standards of the worst of the Scotland–England football matches. The SNP's one-note, backward-looking, anti-Englishness of thought, perennial whingeing and refusal to admit that any other party might have Scotland's good at heart has alienated the majority of Scots.

In Fife, they had a reasonably stable protest vote of 25 to 30 per cent, even though the county was Tory-free for most of the '90s. Campaigning was ritualistic and I concentrated on a positive message, trying to ignore the attacks on the Labour Party and the personal abuse of myself and Labour councillors. No one party can claim a monopoly on patriotism and pride. Their old-fashioned tirades lack ideas and they have exposed themselves as more of an emotional spasm than a coherent ideology.

I am no longer a street-campaigning politician, and I thought I would miss it. In fact, I now realise that there was not a lot of passion nor genuine cut-and-thrust debate with opponents.

When I was elected MP in June 1987, I thought I was the most important person in the world because arriving at Westminster gave you a real sense of place, history and political achievement. My maiden speech on local government finance was made at 1.30 a.m., with only a handful of backbenchers, a lone government frontbencher and the Speaker present. The important thing was getting it over because it meant I had joined what Burns called 'the company of the great and good' and become a member of the club in the forum that had heard Peel, Disraeli, Churchill and Attlee.

In that rarefied atmosphere, it is easy to lose the place, but, if I needed it, I was soon brought down to earth by my first surgery. In a bare room, with four old chairs and a table, my first visitor was a lady from the Kirkcaldy constituency of my newly elected colleague Lewis Moonie. When I pointed this out, her response was: 'I'm coming to see you because I've tried him. He's a doctor, you know.' Lewis was a psychiatrist and could have done her more good than I.

More menacingly, she added: 'I hope we can get on together. I killed Harry Gourlay [the then recently deceased Kirkcaldy MP who had been Deputy Speaker of the Commons] because he didn't take me seriously.'

She then gave me a gift – five plastic pens with the name 'McLeish' wrongly spelled on them – and the advice: 'You had better treat me seriously, because if you don't I'll kill you as well.' She came to see me every second Friday for 12 years with her grievances, requests for advice and even invitations to family occasions. On one occasion, she dumped two bags of partially burned clothing over my head and on another she stopped me in Leven High Street and took her tights off to show me her sore feet.

She was my introduction to the rich pattern of constituency work – and an ever-present reminder. When people talk about the so-called glamour and power of politics, I often think of that lady.

III

The Opposition Years

After the excitement of being elected, the reality was that we remained in Opposition for the next decade. The best Labour could hope for was to land some telling blows on the Tory governments. Especially under Thatcher, they ruled with an iron fist and made no concessions. Even when they knew they were wrong and that their policies were harmful, they would not make sensible changes that we all knew were for the good of the country. It was always tough and often depressing.

Labour were very much a party in transition. We had moved on from the feuding during Michael Foot's years and our chaotic performance in the 1983 election. The manifesto so tellingly described by Gerald Kaufman as 'the longest suicide note in history' was actually entitled 'New Hope For Britain' – but what we needed was new hope for the Labour Party.

Under Neil Kinnock, who was good to me, we were beginning to be transformed. Neil was never at his most comfortable at the dispatch box, never master of the cut-and-thrust, and I noticed that he suffered because of a strange form of racism in the Tory press – they manage to tolerate the Scots, but they do not like the Welsh.

Kinnock was a politician of real stature. Leadership is about vision and courage, and he had both. In that never-to-be-forgotten Bournemouth conference speech in 1985, in which he poured anger and contempt on Militant, he spoke for every decent-thinking member of the Labour Party.

It was a tragedy that he took us so far and came so close, but never became Labour Prime Minister. Had the 1992 general election been held a few months later, I have no doubt Neil Kinnock would have been PM.

Commentators and historians say the notorious rally in Sheffield, a premature exercise in triumphalism, was to blame for what was a shock defeat. On the night it was held, we were seven points ahead in the polls and the rally was meant to demonstrate that Labour were confident of victory and ready to govern, but we had not quite scaled that mountain. We had not completely restored our credibility by then, although in another six months or so we would have done. The effect of the rally was to turn floating voters against us and back to the Tories – which was as big a surprise to John Major as to anyone. The train drivers' leader Derek Fullick put it succinctly: 'You don't belch before you've had the meal . . . '

The one thing that must never be forgotten is that in terms of shaping British political history in the latter half of the twentieth century, Neil Kinnock's impact was tremendous. His political heirs benefited and the biggest landslide in British election history was his legacy.

You cannot win any election unless you have the right policies, consistent with your beliefs, and in modern times presentation is vital. In giving Labour both of these, Neil Kinnock made Labour's success inevitable. I believe we would have won under John Smith and I know that Tony Blair acknowledges his debt to Kinnock.

The Parliamentary Labour Party had its factions but I chose not to join any of them. By inclination, background and training, I was a planner, not a plotter. In politics that can be seen as a weakness and there may also be a bit of arrogance in wanting to say I had done it on my own. In my naivety, I believed that serious politics and hard work mattered most.

I watched the development of significant cliques or partnerships, which became more noticeable at times like Shadow Cabinet elections. To a young, new MP it explained why certain not-particularly-talented politicians (a number of them fellow Scots) had to be found front-bench positions. It was because they were master manipulators in the furtive world of gossip and deal-makers in the tearooms and bars of Westminster, a world in which I was never at home.

In Scottish Labour politics, the factionalism was even more insidious. It should not matter if you are Catholic or Protestant – but in too many constituencies it does. I could not be pigeon-holed as either and had a varied group of friends, which some found baffling. I did not go to Glasgow University, so was not an automatic member of the inner circle, which included John Smith, Donald Dewar and their fellow alumni. Nor did I come from the west of Scotland, so was not part of the Glasgow/ Lanarkshire power grouping which seemed to think it had some kind of hereditary right to control Scottish Labour.

I thought I had joined a party of fraternity and I found it hard to believe some of the things that were done and said by colleagues, about colleagues. Nothing in my political life has ever been so big or so paramount that I would go to any lengths to achieve it. In politics, probably more than in any other profession, you need to have working relationships with people who are outspokenly against you. To me, being respected was always better than being liked. I have worked with many politicians I could not stand personally and they probably felt the same way about me. You develop a thick skin and it helps to take the charitable view that you are all working for the good of your constituents and the country. However, it has to be said that there are leading politicians at Westminster and in Scotland who seem to think nothing can be achieved without doing down others in their own party and who actually relish the role of hatchet man.

When people with something to contribute are frozen out for no reason other than petty partisanship, it is to everyone's disadvantage. A typical example of this was when I left office. The services of our head of strategy, John McTernan, were not required by the new Scottish Executive. However, John is an outstanding thinker and policy adviser whom I first got to know for the contributions he made to our Opposition social security team. He is now in No. 10 Downing Street. It seems strange that the Prime Minister finds him valuable, but he was not thought good enough for the present Edinburgh administration.

Across the floor of the House of Commons the behaviour was so partisan that all they needed were football scarves and an occasional chorus of 'You'll Never Walk Alone'. To my astonishment, the language often heard in the mother of all parliaments was what we knew at home as 'pit language', and the humour could be brutal. One Tory member, who had an altercation with a taxi driver when apparently 'tired and emotional', would be met by shouts of 'Taxi' whenever he stood to speak; another Tory, who had gone on holiday and neglected his flock of sheep, was always greeted with a chorus of baaing. The Deputy Prime Minister John Prescott would inevitably be greeted with an order for 'A gin and tonic, Giovanni' by the Tory MP Nicholas Soames, who would not let the Deputy Prime Minister forget he had once been a steward on a cruise ship. Soames himself seemed impervious to insult – despite (or perhaps because of) being an undistinguished minor member of the Churchill dynasty and a friend of royalty.

In 1987, before devolution and the departure of some Scottish MPs to Edinburgh, the standard of Scottish representation was very high, although there were clearly first-team and second-team players.

I was to discover that on the Westminster benches there were true friends of devolution and true enemies. In a secret ballot in a dark room, a lot of them would not have supported devolution and the Scottish Parliament.

When I was first elected, devolution was not a priority policy, but in a very short time it became one. The longer the Tories were in power, running Scotland with a tiny minority and imposing unpopular and downright damaging policies on a people who had not voted for them, the more inevitable it became. For a party that claimed to protect the constitutional settlement, they seemed intent on dividing and endangering the unity of the UK. If they had shown a little more sensitivity and a lot more understanding of Scotland, I do not believe they would have prevented devolution, but perhaps many Scots would not have been so desperate for change.

In my first year at Westminster, I became a member of the powerful Public Accounts Committee. It was an important cross-party body that showed me the real worth of the committee system, something that became important to me when it came to setting up the Scottish Parliament. A system of committees which need not divide along party lines and is accessible to electors should be the most important mechanism for scrutiny of executive decisions and discussion of issues that matter to the people of Scotland. The Scottish Parliament committees are still too partisan, but they may evolve as the Parliament matures.

Under Kinnock, I was one of the first MPs of the new Labour intake to be promoted to a junior front-bench post. As a member of Shadow Scottish Secretary Donald Dewar's team, I was given Education and my first blooding was on the Self-Governing Schools (Scotland) Bill.

When I say I was 'blooded', I use the word advisedly, because the Tory Scottish Education Minister was Michael Forsyth. He was very impressive, while I was a novice, and I suffered at his hands. Although I disliked all that he stood for, I had a grudging admiration for his political skills.

The House of Commons could also be petty and personal and we were reduced to tactics like forcing Forsyth and his supporters to sit through the night until breakfast. We hassled and harried the small group of Tories because they were running Scotland without a democratic mandate to do so, but we did not really lay a glove on them, apart from making them lose a night's sleep. That way, I learned the difference between substance and posturing in the House of Commons.

It was also the beginning of a long political relationship with Donald Dewar, which was to take us both through the exciting and exhausting process of devolution and into the new Scottish Parliament and Executive. It could never be called a close or personal relationship and, as his subordinate in Opposition and Government, I always felt inhibited. Donald was not good at delegating, and I chafed under the need to report back to him on small and insignificant details.

Early in my parliamentary career, I was one of five new MPs to be chosen for a four-week visit to the United States under their American

Visitor Programme. The others were John Reid, Hilary Armstrong, Doug Henderson and Keith Vaz, all of whom became government ministers ten years later, so the US Embassy were obviously well informed.

Since then, I admit to a long affair with the US. Although many of their attitudes can be baffling and outsiders find some policies highly questionable, there is a lot to be admired in their energy, enterprise, openness and can-do attitude. Most appealing to me personally was their willingness to judge people on what they did, rather than on their origins and backgrounds, and their readiness to give everyone a chance to try again.

I was linked with Mike Synar, a member of the House of Representatives of the US Congress from 1978 who had the distinction of being a radical Democrat in the heavily Republican state of Oklahoma. He was later to be a prominent figure in Bill Clinton's campaign and I joined him on congressional election campaigns in deepest Cherokee country. In Clinton's first presidential campaign in 1992, Mike Synar played the independent candidate Ross Perot's part in the rehearsals for presidential TV debates. Mike, who became a very close friend, was a wonderful congressman with great vision but, sadly, he died of cancer in his early 40s – a great loss to his state and his country.

Because of my frequent visits and lectures at Oklahoma University and more recently 'distinguished scholar-in-residence' at the University's European Union Centre, their *Tulsa World* newspaper headlined me as 'Tulsa's favourite Scotsman'. Because of my involvement with Oklahoma, I was made an honorary citizen of Tulsa by the then mayor Rodger Randle; again a close friendship has been forged with a man who has been in elected politics for nearly 30 years and could have gone on to higher office in the state or even in the US Congress.

One effect of my American experience has been to convince me of the need for more support for our MPs. The House of Representatives is the equivalent of our House of Commons, but there can be no comparison between the staff and back-up available to our MPs and their congressmen.

Each member of Congress in Oklahoma has eight people working in his/her district and another eight in Washington. Some of the offices of elected representatives on Capitol Hill resemble large firms, while an MP is lucky if he has two people between Westminster and his constituency. MPs are vastly under-resourced and members of Congress are able to make a greater contribution on local and national issues, do more research, receive more advice on a wide range of subjects and be accessible to more vibrant and energetic new thinking than we seem to be.

It is true that the average parliamentary seat in Britain has 80,000 constituents and a congressman or woman can serve 500,000, but there should be a great deal more support for our parliamentarians to do their jobs better. The gulf between the abundance of Washington and the meanness of Westminster makes a huge difference in delivering effective representation.

Thanks to Neil Kinnock, Employment became a speciality of mine. With Tony Blair as Shadow Employment Secretary and myself as Shadow Minister, we developed a major crusading tool – a constituency-by-constituency league table of rising unemployment, which brought home the destructive impact of the Thatcher Government in every part of Britain throughout the 1990s recession.

Indeed, when an argument had to be backed up by a blizzard of facts, the word that went out at Labour HQ was: 'Unleash the McLeish!'

The House of Commons library service said I was their biggest customer as I plundered their statistics to deliver a detailed statistical assault on the government. By breaking down the figures, the story became relevant for each constituency, was instantly usable in each MP's local media and made individual communities realise what was happening to them. I notice that technique has now been reversed by Tony Blair, who uses it at Prime Minister's Question Time to remind Tory MPs of the falling unemployment levels and improvements in health and education wrought by his government in their individual constituencies.

By the time I moved to Transport, I had learned to use another weapon in the politician's armoury – the judiciously placed leak. In opposition, we were always being passed confidential documents from various sources, including my links with old railwaymen. I was eventually getting two or three exclusives a week into national papers like *The Guardian* and it became so frequent that my No. 1, Michael Meacher, was annoyed. I regarded it as often more effective than what we did across the floor of the Commons and in committee. I also spent two productive years in two other Shadow teams, Health and Social Security, where I was deputy to Harriet Harman.

By the time our years in Opposition came to an end, I had experience of more departments than any other minister.

In 1995, our family life was shattered by one of those cruel blows which make politics insignificant and put the striving for a career into perspective. My wife Margaret, who had been partner in everything I had done for 27 years and was mother to our two children, Niall and Clare, died of pancreatic cancer. It happened so quickly. Pancreatic cancer often does not show until it is too late. It does not give you much time to do anything.

I was in the Commons, winding up an Opposition day debate on rail privatisation in mid-January and just before I started to speak, I got a message saying she had taken herself to hospital. I made the speech and flew back to Scotland. Two weeks and five days later she died.

We had been on holiday in Newport, Rhode Island, when she first complained of feeling unwell, but then on Hogmanay she had very severe abdominal pains and knew there was something seriously wrong. She had rarely been to the doctor in her life and after New Year decided to visit Victoria Hospital in Kirkcaldy. It is at such times that the true worth of the NHS is brought home to us. The doctors, nurses and all the staff were excellent and gave Margaret care of the very highest order. When the NHS receives so much criticism, it is useful for us all to remember our own experiences.

I was deeply moved by the fact that nearly half of the Shadow Cabinet, including Tony Blair, attended the funeral and Gordon Brown delivered a moving oration. It was also touching that on the same day in Tulsa, Oklahoma, a special service was held by a number of Oklahomans, led by Rodger Randle. It was an example of the friendship that existed between us and said a great deal for the people of Oklahoma. It was a gesture that was much appreciated 4,000 miles away.

It may have been the easy way out, but I submerged myself in work. My mother had died just before I was nominated for the Fife Central seat, my grandmother died after the nomination but just before I was elected to Westminster and my wife died between my being an MP and becoming a minister. It just seemed that at the crucial points of my life, those who had given me so much did not live to see the next step.

IV

New Labour

Neil Kinnock picked out Tony Blair and Gordon Brown because he had an eye to the future and he saw their prime ministerial qualities. Blair was more obviously articulate and smart – a great communicator with a good personality, dynamic and self-evidently a moderniser.

Neil was trying to manoeuvre the party back from the abyss of 1983, when Labour came close to self-destructing, towards a more coherent and electable position. In the eyes of many people, Tony Blair had the advantage of not carrying any ideological baggage. He was a barrister, not rooted in socialism and trade unionism but connected to the broader Labour movement. With his private school and Oxford education, he shared the characteristics of many prime ministers, so that on paper and in person he just looked right.

When he became leader, he said I was the most working-class member of his Shadow team because I had never lost touch with my roots – but we were in agreement on what needed to be done to save the Labour Party from itself.

To those who want to look behind the image, Tony Blair is no lightweight. One of his early positions was Shadow Employment Secretary: crafting new legislation, a strategy to deal with rising unemployment and trade union reform. Although not seasoned in trade union matters, he had a grasp of the issues and an eye for detail and the law. It was exciting to work with him, although I was inevitably in the back room, and it was obvious he was going places.

In politics in post-war Britain, very few people can match Gordon Brown for intellectual rigour, strategy and an unerring ability to look after his constituents. He is dedicated, articulate and passionate. At home, he has been an extraordinary Chancellor, and abroad, he is praised as a true statesman by international organisations like the World Bank because of the reforms he has put in place with regard to international aid and the way he has encouraged the campaign to eliminate Third World debt. I know that the IMF and World Bank regard Gordon Brown as a global leader on these issues.

I have worked closely with him over the years, particularly on matters where our constituency interests in Fife overlapped. He has been a good friend and I will never forget the oration he gave at the funeral of my late wife. Whatever his political opponents and detractors may say about him, no one can ever question his personal loyalty.

From the very beginning, Gordon Brown was in the forefront of the Labour Party commitment to devolution for Scotland. He believed in it, saw the benefits of it and was a great ally to Donald Dewar and the project at a time when there were other Scottish MPs at Westminster who were being obstructive. We were up against English small-mindedness, plus parochialism and spite from the anti-devolution group of Scottish MPs who dismissed a measure of self-government for Scotland as 'White Heather Club' politics.

Gordon was a great background influence in making sure devolution stayed on track, and he and Tony Blair were key players who were very useful in getting things smoothed out.

A lot of nonsense is written and broadcast about Scotland having been Gordon's 'fiefdom'. Of course, a politician of his stature will always be a dominant figure who is valued and supported by Scottish MPs and MSPs, but to say that Scottish Labour is in any way under his personal control is to grossly misrepresent and misunderstand the party, its elected representatives – and Gordon himself.

In any case, the reality is that devolution created a whole new set of MSPs, with whom he had no links and who are quite rightly protective of their own status. He could not dominate them even if he wanted to.

Particularly during the devolution years, Gordon was always careful in his dealings and handled a delicate situation with great dignity. During the Fraser Inquiry, my former ministerial colleague at the Scottish Executive, Sam Galbraith, claimed that Gordon had tried to influence the choice of site for the new Scottish Parliament building. Like myself, Gordon was in favour of a new-build option as being lower cost, better value for money and easier to control. Sam's somewhat snide and unnecessary comment was: 'He may have been Chancellor but we weren't having him tell us what to do.'

Sam was rightly criticised for his attitude – like all other Scottish MPs before the Holyrood Parliament was elected, Gordon had every right to make his opinion known and he was, after all, in charge of the nation's purse strings. I leave it to others, not least Lord Fraser, to decide which would have been the wisest choice.

Just two instances of many show the Chancellor's concern for Scottish interests. If he had not wiped off Glasgow's £900 million housing debt, the transfer of the city's housing stock could not have gone ahead. That was hugely beneficial for Glasgow, the Scottish Parliament and the Scottish Executive.

The Scottish Transport Group pensions settlement, with ex-gratia lump-sum payments for 14,000 bus pensioners and their families, was only made possible by Gordon Brown releasing £124 million. I know it might have been more, but by his action Gordon ended ten years of delay and injustice for a significant group of people in Scotland.

People tend to forget that Gordon has had to overcome a lot of adversity in his life and was nearly blinded as a teenager. That may be one reason why he feels such a sense of urgency and also feels things intensely (I have bitten my nails for 45 years and the only nails which I have seen that look worse are those belonging to Gordon). Yes, he likes to be in control, but that is because he has a clear grasp of what needs to be done and the intellect, drive and political stature to make it happen.

When we were in opposition and I was No. 2 to Tony Blair on the Shadow Employment portfolio, there was no doubt that Gordon was the senior partner.

I had a reputation as the 'number cruncher' who would work up the research and Tony was the ideal front man. When we had the ideas and the facts but were stuck for a press release, we would go into Gordon's office and he would ask one question: 'What's the issue here?' Then he would turn and attack his PC (he never just typed) and would produce exactly what was needed. After that, it was down to Tony's presentational technique and it worked every time. Even then it was obvious that this was going to be a formidable Labour Government team in the future.

I never saw the need to choose between the two and, when in government, never got too stirred up about the so-called Blair–Brown 'feud'. Of course there were tensions, but that was only natural between ambitious, bright, articulate top-rank politicians who cared deeply about the future of the party and the need to be in government.

A lot of it was just gossip and a lot of it was stirred up by hangers-on who thought they were promoting the interests of either Gordon or Tony – or, more likely, trying to make themselves seem important – but were only making mischief and doing damage to both men and to the Government.

John Smith was very different from all the other leading Labour politicians of that time, including Donald Dewar, George Robertson, Gordon Brown and Tony Blair. He came with ready-made solidity which inspired confidence in him as Shadow Chancellor and leader. He was very funny and could speak his mind very forcibly.

On all sides, the Commons appreciated his stiletto wit and his Scottish advocate's ability to think and react on his feet. He could turn any situation on his opponent, as when in a Finance Bill debate the Tory front bench challenged him to give his solution to their financial crisis. In mock amazement, he turned to the benches behind him and marvelled: 'They're the Government and they're asking *me* for the answers!' Of course, it didn't answer the question, but it brought the House down.

He was at his most relaxed when he boarded the midnight sleeper from London back to Scotland at the end of a parliamentary week. He would speak fondly of going home to his constituency to help the less favoured in society whom he affectionately (but never disrespectfully) described as the 'erse oot o' the breeks' brigade. With the sun rising as we passed Carlisle, he would still be holding court with an audience of Scottish MPs. Neil Kinnock had some of the same quality – the ability to be a leader and also be one of the lads. John had natural bonhomie but he could also enjoy a dram of Scotland's national drink.

The obvious and often-asked question is: what kind of prime minister would John Smith have made? He was more favourable to the unions and was a traditionalist by background and culture. That was not a problem, because John had the lesson of 1992 constantly in his mind and was determined not to go down in history as another Labour leader who had nearly made it. There was no stronger supporter of Scottish devolution. John Smith took the Devolution Bill through Parliament in 1978–9, as I was to do 20 years later. He achieved all that was possible at the time and was only sabotaged by a member of his own party, the London Scottish MP George Cunningham, whose '40 per cent rule' effectively delayed devolution for those 20 years.

I believe a government with John Smith as Prime Minister, with Tony Blair and Gordon Brown in his Cabinet, would have had a more mature look and John would have been firmly in charge. A younger, less-experienced politician would have had to find other ways, but John was well versed in the use of power, not least because of his previous experience as Secretary of State for Trade and Industry, and he could be a wily operator.

Although he often appeared to take an old-fashioned view, it would have been a strong and innovative government and he would have carried on the process of modernisation.

Foreign affairs were not a major interest and he would not have been so enthralled with spin. The web that Peter Mandelson wove around Tony Blair simply would not have happened with John Smith.

Behind the scenes, John could be absolutely ruthless and he would use the strongest of 'pit language' when colleagues needed to be sorted out. Because of his personal authority, there would have been discipline in the Cabinet and the party.

On the day of John's tragically early and sudden death, I had never seen Westminster in such a state of absolute shock and disbelief. There was genuine grief and a great sense of loss, not just in the political world but throughout the whole national community. The House of Commons was an eerie and sad place throughout that mourning period.

His last appearance was at a dinner for a European conference when, with every expectation of becoming prime minister, he said all he wanted was the chance to serve. By the cruellest of tragedies that chance was taken from him – and him from us.

When John died, the key difference between Tony Blair and Gordon Brown was that Tony – for good or ill – was better and more effectively organised. He was quicker out of the traps and within days the succession was almost a fait accompli.

The day after John's funeral, Anjie Hunter phoned me and said: 'Tony would like your support.' Immediately, I replied: 'He's got it.' I had not spoken to Gordon Brown, but it was clear that the Tony Blair bandwagon was already rolling. Gordon had impressive backing in the trade unions but had not even started rallying support in the party. Whether Gordon wanted to stand or not, Tony was already in pole position and it was clear that a leadership contest between them would have been divisive. People forget that Tony has a ruthless streak when he is in pursuit of an objective in which he believes.

Gordon, a son of the manse, is steeped in the history of Scottish politics and has a reputation for being able to connect any audience, especially at conferences, with the traditional roots of the party. Because of this, and his strong links with the trade unions, some regard him as less of a moderniser than Tony Blair and this has figured recently in the speculation about who will be the next Labour prime minister.

In fact, Gordon Brown is the arch-moderniser – an admirer of the enterprise culture of the United States and the architect of welfare-to-work. In many ways, the modernisation of Labour Party policy would not have happened without his commitment and his connections.

New Labour was more than a tag, it was branding. But it was also more than spin. It was good Labour policies made relevant for today's Britain. It was also provocative, because it said: 'You have been Old Labour for 90 years and look where it has got you.'

We are not good with change and the more radical the change, the more we look backwards. People embrace the past in times of uncertainty, when they are insecure and lack confidence, and they find it very difficult to embrace the future.

I was one of the group that were fed up with what the Labour Party had become. Those harbouring self-righteous and sterile attitudes within the party believed we were setting the public an examination at elections and it was the public who were failing the test!

In Opposition, it just became hard going. Although you could be on different wings of the party – left or right, traditionalist or moderniser – being in Opposition is only good if it is in preparation for being in Government. You can preserve your principles and values, but you also have to be in tune with a changing electorate and a changing world. After 'the longest suicide note', it was obvious we had to update our policies, create an efficient party machine and adopt new campaigning techniques. In the 1983 election, Labour's share of the vote was the lowest since 1931, the lowest actual vote since 1918, and UK-wide we lost 119 deposits. Although we won nine times the number of seats that the SDP–Liberal alliance won, in terms of votes cast we were only 700,000 ahead of them.

People, not least those who claim to be keepers of the flame and custodians of 'real' Labour, tend to forget that the truth was simple and stark: we had to modernise to win.

In the last two or three decades of the twentieth century, most people in the Labour Party survived on passion and rhetoric, but the language had become meaningless. If a party sentences itself to 18 years in Opposition, it is because it is a party of political puritans who have been ignoring the electorate.

Some people are uneasy about New Labour because for them it conjures up images of Peter Mandelson – manipulation and image over substance. They are also confused between modernisation and issues like privatisation, when the key issues are the economy, social justice and a modern welfare state.

I am irritated by those who say that modernisation was a sell-out. The 'Sour Grapes Tendency' has always been one of the most insidious factions in the Labour Party. Instead of talking up our achievements, they prefer to pick on small flaws. They deliberately forget the Labour Government has delivered a great deal for every section of our community. They remain rooted in nineteenth-century ideologies, yet nobody is a Communist any more: Marxism, which was supposed to be the world's most important doctrine, only survives in Cuba and some African states.

In the 1997 election, we knew our vote was there, so the tactic was to make no mistakes. The press commented that it had been one of the most boring, unexciting and gaffe-free election campaigns ever held in Scotland and, as the campaign coordinator north of the border, I took that as an enormous compliment. Some people find election campaigning enjoyable, but, as with football, for me it was winning that mattered.

Scotland was no different from the rest of the UK – people were desperate for change. It was a watershed for British politics, because the Tories had lost what they had come to see as their automatic 'right' to govern. Meanwhile, we had modernised, become relevant and turned ourselves into an imaginative, forward-looking party with a smooth-running campaign machine, and we had charismatic leaders.

There was one special dimension in Scotland. Devolution had been an issue since Keir Hardie became vice-president of the Scottish Home Rule Association in 1886 and made it an important part of the platform for the new Scottish Labour Party in the 1888 election. Now, its time had come.

The Nationalists had taken their revenge after the disappointment and disillusion of the 1979 referendum and the result was 18 years of Tory rule. We were determined that the wrong that had been done in 1979 would be put right, and that gave an extra commitment to our election effort in Scotland. With the full support of civic Scotland and the trade unions, devolution would become a reality. We knew that would result in Scotland being in the forefront of the biggest shock to the UK constitution for a century or more and we were prepared for whatever that meant.

The result was a fantastic success in Scotland, when the great and the good of the Conservative establishment disappeared like snow off a dyke and Scotland became Tory-free. I admit that it was a surprise because we had not fathomed the full depth of Scotland's anger and disgust at the Tories. Nor was it an entirely desirable outcome, because it gave the Nationalists a glimpse of being the official Opposition in Scotland. I did not really mind who lost seats as long as it was Labour who won them.

The weekend was spent savouring our victory, broken by a phone call from No. 10 Downing Street to say Tony Blair was sorry for not getting in contact but 'the Prime Minister will be in touch with you'. The words 'the Prime Minister' brought home to me that at last Labour were back in power. On Sunday, there was a similar phone call and it seemed obvious that there might be a surprise in the Scottish appointments. On Monday, the PM phoned to say he wanted me as Minister of State for Devolution and Home Affairs at the Scottish Office under Donald Dewar. I was delighted. After ten years in Opposition, we were the Government of the United Kingdom and I was one of the team charged with putting Scotland back on a proper footing, with special responsibility for introducing devolution.

Amid the euphoria, the realities of being in power came too thick and fast to appreciate them: moving into St Andrew's House in Edinburgh; the amazing office in Dover House in Whitehall looking out onto Horse Guards Parade; the first blue boxes as confirmation of ministerial status; briefing notes from civil servants; the first appearance at the dispatch box for parliamentary questions.

In a curious way, the civil servants were pleased from a work point of view. They relished the change from ministers who were exhausted and had run out of ideas, and it was exciting for them to have a new government with a huge programme, a raft of legislation and the massive challenge of devolution to be completed within two years.

It was a huge and daunting challenge for an untried minister, but I was aware that the greater danger was opting for the easy life by failing to exercise power. In government, if you keep your head down and do nothing, you are not creating difficulties. For some ministers, that can become a way of life.

Civil servants like you better when your diary is full of official openings, launches and visits. They are less happy when you have time to reflect and come up with new ideas. If they describe what you are doing as 'interesting', in the true spirit of *Yes, Minister* it means you're one step short of the psychiatric ward.

In Opposition you can argue and urge solutions on those in power, but in Government what you say matters and, more importantly, it is put into practice and can have an impact on your country and the lives of those you represent. Just how great the impact would be on Scotland – and, incidentally, on my own life – was yet to be seen.

PART II

Delivering the Dream

V

'There Shall be a
Scottish Parliament . . .'

Devolution, decentralisation of government and home rule have been, to a greater or lesser extent, on the agenda throughout the twentieth century since the days of Liberals in Government and Keir Hardie, founder of the Labour Party in Scotland. We were working against the background of nearly a century of ebb and flow of debate in Scotland.

That debate has had many facets and parties have had different views at different times, especially Labour. The Scottish Nationalists had talked about independence and separation since the 1930s. The Conservatives, apart from glimmers of sense, like Edward Heath's 'Declaration of Perth', were always steadfastly opposed to devolution and wedded to UK centralisation. Margaret Thatcher, in her book *The Path to Power*, writes: 'Ted had impaled the Conservative Party on an extremely painful hook from which it would be my unenviable task to set it free. As an instinctive Unionist, I disliked the Devolution commitment.' The Liberals campaigned for federalism and, of all the parties, had a properly worked-out devolution agenda through the years.

The other dimension is the Scottish people. There were times when Scots had a greater sense of belonging to their own culture and a pride in their nationality. But – despite high points of Nationalism provided by the Hamilton by-election and personalities like Winnie Ewing and Margo Macdonald – it has often been an issue that failed to engage the public in any significant way.

Many within the Labour Party are still not totally committed to a devolved Scotland although, thankfully, their numbers are now fewer. There was a long debate in the party about whether any form of devolved government would be appeasement of the Nationalist party. There were also those who believed it would be the 'slippery slope to separation' and others who argued that socialism could only be delivered to the whole of Britain.

Often, the argument was bedevilled by bitterness and downright hatred between nationalism and socialism in Scotland and between individual personalities. This was reflected in the early days of the Scottish Parliament, when devolution was a fact. Even then, the vitriol was much more tangible than the consensus.

Devolution has always been much more than a powerful idea being powerfully advocated by politicians and people. There have been influential contributions from key figures in Scotland's modern political history, the rise and fall of the Nationalist vote and the debacle of the 1979 referendum. Although Scots were robbed by an artificial hurdle erected by a Scottish MP with a London seat, it has to be said that the proposed Scottish Assembly would have been much more limited than the Parliament we now have. It would have been a much weaker, less ambitious, less comprehensive devolution of powers than under the 1998 Government of Scotland Act.

The 1979 referendum was an important factor in the fall of the Callaghan Government, with the SNP effectively voting for 20 years of Conservatism. Despite knowing that Scotland was slipping away from them politically, and despite the fact that many of their Westminster policies were fundamentally out of step with Scotland's needs, the Conservative Government persisted with the ravages of the '80s, the job losses and the deliberate decline of our traditional industries. We have the self-destructive spite of Scottish Nationalists to blame for all of that – although it must be admitted Labour's own debilitating internal civil war made us a less effective Opposition.

All of this reinforced the widespread belief among those who had previously not supported devolution that it was time for a constructive reaction. The 1988 *Claim of Right For Scotland* tried to build, for the first time, a consensus of the friends of devolution. It did not have the support of the SNP and Tories, which was a weakness, but it did have Labour, as the only party which could form a government, forming a public alliance with other political parties, MPs, councillors, the STUC, churches and civic Scotland.

That spirit of unity was reinforced by Thatcherism, which, in a negative way, encouraged the development of a comprehensive plan for devolution. The more the Prime Minister ignored the Scottish people, the more she fuelled discontent with the existing form of government. After the Second World War, the Conservatives still held the majority of Scottish parliamentary seats, but the actions of the Thatcher and Major governments punished their own party and brought it to the edge of extinction north of the border. History will show that the inflexible and damaging policies of the Conservative Party led directly to devolution. In effect, the party who claimed to be the defenders of the United Kingdom were actually undermining it.

Even in 1997, when we had a Labour Government committed to devolution, it still left the question of what the people meant by devolution and what they thought they would be voting for. There were confirmed Nationalists who wanted to break away from the United Kingdom. Some wanted a reflection of our distinctive culture and historic nation status reflected in changes in government and were 'small-n' nationalists who wanted a parliament in Scotland, but not full separation. Others set aside these issues and genuinely thought it would improve government. A growing number were beginning to realise that Scotland in the latter part of the twentieth century should reflect the regionalism that was happening in other countries.

Most people were heartily sick of Toryism and a form of government by a minority in Scotland and saw devolution as a bulwark against the excesses of an inimical Westminster government.

The 1988 *Claim of Right*, with its echoes of similar claims made on behalf of our nation in 1689 and 1842, voiced this discontent with what came to be known as Scotland's 'democratic deficit':

> In the last election, political parties expressing the intention of creating a Scottish Assembly won 57 per cent of the United Kingdom votes cast and 76 per cent of the Scottish votes cast. In spite of which, there is currently a Prime Minister dedicated to preventing the creation of a Scottish Assembly and equipped, within the terms of the English constitution, with overwhelming powers to frustrate opposition to her aims.

It went on to say that the spirit underlying the Treaty of Union had been 'eroded almost to the point of extinction' and 'the wishes of a massive majority of the Scottish electorate are being ignored'. More ominously, it warned: 'In such a situation, one would expect to see signs of a breakdown of respect for law. They are beginning to appear.'

It was hard to take the nation's or the party's pulse on devolution, because the Labour Party reflected the mood of ordinary voters at the time – equal measures of deep scepticism, anxiety and indifference.

One of the great problems in any discussion of the issue is that it so often becomes rooted in nostalgia, sentiment, historical grievances and national pride. That is a heady mixture which the Nationalists stirred regularly because of its all-too-easy appeal. We are all patriotic, but for the other political parties, particularly Labour with the prospect of being in government, it had to be about more than that.

Donald Dewar, who was then Shadow Scottish Secretary, was content to see the cross-party Scottish Constitutional Convention go ahead with the preparation of a plan for devolution. Bearing in mind that we were the party that would have to implement it, he expected and got strong Labour representation on the Convention.

When he made a public commitment to the Convention, he said Scottish politicians would be 'living dangerously' – and Donald was not, by nature, a daredevil. The main danger was that if the Convention again raised expectations which came to nothing, it would make Scotland fertile ground for the SNP. This was a real danger for Labour.

The SNP and the Tories were the only parties missing from the meeting which created the Scottish Constitutional Convention on 30 March 1989 in the Church of Scotland's Assembly Hall in Edinburgh (the very building which was also to be the setting for the restoration of the Scottish Parliament and which became its temporary home). I was one of the 58 Westminster MPs who attended and I was heartened when my fellow-Fifer and political mentor Harry Ewing from Leven in Fife, a former Labour Scottish Office Minister for Devolution, was elected by acclamation as co-chairman with David Steel.

Jim Sillars (at this time in the guise of a senior figure in the SNP) described it as 'Labour's rigged Convention', but, as so often in his career, he was hopelessly wrong. It was a breakthrough because it was the first time political parties and a broad range of interests had come together to make common cause in the interests of Scotland.

Some years later, when I was Minister for Enterprise, Sillars' position on the board of Scottish Enterprise came up for renewal. Despite noises in the system and the hostility of some colleagues, I was convinced he had done a good job and his appointment was renewed, with the support of Donald Dewar.

The Convention brought together people of different strands of thought to produce the substantial blueprint for devolution, complete with proportional representation and gender equality.

It was the Convention that influenced Labour on electoral reform, not the other way around. If you look at the history of the Labour Party, our support for first-past-the-post voting (FPTP) and our hegemony in national and local government politics in Scotland, Labour had no need to commit to proportional representation. Some feared that the SNP could become the majority party but there is no real prospect of that. Under first-past-the-post voting, Labour would have the majority in the Scottish Parliament. Yet we committed ourselves, albeit by a narrow margin at the Scottish party conference, to a future in coalition. No one should underestimate the importance of that step.

Now, councils are kicking over the traces of the introduction of PR voting in local government and it is clear that a number of MPs and party members do not like PR. At the time, we believed we should have the courage of our convictions and that the Scottish Parliament should be different from the Westminster model. The geography of Scotland was also important. Rural areas above and below the Central belt had to feel included. A Parliament dominated by Labour and the Central belt would not have acheived this.

It is only fair that the composition of the votes cast is reflected in the make-up of the Parliament and the Executive. The fact that Scottish Labour had 55 seats of 72 at Westminster, with just over one-third of the vote, spoke for itself.

George Robertson had become Shadow Scottish Secretary and George was nothing if not a pragmatist. There was a significant return to common sense in the Scottish Labour Party between 1992 and 1997 and much of that had to do with him. Later, when he was Secretary-General of NATO, George was asked about the difficulties of dealing with the Bosnian Serbs and he replied that after dealing with the Scottish Labour Party and the Scottish media, anything else was a cakewalk.

One indication of Labour's commitment to devolution, while not having thought the policy through, was on the future Scottish Parliament's financial powers. Our 1992 manifesto actually said: 'The Scottish Parliament will be assigned all Scottish tax and VAT receipts from Scotland.' It went on:

> These monies will not be the foundation of the parliament's financial base but in addition Scotland will receive any sum required to meet Scotland's financial needs. It will have the right to vary its own revenue by adjusting the basic rate of income tax up or down by 3p. Our proposals will make the Scottish Parliament financially responsible without fundamentally altering the tax structure.

Giving the Scottish Parliament all the tax and VAT money raised in Scotland would have been effective financial autonomy – and although it was a manifesto statement, it went much further than many pro-devolutionists were prepared to go. If you take all of Scotland's tax receipts from London, why not collect them yourselves? If you take all the VAT from London, why not collect it yourselves? From that position, it is a very small step to independence.

Donald Dewar signed off that manifesto, although for many who fought that election the concentration was on other promises like the anti-poverty programme and a national minimum wage. Nonetheless, the intention was clear: 'Our Scottish Parliament will have all the effective economic powers – tax powers, PR, foreign policy, representation in Europe.' This was going to be a much more nationalistic (with a small 'n') form of government for Scotland. It was much more radical than the current financial powers of the Scottish Parliament and the Executive.

Had we won on that manifesto, it could not have been fully implemented with all the income tax and VAT receipts handed over to us instead of the block grant and Barnett formula, which is an assessment of Scotland's needs from the general UK taxation fund. It simply shows that the thinking on devolution and all its implications had still not been fully developed.

Three years later, the Constitutional Convention's historic document *Scotland's Parliament, Scotland's Right* amended the financial powers to 'a continuation of the principle of equalisation of expenditure within the UK (through the Barnett formula); autonomy for the parliament in relation to its expenditure; and the limited power to vary the basic rate of income tax'.

Another promise in Labour's 1992 manifesto was this one: 'In years to come, there can be further evolutionary change as the role of the Scottish Parliament develops.' Watch this space . . .

Any doubt about the importance of devolution to a significant section of Scottish society and its ability to cause controversy was removed by the furore over Labour's announcement in June 1996 of a referendum with a second question on whether the Parliament should have the tax-varying power.

People were concerned and pointed out that John Smith would not have held a referendum because, as far as he was concerned, it was the 'settled will' of the Scottish people. However, I thought that, in principle, it was a good idea.

When he became leader of the Labour Party, Tony Blair accepted the commitment in John Smith's declaration that the achievement of the Scottish Parliament was 'unfinished business'. However, although born in Scotland, he was not so in touch with how deeply this was felt; he was being advised by English MPs and staff who had no idea of the outcry there would be if the Parliament was not delivered.

Devolution was something that had been handled by a Welshman, Neil Kinnock, who was not too sympathetic to the idea and opposed to it for Wales, then by a Scotsman, John Smith. From then on, it seemed to become a peculiarly Scottish affair and there was very little understanding of it elsewhere. Tony also wanted to be absolutely clear that the Scots sought devolution and he determined to test that before a commitment to legislation. The logic was that if Labour or the nation were afraid of a referendum, it could throw some serious doubts on Scotland's commitment.

When the double referendum was announced, Scotland flew into a flap because this had not been on the political horizon. The fear was not that Scots would reject it, but that the margin might not be big enough. If there had been a 52 per cent 'Yes' vote, Labour would claim the victory, but the Tories could claim with some justification that it was not decisive enough. It should also be remembered that this would be the first time that people would vote to have their income tax raised or lowered by a new parliament.

Significant changes were already appearing in the devolution scheme. There was the re-think on the financial regime and doubts were emerging about the wisdom of the Royal High School (RHS) as a potential parliament building.

The surprise announcement of the referendum dropped like a bombshell. It was also badly handled by Labour in London, and what should have been presented as a positive policy caused needless offence and alarm in Scotland.

Many in Scottish Labour, scarred by the debacle of the 1979 referendum, wanted to take no chances this time. Some suspected – quite wrongly – that Tony Blair was unhappy at inheriting devolution and was looking for an excuse to ditch it. There were other unfounded suspicions that the second question was a way of shackling the Scottish Parliament and keeping full financial control in London.

The Labour leadership's aim was to pre-empt a Tory summer offensive against Scotland's Parliament and constitutional reform to be launched by John Major with a strongly worded 'defence of the Union' speech in London. In an attempt to bolster the Tories' Scottish credentials, this was to be followed by an unprecedented Prime Ministerial appearance at the Scottish Grand Committee meeting in Dumfries, followed by a speech at a Burns Supper. Major's close advisers, including Scottish Secretary Michael Forsyth, had persuaded him that the anti-devolution platform could be a last-ditch vote winner in the coming general election. It proved to be yet another example of the Tories' total misjudgement of Scotland.

However, Labour in London almost blew it with a cack-handed spin operation. After dismissing the referendum as mere speculation, they leaked its announcement in advance to *The Independent* (bitterly dismissed by one Scottish commentator as 'The Insignificant'). The leak was so ineffective that it went unnoticed and had to be repeated! The real damage was that the lack of consultation was seen as a snub to Scottish MPs and the party. Instead of delivering the message that Labour really meant business in Scotland, the opposite was suspected.

The first our Scottish front-bench devolution spokesman John McAllion knew of the referendum was when he was told about it by the furious Scottish Liberal Democrat leader who had read it in *The Independent*. Damagingly, but not surprisingly, McAllion resigned.

My old friend Lord Ewing resigned as co-chairman of the Convention, saying the policy reversal was an insult to the Scottish people: 'I have had a bellyful of all this frustration and delay. I have been at this now for 30 years and through this twice before and I see all the signs of the whole thing running into the sand.'

Dennis Canavan fumed that there would be a 'huge backlash' on the Labour backbenches by those who believed 'being voted into power would give us a full mandate to set up a Scottish Parliament as soon as possible'. The revolt was prevented by George Robertson addressing a meeting at Westminster and the next day he faced a hostile reception at a hastily convened media conference in Glasgow. To show that the strategy was being led from within Scotland and not by London, he was flanked by the heavyweight Scots team of Chief Whip Donald Dewar, Shadow Chancellor Gordon Brown and Shadow Foreign Secretary Robin Cook.

The Scottish media, understandably resentful that this new Scottish policy had been leaked to a London paper, described it as a 'U-turn' and 'Blair's retreat from Scottish devolution'. The attitude of the opinion-formers, reflecting the general feeling, was: 'We should have been told about *our* referendum for *our* Scottish Parliament first.'

Tony Blair was subjected to an even rougher handling at the hands of the Scottish press, an experience which for ever after left him wary of the Scottish media – and was responsible for Alastair Campbell's typically contemptuous reference to them as 'unreconstructed wankers'. More importantly, Tony had to face a grilling by the Scottish Labour Party's national executive at a specially convened meeting in Edinburgh. The referendum plan was opposed for two hours of sticky and often acrimonious debate, but in the end they voted 20–4 in favour in what was a loyalty vote for the good of the party.

The referendum policy was introduced (some would say sprung) late in the day, extraordinarily hurried and badly organised. It injected into the debate something most Scots did not see as essential. People like George Robertson and myself did not see the fiscal arrangement as a problem and we were uneasy about the second question. It seemed obvious that the majority for the second question would be less than for the first or you might not have a majority for the tax-varying power at all (as in Shetland and the Borders). As it transpired, the result of both votes was an overwhelming endorsement that reinforced the 'settled will' of the Scottish people.

However, the affair showed an ignorance about Scottish affairs in general and devolution in particular that is still evident in London, often in the House of Commons. There are many misunderstandings, some based on genuine ignorance and some which result from genuine malice. Westminster and England need to have devolution explained, with its relevance to them and the benefits for other parts of the United Kingdom made clear.

Scotland is different, with different churches, education, law and history. Devolution is regarded as something which, having been given to Scotland, Wales and Northern Ireland, does not matter further. It does matter, however, because England will also change over the next 20 or 30 years. We should educate them and articulate devolution, particularly amongst northern Labour MPs, who always complain that Scotland is treated too well.

With the benefit of hindsight, the referendum helped – as Tony Blair, in the teeth of much criticism, said it would. When there are no constitutionally guaranteed safeguards for devolution, the will of the Scottish people as declared in the referendum is now the strongest defence against any future meddling or mischief-making by anti-devolutionists at Westminster.

The unnecessary flurry over the referendum was a testing time for devolution and its supporters, but we came through it. Any heartaches and anxieties were more than countered by the quality of the product we took from the Scottish Constitutional Convention to Westminster.

As a result of this, in less than two years, we delivered a White Paper, two referendum results, a Consultative Group report that laid down the procedures, a parliamentary bill that became the Scotland Act and the first election for the Scottish Parliament. The referendum row strengthened the process and massively improved the credibility of the financial regime. It was a very professional effort by Labour and we felt much more confident in taking it forward from that point onwards. There had been a lot of blood on the carpet, but it was all expended in a good cause.

The prospect of being in government for the first time in 18 years, implementing such a historic policy for Scotland and making a success of it made us focus on getting it right.

The Tories paid for ignoring that Scottish spirit by the total loss of their MP-base and humiliation in elections thereafter. Their political behaviour ensured the destruction of their own parliamentary force in Scotland and reinforced the importance of the Scottish Parliament in the minds of many Scots who had at best been sceptical about devolution.

Many people were puzzled when George Robertson did not become Scottish Secretary after our victory in the 1997 general election and Donald Dewar came to Scotland instead. There was a very real sense that

George took the pain and Donald got the gain, but I do not think that was the whole truth.

Donald Dewar was through and through a Scot and when asked, he was very positive about coming back to Scotland to deliver devolution.

George was a centrist, slightly on the right politically and very pragmatic. I always found him a delight to work with, because he gave his team a very free rein. He has always been a strong supporter of the US, always did a lot of travelling in Eastern Europe, was strong on modernisation of the armed forces and not anti-nuclear. I believe he was someone Tony Blair always had in mind for the wider role, and after discussions between Blair and Clinton he became Secretary-General of NATO. With his track record, making him Defence Secretary showed there was a plan to put someone like him in the job: trustworthy, loyal and a safe pair of hands. That has been proved by his leadership of NATO through years of crisis. His reward of the US Freedom Medal was well earned.

Also, George was a head-on opponent of the SNP, who, however unlikely it seemed, would be our allies in the devolution referendum. He had good reason to detest them by conviction, through years of opposition in his Hamilton constituency, which had been a Nationalist prize in the '60s, and because of the insults and personal abuse he had received from the Nationalists. He was once disgracefully described by the SNP's Alex Neil as Scotland's 'Lord Haw Haw' – a despicable slur on a patriotic Scot who has done so much for his country.

Where George could be brutal, Donald was more subtle and erudite. Donald did not like the Nationalists, but was more circumspect about it. He was steeped in Scottish culture, books, poetry and art, and he had a lofty disdain for the SNP, who tried to hijack Scottish pride for narrow-minded reasons.

George, Donald and myself were all small 'n' nationalists and I believe that George's famous comment about devolution killing the SNP 'stone dead' is right. I believe it will – in the long term.

In Government, with the help of the civil servants, we developed the thinking from the Constitutional Convention into a White Paper. With the authority from the referendum, it became the bill which had to be argued on the floor of the House of Commons and in committee until it became the Scotland Act.

Running parallel with all that was the Consultative Steering Group, which I chaired. It was charged with setting up procedures and working arrangements for the new parliament. That was a formidable piece of work when one considers that the Secretary of State and myself had other responsibilities in London and Scotland.

The White Paper was the key to what I regard as the success of the Scottish Parliament. It was acclaimed by most people as a very serious and accurate reflection of the debate in Scotland and also set out clearly how the Parliament of 1999 would be significantly different from the Assembly of 1979.

For me, the crucial issue was how the proposals we had framed in the manifesto would stand up to the political and bureaucratic scrutiny of Westminster. The key to this was the Cabinet sub-committee called Devolution – Scotland, Wales and the Regions (DSWR). This was the forum in which every line, every paragraph, of what was to become the White Paper was debated and scrutinised. DSWR had the heavyweights of the Labour Government – the Lord Chancellor, Derry Irvine, along with Jack Straw, David Blunkett and John Prescott – and each had a strong view on devolution. The committee met frequently between the election in May and the publication of the White Paper in July 1997. The proposals would be discussed with the Scottish Office, with ministers and civil servants and would be sent to all the UK departments, as they were affected, before returning to the DSWR for approval or change.

Despite the quality of the proposals we had put forward, it quickly became clear that there still remained much work to do in addressing the details of what was to be the biggest upheaval of the British constitutional landscape for nearly a century.

Donald Dewar was joined in battle sometimes twice a week, fighting Scotland's corner with the other Cabinet ministers. He would often come back dispirited and discouraged after these long and tiring sessions, saying in his usual unassuming fashion that it had been tough and he felt he had not got what he wanted or made the points effectively. Civil servants would later tell us privately that Donald had argued brilliantly and literally wiped the floor with those who wanted to weaken the devolution settlement. He made sure that nearly everything in our initial submission was either retained or improved.

As someone who was never personally close to the Secretary of State, I admired the remarkable focus and, in his own way, ruthlessness which were absolutely essential in making sure we got the White Paper Scotland wanted, rather than the watered-down version many in the Cabinet wanted to see.

Some of the Cabinet were not naturally devolutionist and were reluctant to concede power from the centre. Coalition was not in their political vocabulary and they were suspicious of the deals and concessions we had made with other political parties in the Constitutional Convention before we gained power. While they acknowledged devolution had been an important part of Labour's manifesto, some proposals were designed to cause difficulties and the discussions could be belligerent.

All of this was happening against a background of English MPs supporting the Labour manifesto, but the majority of them were not great enthusiasts for devolution for Scotland. A number of them, particularly in the north of England, thought it would reinforce all the advantages Scotland had over them. They were always uneasy and sometimes downright hostile.

Our strength was that we had two powerful allies in Cabinet – the Prime Minister and the Chancellor. While Tony Blair and Gordon Brown both had strong views on preserving the integrity of the UK, they were always ready to intercede when it was to Donald's, and Scotland's, benefit.

Some have tried to assert that Downing Street attempted to contain and control devolution. It was important to Donald Dewar to get it right for Scotland and just as important for the Prime Minister to get it right for the United Kingdom.

Soon after being made Secretary of State for Scotland following the election, Donald had a series of meetings with Blair, during which they firmly established the essentials of the devolution scheme. From then on, the Prime Minister regarded the agreements they reached as 'non-negotiable' – including issues on which other Cabinet Ministers profoundly disagreed.

The main difference from the failed Scotland Act of 1978 was in the devolved and retained powers. Whereas the previous act listed all the powers that were to be given to the Scottish Assembly, the 1997 version detailed all the powers that were to be kept by the Westminster Parliament and these were enshrined in 'concordats' with the various UK departments.

This, in fact, made the negotiations more straightforward, but did not make them any less bruising. There was conflict with the Department of Trade and Industry over aid for enterprise and industry, because of their fears that Scotland could gain what they saw as unfair advantage over the English regions on inward investment, as well as hard negotiations over energy, transport, the environment, equal opportunities and race relations, and relations with Europe.

Throughout, the substance remained: the Scottish Parliament, with a budget of £15 billion, would be responsible for the issues which most directly affected Scots from the cradle to the grave in their daily lives. The devolved powers included all aspects of healthcare; education from nursery to university and lifelong learning; law and order; housing and the whole range of local government, including social services; transport; enterprise, business and tourism; the spending of European regional funds; the environment, agriculture, forestry and fisheries; and the arts and sport.

And, of course, the fine detail of the power to vary plus or minus 3p in the pound income tax for which the Scottish people had voted in the second question of the referendum. There were endless lawyerly wrangles over the tax status of people who lived on one side of the border and worked on the other, Scots residents who worked for English-based companies, private pensions paid to Scots from UK funds and so on and so on. But this was really only political knockabout with no real practical purpose.

Some people say the decisions on the Scottish Parliament building, which have since caused so much trouble, expense and controversy, were taken in London and should be paid for by Westminster. In fact, the new parliament building was only ever raised once in the DSWR committee and the issue was whether or not we could get extra money for it from the Treasury or whether it would be from the block grant. Donald Dewar had assumed it was a block grant issue and did not believe it was worth pursuing. I agreed with him.

The Treasury insisted that there should be a sentence in the White Paper saying it should be paid for out of the block grant. That reinforces my view that Chancellor Gordon Brown was not seeking a low-cost option and was not seeking to meddle, as was alleged by Sam Galbraith at the Fraser Inquiry. To have done so would have been inconsistent, because once it was accepted that the building would be paid for in Scotland, it was also accepted that the decisions would be taken in Scotland.

There is no doubt in my mind that in all the time I knew Donald Dewar as Secretary of State, minister and MP, the achievements of the White Paper were his finest hours. While I am critical of Donald in other areas, I have nothing but praise for him with regard to devolution and the White Paper.

I saw at first hand, for the first time ever in British political history, the process of devolution evolving. I saw a Secretary of State who was on top of every detail of a hugely complex subject, deploying his extraordinary knowledge of Westminster and not just his intellectual input but also surprising energy, enthusiasm and dedication.

Scots owe Donald Dewar a debt of gratitude for taking on Westminster and delivering a White Paper that was true to Scotland's aspirations.

The White Paper was everything, because it decided how much Westminster lost and how much Scotland won. If we had not produced a White Paper of that quality, we would have been seen to have failed to deliver on our manifesto and would have been berated by the political parties, the media and the public in Scotland.

Derry Irvine was forensic in his approach. Of all the people on DSWR, he subjected the issues to detailed logical analysis. After sessions with him, Donald Dewar could come back despondent, limp and wrung out like a wet rag. The then Lord Chancellor is an exceptional personality and, having been on sub-committees chaired by him, I can say it is not an experience for the faint-hearted.

Their personal history is well known and I have no knowledge of their relationship, but there was never any sign of animosity between the two men. Those who thought it was a piquant situation and a source for Westminster gossip could not have been further from the truth.

I do know that while Donald found it energy-sapping on an intellectual level he came through with flying colours against one of the foremost legal brains in Britain. Lord Irvine gave no quarter, but the same could be said of Donald.

While I was involved to a large extent with civil servants and advisers, Donald's role was really decisive. This was high politics, Westminster-style. The stakes were high because the Lord Chancellor was custodian of the UK constitution and Donald was in new territory, opening up a new future for Scotland and Britain. There was a lot to be gained and a lot to be lost.

The White Paper on Scottish devolution was published on 24 July 1997 and immediately became the best-selling government document ever. It was the subject of a double launch – in the House of Commons and later the same day, with much more jubilation, in Scotland. There was excitement at such a historic achievement and the fact that the first two months in government had been so productive and positive for Scotland. As professional politicians, along with the civil servants, we could feel it was a job well done and that we were part of something historic.

Donald Dewar was never overtly demonstrative. Modestly, he began his speech to the Commons: 'I am a little nervous about my place in history.' Later that day, at Edinburgh Castle, he admitted in his dry and droll style that he had been 'enormously encouraged, almost enthused', but he was in good form and he had every right to be so.

Naturally, the only sour note was struck by the Tories on the Opposition benches who heckled Donald and, with no sense of occasion, put him off his stride. I remember being so angry that I shouted across at them: 'You're pathetic!' It was then that Donald came up with one of the best parliamentary put-downs I have ever heard. Michael Ancram, who had been ejected from his Scottish seat and now represented Winchester, pulled him up for using the pronoun 'we' and wondered whether the Secretary of State was speaking for the people of Scotland or the Government of the United Kingdom. Donald replied with withering sarcasm: 'I am sorry. I made the cardinal error of assuming I was a Scot for the moment. The Right Honourable Gentleman may have suffered some psychological amputation that removed him from Scotland, but I have not.' In one off-the-cuff remark, he encapsulated the hypocrisy and the dilemma of the Scottish Tories and made clear that devolution was now unstoppable. No wonder we were all in triumphant mood when we left the Commons and took a plane from City Airport in London's

Docklands on what was dubbed, with some exaggeration, the 'Freedom Flight' for the celebration of the White Paper at Edinburgh Castle.

Polling focus groups showed that a 'yes, yes' vote was by no means certain. When the referendum was set for 11 September 1997, I cleared my ministerial diary and took charge of the campaign team in Keir Hardie House in Glasgow that had worked so well in the 1 May general election victory. Once again, it was strengthened by staff from Millbank including David Hill, who is now Tony Blair's head of media relations at No. 10 Downing Street.

The last thing we needed was any doubt which would be exploited by the Opposition, the media and the public. We needed an unequivocal 'Yes' to the second question on tax-varying power for the credibility and integrity of the Parliament.

Regional parliaments in Europe have financial powers, whether they are sales taxes or other forms of revenue. We believed that we would not have to use it in the short term, because the block grant would meet our needs – as has been proved by the Scottish Executive's underspend in successive years.

It was a power we would not use because it would make Scotland the highest-taxed part of the United Kingdom, with all the disadvantages that would mean in practical political terms and within industry and investment. It would have made Scotland uncompetitive against other areas of the UK and would have raised demands at Westminster to cut the block grant by the amount of extra tax we raised.

The most serious opposition to the tax power came from an unexpected source. Sir Bruce Pattullo, governor of the Bank of Scotland, quite rightly held himself aloof from politics throughout his term of office. In the middle of the referendum campaign he gave a rare newspaper interview – with the backing of the bank's board and obviously timed for maximum impact – in which he said that the tax-varying power would be dangerous. While the Bank of Scotland was neutral about a Scottish Parliament in principle, it was concerned that a higher tax regime in Scotland would be damaging for business and jobs. Giving the worst-case scenario, he warned that if the full 3p was levied, it would cost the average Scottish wage earner £6 per week.

Donald Dewar and I countered with a damage-limitation strategy in which we spoke to business audiences and individuals, reassuring them that the Parliament and Executive would help, not hinder, enterprise and in any case the power would not be used. The 'Scotland Forward' campaign also paraded a formidable group of businessmen, job creators and entrepreneurs who said they had nothing to fear from devolution.

On the popular front, Deputy Prime Minister John Prescott came to

Scotland to show his support for devolution and, in typically blunt fashion, told Sir Bruce to stick to banking and stay out of politics: 'Play around with your money and just leave us to get on with the politics.'

It was a timely reminder that, under the old way of doing things in Scotland, a small Establishment clique felt it had the right to exercise disproportionate influence over Scottish affairs. The interference from the top of the Mound might have been damaging, but, if anything, it caused resentment and reinforced the 'yes, yes' vote.

In these circumstances, it is reasonable for opponents to ask: why have the tax-varying power in the first place? The answer is that you can never say 'never'. When the rest of the United Kingdom changes, as inevitably it will, other regions may well have fiscal powers and start to use them for their own local reasons. That is the only circumstance in which I can see the Scottish Parliament's tax-varying power being invoked – but we should continue to debate this issue.

In Scotland, 1p on tax would raise £250 million. It would be possible for the Parliament to use the tax for one year only to raise that sum for a single specific purpose. They might put the proposition to the public in a referendum to see if they agree. If it were simply for unspecified spending, I believe the answer would be 'no', but if it were for a one-off project which had public sympathy or was to be levied over a specified time, Scots might well agree.

The tax-varying power allows us to think creatively, but our thinking remains too narrow and the debate on its use has too many distractions. The Nationalists simply see fiscal autonomy as independence; the Tories do not want Scots to have the power and certainly do not want it used under any circumstances; and it is difficult to know what the Liberal Democrats think. It requires some openness of mind and imagination to see circumstances in which the use of the tax-varying power might be possible and might even be beneficial. Most emphatically, one thing I would not recommend putting to the Scottish people is the use of the taxation power to pay for the extra cost of the new Holyrood building!

In the referendum campaign, there was a surprising unity between Labour, the SNP and the Liberal Democrats. There was an unspoken agreement between the three parties that we had to win the referendum.

There was never any doubt about the Liberal Democrats' stance, since their Scottish leader Jim Wallace had already said that a Parliament without tax powers was 'not worthy of the name'.

The Nationalists under Alex Salmond played a praiseworthy part, because there was heated debate in their party about the tactics for the vote. Although the SNP might poll only 20–25 per cent on a good day, it would have been deeply damaging if they had told their supporters to abstain or vote 'no'.

All other issues were secondary to getting a clear majority on both questions. There was an acknowledgement by the SNP that a defeat for the proposed devolved parliament would be a huge setback for any dreams of independence. There was also the very realistic consideration that if they had abstained or not supported the setting-up of the parliament, how could they have stood in the elections to it?

That was not a consideration that seemed to trouble the Tories. Their 'Think Twice' campaign calling for a 'no, no' vote had been launched by Brian Monteith, who later became an MSP. He was to be replaced, and later in the campaign the Conservatives' constitutional spokesman, Michael Ancram, scion of a long line of Scottish aristocrats, stupidly compared his party's stand against devolution to Churchill and Nazi Germany.

On Sunday, 31 August, with 11 days to go, the nation was hit by a tragic event which brought normal life in Britain to a bewildered halt. The death of Princess Diana in a car crash in Paris overshadowed everything and there was no point in campaigning, even if anyone had wanted to go against the general mood.

I agreed with the feeling that a period of mourning and respect was the proper response. Although I had some concerns because this was new territory, I did not think the break was as significant as some people feared, although politicians and party workers get carried away at elections and think it takes four weeks to get the message across. In fact, there is usually a lull in the middle and campaigners have to work hard to hold the public's attention.

Long campaigns are not necessarily more effective, with the final few days always the most crucial. The resumption of campaigning after Diana's funeral left only three days to make that final impact – and we were fortunate to be able to call on the world's best-known living Scotsman.

No one should underestimate the pull of an immensely popular figure like Sean Connery – I have always had the view that you are in a contest to win. The main thing is to get the voters out and you should field the best Scottish team you can.

On the Sunday campaigning resumed, Sean Connery took a symbolic boat trip across the Forth with Gordon Brown. The photograph of the two most prominent Scots with the Forth Railway Bridge in the background and a Saltire flag streaming out behind them was the best relaunch we could have had. It carried all of the vital messages, some of which have been described as corny, in an effective and widely used image – historic achievements behind us, in the same boat together, for the good of Scotland and its future.

Sean, Chancellor Gordon Brown and I had breakfast at the Hawes Inn in South Queensferry. His status as the most popular Scotsman alive was clear and well deserved. He was charming, particularly to the staff, and we talked about America, milk rounds and football (he had played for a Midlothian junior team).

Later that day, he addressed an all-party meeting in the Royal High School building (which everyone still assumed to be the potential parliament building) along with Donald Dewar, Alex Salmond and Jim Wallace. There was awed silence when he read from the Declaration of Arbroath and, sealing the mood of unity, added: 'This issue is above and beyond any political party.'

Despite the misgivings and concerns expressed by some Labour MPs, because of his avowed allegiance and financial support for the SNP, Sean was wholeheartedly on-side in the cross-party campaign for a Scottish Parliament.

It was a consultative referendum, not binding on the government. I suppose in the darkest reaches of my mind I thought that if we lost the vote we might still go ahead, although realistically that was never an option.

The turn-out in 1979 had cost us devolution. The pattern of ever-lower turn-outs in elections was already clear in 1997 and there was always the worry that a poor vote would undermine the credibility of the result. People were uneasy with the referendum because it is not part of the normal democratic process in Britain. Apart from the 1979 debacle in Scotland, there had only been two in the UK, on Europe.

In general elections, the electorate vote for a wide variety of reasons and they are influenced by different issues. The referendum was to be the biggest test of Scottish opinion on the single issue which had been biding its time for nearly a century. For many of us, there was a 'now or never' feeling because if devolution failed this test it would not come again in our generation.

The 60.1 per cent turn-out was not up to general election standard, but was enough to put the credibility of the result beyond question. An overwhelming 1,775,045 (74.3 per cent) voted 'Yes' to the Parliament, a 3–1 majority, and a similarly positive 1,512,889 (63.5 per cent) answered the tax question in the affirmative, a 2–1 majority.

Both votes were substantial enough to silence the critics and there was huge satisfaction, with quiet relief, at the solidity of the second vote. Democracy provides people with the opportunity to vote, especially for the power to raise their taxes.

Along with the result we had worked and hoped for came the realisation that it was only the beginning of a hard slog. No matter how good your campaign or how high your aspirations, if it is to be more than rhetoric there must be a totally workable and practical end product.

When Donald Dewar introduced the Scotland Bill on 18 December 1997, underpinned by the authority of the referendum result, he voiced the satisfaction of us all by quoting its opening words to the Scottish media with some relish: "'There shall be a Scottish Parliament" . . . I *like* that.'

Although the Secretary of State was in overall charge, I was politically responsible for getting the bill, with its 116 clauses and 8 schedules, through its parliamentary stages. Because it was a constitutional bill, every stage was in the main chamber and I spent 120 hours debating the bill on the floor of the House of Commons in sessions that would last from 3.15 p.m. to 10 p.m., two days and nights every week.

I was doing something in the House of Commons which I had never imagined I would be doing when I first entered it. It all stemmed from that phone call from Blair, and I began to realise that he had wanted someone who was committed, with proven experience, managerial, with an eye for detail – and a workaholic!

There were some bizarre debates on subjects like responsibility for seed manufacturing, but, because of the nature of the business, I had to be alert at all times, understand what every line of every clause was about and be prepared to examine every objection.

With our massive majority, the prospect of a defeat was remote, but I had to work with the whips to make sure we had divisions at the right time. Much of the debate was conducted in a near-empty House because, despite its importance, English (and many Scottish) MPs were not particularly interested in the technicalities and there was always the possibility for ambush or embarrassment. Because the bill was guillotined, the timetable put pressure on the Opposition and many of the debates and votes were on what they thought was important and the rest went through on the nod.

Much of the serious concern came from the Labour backbenches, and the most persistent and difficult of the critics was the indefatigable Tam Dalyell. He was always most courteous and deeply committed, but there were times when he could be mulish in his determination to find fault with devolution. Tam has the most remarkable antenna and a wide range of contacts among academics and experts on every subject, and he raised many pertinent questions. Often, it became wearying as he bogged down the committee in obscure detail and would read out, in full, letters he had received – but that is democracy and there is no greater exponent of it.

In the light of the referendum result, there had been an undertaking of no unnecessary obstruction by the Tories, but they had no clear opposition strategy other than striving for cheap political points. Over the decades, they had simply learned nothing and were utterly devoid of any interest in devolution. Despite their electoral wipe-out in Scotland and despite the clear declaration of will by the Scottish people in the referendum, they were ill at ease with the idea of conceding any form of responsible government to Scotland. Their jibes about the 'tartan tax' were no more than typical Tory alarmism, and, under the leadership of Michael Ancram, they were reduced to isolated forays and ambushes on issues which were, at best, marginal. They were intent on trivialising important subjects and exploiting obscure matters to gain publicity for scant political advantage. Their contribution was summed up, in my opinion, when one frustrated Tory MP threw a copy of *The Scotsman* across the floor of the House – the first time the paper made any impression on me – and the Speaker forced him to apologise.

In a curious way, the Scottish Parliament saved the Tories from extinction in Scotland. Under proportional representation, which they despised, they were able to rise from the rubble that was all that was left of their party and were elected to the very Parliament they had denigrated. Their conduct during the passing of the Scotland Act showed they were so short-sighted that they had no concept that devolution was not only good for Scotland but might also be good for them. Despite their worst efforts, we managed to pass an act which brought them back from political oblivion. I like to think their ambivalent and unsure contributions in the Scottish Parliament show they have the decency to be embarrassed by this rich irony.

The SNP cooperated with the guillotine, so we had an even larger majority behind us if we needed it. Much of what the Nationalists said was dated, tired and plain wrong, but they could not be seen to be obstructionist.

Our timetable was to have the first Scottish Parliament election by January 2000, but we were able to bring it forward to May 1999. We thought the process had gone so well that it would be useful to have as short a time as possible between referendum and full election so that we could built on the momentum created by the vote for devolution. In politics, the longer things are drawn out, the greater the chance of ambushes, skirmishes and what Harold Macmillan described as 'events, dear boy'.

Personally, I felt a sense of urgency. After all the expectations we had raised in the campaign for devolution, the Scottish people would be unforgiving if we allowed it to become bogged down at Westminster. We all wanted to see the White Paper tested in reality and to have our own Scottish Parliament up and running. I had a great sense of being part of history and, with the Secretary of State, helping to shape it. When you have a great sense of achievement, I have found it is often only the starting point for the next challenge.

VI

More to Life than Devolution

During the period from 1997 to 1999, devolution was dominant, but Scotland still had to be governed under the old system. From the May 1997 UK general election until the May 1999 Scottish Parliament election, my Scottish Home Affairs portfolio involved me in a darker side of Scotland which I had not fully experienced before.

What became known as 'the Jason Campbell affair' was the first and most instructive lesson I learned as a new minister – indeed, it could have been my last.

In the excitement of becoming a minister and dealing with important constitutional issues, it was easy to respond far too quickly and unthinkingly to a request from a Westminster colleague.

Campbell had been imprisoned for a particularly vicious murder in Glasgow against a background of sectarian hatred, and the Northern Ireland Secretary Mo Mowlam was seeking his transfer to a prison in the province as part of the peace process. When she telephoned, I was in a ministerial car and I agreed without any real knowledge of the ramifications of that off-the-cuff decision. In the mood of the time, we all wanted to do anything to help the new deal in Northern Ireland. Had I given more thought to the background of Campbell's crime, I would have realised the offence it would have caused for many people, especially the victim's family.

I quickly came to realise the harm that would be done in Scotland by giving the appearance that a murderer, who had viciously attacked an innocent young man on a Glasgow street and was motivated by the religious bigotry surrounding an 'Old Firm' football match, was somehow a 'political prisoner'. It would also give the impression that Scottish justice was somehow subservient to political interests in Northern Ireland.

On my own, I was determined to have the decision reversed, but Mo was completely uncompromising. She would not change her mind because she wanted this to be seen against the background of the peace process and said I would have to explain my attitude to the Prime Minister. After 40 minutes on the phone with Tony Blair, I took the decision that Campbell must stay where he was in a Scottish prison and I then imparted the outcome to Donald Dewar.

It was one of those situations that come at a minister out of the blue and had been a decision taken far too quickly on the basis of a mixture of friendship and unfamiliarity with the subject. From then on, I was ultra-cautious with any requests affecting prisoners, especially when dealing with 'lifers' and those being considered for parole.

I did not think Home Affairs needed a lawyer; in fact, I was happier not to be a lawyer. A lawyer's training, career and absorption into the legal establishment would have made it difficult to get a new perspective on law and order issues. I was able to look at them from the people's perspective, as they affected my constituents, and I was able to have a much more open and flexible mind on the changes that were needed. I often had differences of opinion with Donald Dewar, who was a lawyer, on things like sentencing policy, particularly regarding drug offences, and what I and many other people regarded as the 'soft' approach of the Liberal Democrats.

Making policy changes was difficult enough in this area, with an impressively wise and powerful Scottish legal establishment to cope with. The legal world is governed by precedent and a minister always has to respect the separation of powers between the government, which legislates, and the legal system, which oversees and administrates justice and protects the rights of the individual.

Home Affairs is an area of public policy affecting the nation's quality of life, in which a remarkable amount of work still needs to be done. We should be asking ourselves, what kind of Scotland do we want to live in?

The first priority was the ever-growing menace of drugs. Communities in virtually every part of Scotland are blighted by drug abuse, but it was in Easterhouse in Glasgow that I became involved with Mothers Against Drugs and met women who had lost sons and daughters to what was now a national scourge. I was struck by the disastrous effect drugs had on individuals, but also the impact on families and communities. This was one of the main reasons why I became closely involved with the setting up of the Drug Enforcement Agency to reinforce the work of the police in what is an ongoing war. In Scotland, many of the 'Mr Big' figures at the top of the supply chain are apparently upstanding members of the industrial and business community, whose seemingly respectable and legitimate businesses are used as fronts for laundering drug money.

Political parties are agreed on the need to tackle this social evil but differ on priorities and on how much emphasis should be given to punishment versus prevention and rehabilitation. One major conflict within the Scottish Parliament is over the legalisation of so-called 'soft' drugs.

Any movement on the legalisation of cannabis or changing drug classifications is a matter reserved for the British Government. What struck me in the debate was that we hear a great deal about 'recreational' use of drugs and it is argued that, unlike other drugs, cannabis does not harm people. I did not believe that when I was the Minister for Law and Order and I do not believe it now. International research has shown that prolonged use of cannabis can have detrimental effects on individuals and that it can act as a 'gateway' to abuse of hard drugs. I applaud the steps taken by the Government into further research of the use of cannabis for medical conditions, but careful balance is required. I believe the legalisation of cannabis would be a distortion of any serious approach to tackling drug abuse in Scotland.

There was also much agonising about the urgent need for more detoxification and rehabilitation facilities in Scotland. Although they are very expensive, they are the most effective means of getting people unhooked from addiction.

A harrowing but important 'wake-up' call for me was my ministerial involvement with prisons, particularly my experience in dealing with suicide victims at Cornton Vale, Scotland's women-only prison. An unacceptable proportion of Cornton Vale inmates – mainly young women and teenage girls – were serving sentences for crimes and non-payment of fines which were really the result of their addiction to drugs. By imprisoning them, we were punishing them for their crime, but – to coin a phrase – we were not dealing with the causes of their crime. It was a revolving door, because they were going into prison then coming out and re-offending.

This is not an easy problem to tackle because society has the right to expect that crimes will be punished, but sentencing these women to prison does not make much sense. Prison sentences handed down by courts, with a remarkable degree of discretion as to what they can impose, are no solution to the long-term problem. They have a disproportionate effect on these women and their families, with dire social consequences and serious implications for social work and childcare. In addition to their mental disintegration and the agonies of drug withdrawal, these women are deeply distressed about their children and their families.

In a short period, there were six suicides at Cornton Vale and, because I had taken such a high-profile interest, I had to respond to each suicide.

I made a number of visits to the prison and the suicide cells, which are clinical but grim and forbidding places. To prevent them from harming themselves, the inmates were given cardboard furniture and stripped of anything they could use as a ligature. Despite this, the woman were at such a low emotional ebb that they still managed to find ingenious ways to end their lives. The governor explained to me that they had tried everything, including virtually 24-hour surveillance, but some prisoners were so desperate that they managed to unpick every thread in their clothing to spin into a ligature. I am no psychiatrist but as a human being I can guess at the depth of despair that requires. I had conversations with young women who seemed pathetic, lifeless and absolutely forlorn.

We could encourage and exhort the courts to think of non-custodial detox-and-rehab options, although, to be fair to the legal authorities, there are many players in the system and there are still too few of these options due to lack of investment. I said at the time we should plan to halve the number of women going into Cornton Vale by providing more non-custodial facilities, but, sadly, there has been an increase in the population in that prison and no significant improvement in the available options.

On a visit to Finland, I learned they had halved the number of inmates in their prisons. Some of this was due to a change in the law so that some crimes were no longer automatically punishable by prison sentence, but they had also instituted more drug rehabilitation schemes.

As Home Affairs Minister, I was very conscious of trying to reflect the fears and concerns of the public on violent crime, antisocial behaviour and sex offenders. I was also conscious that we have a hard punitive culture in Scotland. That is easily understood because the notion of crime and punishment and the Calvinistic ethic still permeate our culture and attitudes.

Crime and punishment are firmly linked in the public mind, but if you have a punishment that does not reduce the incidence of that crime, costs vast amounts of taxpayers' money and does not deal with the causes, that should be a reason for national debate. Instead, the argument is over 'soft' and 'tough' options. To me, the soft option is to lock people up for no better reason than to satisfy a public urge for revenge. The really tough option is to find a more civilised but also more effective way of dealing with drug-related crime – which means much of the violence and many of the car thefts and crimes against property that plague our society. That is the debate we must have.

The conditions in some of our prisons were, quite simply, a disgrace for a supposedly civilised country. On my first visit to Perth, I held an impromptu press conference and, perhaps uncharacteristically for a minister, told the media what I thought of the atmosphere, the physical fabric and the unimaginable squalor. There was no slopping-out in English prisons and I found it intolerable and difficult to understand why we still had such a degrading practice in Scotland's jails. It was a failure of investment but it was also a failure to take seriously a gross infringement of human rights.

In Scotland, we have a hard core of serious male offenders who have to be imprisoned for public safety and for punishment. At the same time, the long-term futures of a significant number, often drug addicts, would best be served by a more intense rehabilitation regime. Anyone who advocates that is up against a very hard-line populist culture, the sentencing discretion of the courts, the constant squeeze on public resources and an unforgiving media.

Although Home Affairs brought me into contact with the darker side of Scottish life, it also had its lighter moments. In Barlinnie Prison in Glasgow, I sat on a bed and had a chat with one of the more difficult prisoners in the long-term wing. I was media-savvy enough to notice when the photographer was lining up his shot that the image he would get in his lens was my head between a pair of outsize breasts in a pin-up on the wall behind me. These are the things of which a politician has to be constantly aware!

Another inmate and I had an interesting chat about his personal history. He had smashed a bottle in a pub and slammed it in someone's face for no better reason than 'he was getting on my nerves'. As I left, he asked me: 'Is it true you're the Minister for Women?' This was during the time when Donald had given me additional responsibilities. When I said I was, he said: 'Well, next time you come, bring in one for me!'

There is one area in which I do believe a hard line should be taken. I fully sympathise with public concern about sex offenders and paedophiles, and support the strongest possible measures to protect women and children. I see nothing wrong with long sentences for such offenders and believe we must be very wary about their rehabilitation and release. That is why at Westminster I worked on the legislation involved in setting up a register of sex offenders and in making sure that the overriding consideration was public safety.

As the minister responsible, I took a very dim view of the unfeeling remarks made by the Chief Constable of Grampian Police, Ian Oliver, in a particularly harrowing child murder. He appeared to be blaming everybody, including the bereaved family, while shifting responsibility from his force and those who should have kept watch on a known paedophile. His comments were hurtful and insensitive, and took no account of the loss suffered by the victim's family or the sense of tragedy, outrage and alarm felt within the local community.

When children become victims, it evokes enormous natural concern.

There can never be 100 per cent protection, but we should not give vigilantes the opportunity to arouse fears in local communities and punish beyond the bounds of the legal system. Those who are responsible for close surveillance should make sure it is effective, and schools and other organisations should be alerted on a need-to-know basis.

Serious offences always loom large in the criminal justice system but to me what lacked sufficient attention was the whole question of antisocial behaviour. The general view of the ordinary people I represented, reinforced by comments I heard on my travels around Scotland, was that the police and courts were not doing enough to deter this kind of crime. In the minds of the public, there was a failure to understand the sheer hell people could experience as a result of a build-up of offensive behaviour.

My own experience was very real and personal. In my constituency in Glenrothes, the Graham family – known locally, and later nationally, as the 'Family from Hell' – had terrorised the community for years. People were afraid of the father and sons after a series of serious crimes committed against a background of prolonged and intense antisocial conduct. The lives of those who lived in their locality became absolute misery and finally they had had enough.

When eviction procedures were brought against the entire family, the community needed strength and leadership. I spent two hours in the witness box in the Sheriff Court as a witness against the Grahams, during which I was interrogated by Mr Graham, handling his own defence. The remarkable thing was that these were not ignorant people; there was intelligence in the family and two of the daughters were making respectable lives for themselves. The father and sons were simply malicious and irresponsibly wicked, intent on terrorising those around them. The most appalling example of this was when one of the sons on a joyriding spree in the neighbourhood ran down a young girl, whose leg had to be amputated. We won the eviction case and the family were evicted. Some people may say evictions do not solve such problems, but merely move them on. As far as the long-suffering residents of the street in Glenrothes were concerned, they not only won a victory but also rid themselves of an utterly destructive and evil force in their midst.

During all that time, I had police surveillance cameras at my home in Glenrothes to give protection against the possibility of reprisals against myself and my family. It was especially worrying because I spent so much of the week away from home at Westminster and in Edinburgh.

Throughout Scotland, I had no doubt similar families, gangs and individuals were creating the same kind of misery for others, especially old people. I was the minister responsible for putting legislation through the Westminster Parliament, for the first time creating antisocial behaviour orders and making this a recognised and serious issue. The new law offered the prospect of some hope for decent people whose lives were being ruined by this type of behaviour. It was also a strong message to the malicious and mindless who have this kind of so-called 'fun' at the expense of others. Disappointingly, local councils have not used this measure as much as they should do.

Crime and its consequences were also brought frighteningly close to home as a result of a decision I made in the 'Ice Cream Wars' affair. The cases of Thomas 'T.C.' Campbell and Joseph Steele, who had been found guilty and given life sentences in 1984 for the murder of six members of a rival family in Glasgow in the vicious war for the city's lucrative ice-cream van trade were up for review. Although both men constantly protested their innocence, I felt there was no reason why there should be any change in status and Donald Dewar agreed.

I was then alerted by the security services that threats had been made by unknown sources. At the same time, when I was on an official visit to Grampian region, I was informed that Tommy Sheridan and his Scottish Socialist mob had taken over my office in St Andrew's House in protest at my decision. They left after negotiations with the police and their only achievement was to empty the drinks cupboard.

My wife Julie and I went away for the weekend and when we returned to our home in St Andrews on Sunday morning, there was intense police activity in our street. The property of an older couple who lived in our cul-de-sac had been trashed and scrawled on one of their cars was 'McLeish you bastard'. They had got the wrong house, causing tremendous distress for the couple and £5,000 worth of damage to their home. Police intelligence, after checking surveillance cameras at our home and on the Forth Road Bridge, suggested this was another reprisal for my decision in the Ice Cream Wars case. The most spine-chilling aspect was to see police pictures of a strange-looking individual peering through the windows of our home.

In politics, you may not think you deserve some of the things that happen but you accept that a certain element of risk comes with office. What caused me great anguish was that my neighbours had to suffer and from then on had to put up with an obvious police presence and constant surveillance.

The general population are concerned and alarmed by the continuing high levels of violent crime, serious offending and property crimes, but antisocial behaviour encompasses a huge range of activity which can affect and harm ordinary people – vandalism, graffiti, foul language and lack of respect for elders.

In Scotland, there has been a breakdown of respect and rising levels of intolerance and insensitivity towards others. Like most Scots, I grew up in a society in which there were rules and norms which were never contravened; communities were self-policed by the local community. Today, people are more self-centred, less collectively and community minded; there have been traumatic changes in family structure and a loss of self-imposed community discipline.

Our present-day society is in danger of losing the values of respect and tolerance, a sense of community and helping others. Citizenship should be a way of life, not merely a subject taught in schools, but it starts in the home – and the most noticeable trait in modern Scotland is the shirking of responsibility within the family.

I have spent many hours in my surgeries with parents who complain about police, social workers, housing officers, teachers and anyone who may have something to do with their children. When I have confronted these parents with the uncomfortable truth that they are responsible for their children, it was usually met with anger and disbelief. Over-dependency on the State and official agencies allows too many people to evade their own responsibilities to their family and their community. I acknowledge that society has changed dramatically over the last two decades and that some families need real help in coping with their lives. That should not blinker us to the fact that a liberal and tolerant society can still be based on rights and responsibilities, and high community and personal standards.

Certain 'isms' – racism, sexism, sectarianism – are all forms of intolerance and narrow-mindedness. After 11 September 2001, outrageous and ill-informed comments were made about Muslims and I thought it important to visit a mosque in Glasgow, and then undertook to finance CCTV cameras at mosques across Scotland. There was, and still is, a feeling of vulnerability among the Islamic community that they are being affected by antagonism which should be directed against Al-Qaeda. They needed reassurance that their immensely valuable contribution to Scottish society is understood and that they are respected along with other religions. We have a good record of racial tolerance, and the more sensitive approach in Scotland contrasts favourably with the approach of some UK politicians. However, the issue of asylum seekers and the aftermath of 11 September show we must not become complacent.

Much good work is being done by the Scottish Executive on problems such as domestic violence, knife crime, alcoholism and what has become known as 'yob culture', but civilising Scotland is a long-term programme.

Among the areas requiring change is our 'macho culture' with its violence, domestic abuse and alcoholism, largely the legacy of our industrial history. Scotland remains a male-dominated society, but we are reaching the point where there are more women working than men. The impact of that on family life and society remains to be seen. Under devolution we have seen changes in the representation of women (for which Labour, of all the Scottish parties, deserves most credit) and their appointment to the highest offices. These are trends which have to continue, because they are important in themselves and because we have to keep changing that harder, tougher side of Scottish life which does not sit easily with other societies in Europe.

'Yob culture' is a highly charged term to describe young people behaving very badly. Some people say that it is a slur which stigmatises the younger generation. Of course, it is not a true picture of the majority of young Scots, and we have to accept that long-term policies are required to improve the opportunities available to young people in certain parts of Scotland. However, it should also be looked at from the point of view of those who have suffered – older people and law-abiding citizens who simply want to get on with their lives without harassment and intimidation. While understanding the problems of young people and making better provision for them, we cannot dismiss the suffering that is caused to others by taking an over-sympathetic view of those who are causing the problems.

It is a question of balance. The people I met in my constituency and on my travels were not anti-youth but had simply had enough of this type of behaviour. We do not want Scotland to be perceived in the twenty-first century as a mean-spirited country in which low standards are accepted.

Scotland can become a society in which everyone is valued and makes a contribution, reversing the undesirable social changes in which people feel they can pass responsibility on to others. There has to be a return to the common-sense realism, responsibility and sturdy self-reliance that used to be the hallmarks of the Scottish character.

While serving as Minister for Law and Order, I had the opportunity to visit Oklahoma State Penitentiary in McAlester. Oklahoma executed more people in 2001 than any other state in the US, and in 2003 was second in the national league tables. Oklahoma is located in the middle of the Bible belt, where there is a strong religious fundamentalist streak. Execution is by lethal injection and the execution chamber has the appearance of a hospital ward. As someone who is totally opposed to the death penalty, I was almost physically sick amid the surroundings where judicial killing takes place.

Americans know it is not a deterrent and that it has no role in penal policy in bringing down the murder rate. It is simply revenge.

I was horrified by the story of one of the supervisors of the execution unit, who told me that not long after getting the job he had suffered psychological problems. He was told to look at pictures of crime locations, including those of murders, rapes and other horrific crimes, and that would ease some of his concerns. He said it worked.

To me, the unit had a sinister and intimidating atmosphere. In addition to the death penalty, the state has life sentences without parole, so that as well as bodies being taken out after execution there are people dying of old age and natural causes – the only way their sentence is going to end.

I was struck by the fact that the inmates of death row were nearly all black and aged between 18 and their early 30s, having committed some of the most heinous and horrendous crimes imaginable. Most were locked up for 23 hours a day.

The death unit looks exactly like an operating theatre, but the clinical conditions do not change the fact that this is state-supported killing.

Those receiving the death penalty are strapped to a cross-shaped gurney and tubes are inserted through which they receive three injections – one to relax the muscles, the second to anaesthetise and the third to kill. The orderlies administering these doses are behind a screen. They are not doctors because under the Hippocratic Oath members of the medical profession cannot take life. The horror is that the second injection is supposed to put the subject to sleep, but new evidence suggests it shuts down the body but not the mind.

Above the head of the condemned person is a microphone and before the execution starts, he is asked if he has any last words. Frequently, one of the things the murderer says to the viewing audience, which can include the family of his victim or victims, is: 'You may think this will draw a line – but tomorrow morning you will still wake up feeling the same.' The tragic truth is that killing the killer may exact vengeance, but it does not bring closure to the bereaved.

Only the Iranians and Chinese are executing more people per head of population than the Americans and it is shocking that in a civilised society, such as the USA, this practice is still widespread. It is part of the 'High Noon', 'Wanted Dead or Alive' culture in a land of high gun crime and gun ownership, where – even after the slaughter of Columbine and the Washington sniper – the National Rifle Association are opposed even to checks on people buying weapons. In that kind of culture, American citizens become very protective of themselves and their families.

The visit to death row only confirmed in myself my opposition to the death penalty. I can accept heavier sentences, perhaps even life without parole, but I do not believe any government can judicially kill people. It is totally abhorrent and there is no dignity in the process for the executed, for those doing it, those witnessing it or for society as a whole. It begs questions about the social context of those who commit these crimes and the acceptance of a regime that is unforgiving, punitive and in no way prevents these crimes. Nor does it console those whose lives are shattered by the loss of a much-loved member of their family. Of course, the advent of DNA testing in America has confirmed that many innocent people have been executed. For them, there is no redress. The full appeal procedure for each death row inmate is estimated to run for ten years and cost nearly $11 million.

I recalled voting in the last Commons vote on the return of capital punishment. I have always taken a tough view on law and order and when I voted I remembered Peter Manuel, Scotland's worst mass murderer up to then – the appalling massacre of the innocents at Dunblane had still to happen – but still voted against the restoration of the death penalty in Britain.

VII

Creating the Parliament

We had an electoral system that was going to deliver 129 MSPs. We then had to fix up a temporary building, devise a blueprint for working procedures and the structure of the Scottish Parliament: the nuts and bolts of its daily working, its hours, standing orders, debates and everything that makes a modern parliament function. We set up the Consultative Steering Group (CSG), a committee with representatives of the political parties, industry, the STUC and other representatives of civic Scotland, which met at the Scottish Office at Victoria Quay in Leith and which I chaired. Our aim was to create a different kind of parliament with different procedures and a different atmosphere. We had a look at one or two other parliaments and were guided by some new thinking to the decision that this was going to be a family-friendly parliament with normal working hours, less formal and deferential, and more open, accountable and accessible.

The aim was to prepare for the new Scottish Parliament a document which it could either accept or reject. While all of that could have been done at Westminster, it seemed important that we should do it ourselves in Scotland. It made sense because it gave Scotland direct input into its own Parliament through an impartial, many-faceted group, which gave a sense of national ownership. There were some fierce debates, but in the end we were all satisfied with the pioneering role the CSG played.

Its blueprint was accepted as the basic structure of the Scottish Parliament and has stood the test of time. The physical appearance of the Scottish Parliament, with its non-confrontational horseshoe-shaped layout in deliberate contrast to Westminster's archaic 'two swords'-length apart' chamber, may be different, but most of the occupants of the Edinburgh Parliament still want it to be as adversarial as Westminster, perpetuating the knee-jerk divisions between parties with cut-and-thrust and generating more heat than light.

That may have been idealistic, but politics in Europe, North America and elsewhere are increasingly about values, ideologies and reasoned debate. Regional parliaments throughout Europe are more about achieving consensus where possible, more focused on issues that matter and more willing to involve those outside narrow politics. The Scottish Parliament should be closer physically and psychologically to the people and should be able to allow the whole of Scotland to become involved. Unfortunately at this stage, Holyrood merely replicates old-fashioned deep-seated political prejudices. Most of the differences between the political parties are small, especially on day-to-day issues, but a great deal is made of them. In particular, the enmity between Labour and the SNP is unnecessary and harmful. Role-playing is no substitute for converting devolution from mere constitutional change into a force for Scotland's general good.

Since it is elected by PR and no party has an automatic majority, individuals become more important and the Executive answers to Parliament in a way the Westminster Government does not. Scotland's First Minister is much more subject to control and scrutiny, and can lose votes in Parliament in a way that does not normally happen at Westminster. That parliamentary control is strengthened by having to submit the appointments of Scottish Executive ministers and deputies to the approval of the Parliament. While Parliament cannot reject one minister, if it is unhappy with any appointment it can reject them all.

Thanks to a more enlightened attitude by the parties, particularly Labour, the Scottish Parliament has the second-highest proportion of women among the world's parliaments, after Sweden. The committee system broke the Westminster mould by combining select committees and bill committees into what has become a highly effective and much-praised single committee system, including a Public Petitions Committee, which gives the ordinary Scot direct access to the Parliament.

I always knew it would be a difficult choice about whether to remain at Westminster or leave and make my future in the new Parliament. Politicians are no different from other people when it comes to change in their lives, and I was quite apprehensive about the decision to leave for Scotland and the uncertainty of the new era.

I enjoyed Westminster not only because of its political importance and, latterly, the challenge of being in government but also because of the comradeship. I have reason to know that the Prime Minister had reservations about my decision to go to Edinburgh. I worked closely with him in Opposition, as I had with Donald Dewar, George Robertson, Michael Meacher and Harriet Harman. My experience of more departments than anyone in Labour, having specialised in employment, social security, health, transport and Scotland, had given me a good grounding in the practicalities of our trade. I might have had a ministerial future of some kind at Westminster, but there was an inevitability about my decision to become an MSP. The decision was really made the moment I accepted the brief as Minister for Devolution.

There was an expectation that I would put my faith in what I was helping to create, and I accepted it would be seen as inconsistent to be so directly involved in setting up a new parliament without wanting to be a member of it.

The most important consideration was that the Secretary of State and I had worked hard in a very serious way to get to 6 May 1999, when we would have the first-ever election for a Scottish Parliament. I had been in from the beginning of the process, saw it through at Westminster and it would be exciting to be in at the start of the new Parliament. I had to see how my theories and proposals would work in reality.

These were overwhelming reasons for me to relinquish Westminster. I simply saw it as my duty and responsibility.

Soon after going to the Scottish Parliament, having been at Westminster, I recognised a factor which worries me about politicians at different levels of government. In the minds of many, there are 'first-' and 'second-class' representatives and a pecking order in which MPs look down on MSPs (who can forget or forgive the jibe by a Scottish Westminster MP about the 'White Heather Club' Government in Scotland?). In turn, MSPs look down on local government and all three have deep suspicions about Europe and MEPs.

We need to get to the point, as in other European countries, where there is a parity of esteem between politicians and where moving between regional, national and international bodies is regarded as natural. It should not be regarded as somehow more important to go to Westminster than it is to go to Holyrood. The responsibilities may be different, but they are still vital to the people they both represent. Holyrood has a £26 billion budget for 2005–6; the biggest councils in Scotland spend over £1 billion each; and Fife's budget is £½ billion. The leader of Glasgow Council has greater responsibilities than any MP or MSP, but to make such comparisons is to sow the seeds of division and unhealthy rivalry. The sensible view is that it is all taxpayers' money and it is all representative politics.

When I came back to the Scottish Parliament, I had no idea of the transformation that would be necessary. A new political theatre was opening up and regional government was going to be very different from the national Westminster government. The Westminster Parliament is sovereign and could question, control and constrain every aspect of British life. However, a powerful Prime Minister and party with a working majority rules absolutely, and the balance has shifted to Cabinet government.

That was no longer the case in Scotland, and I do not think Donald Dewar found it an easy transition. He enjoyed being the creator and custodian of devolution, guaranteeing his place in history, but he never settled to the new style of government. As someone conditioned by long years at Westminster, he did not have a particularly high regard for many of the new parliamentarians in terms of ideas and political quality. Often, he did not conceal his disdain – but then, they often deserved it.

Donald was also rattled by the media blitz to which he was subjected, and he hated the essentially unforgiving nature of sections of the Scottish press.

The sniping and snide criticisms by Labour MPs at Westminster were malicious and mischievous. Part of it was (and still is) ignorance of this new form of government. At least with Scottish MPs, you would expect them to speak to their MSP colleagues to gain some appreciation, but there are those who do not want to learn how devolution can work to everyone's advantage. No one should be in any doubt that there is a residual ill will at Westminster about devolved Scotland and, naturally, issues like the cost of the Holyrood building stoke the flames. At times, the ignorance among some MPs – whether wilful or not – is astonishing and, because of the fragility of the new constitutional settlement, it does untold damage. The precarious lack of constitutional safeguards means we must constantly be on our guard against the enemies of devolution.

Many Scottish MPs at Westminster feel the new Parliament has undermined their position and curtailed their media exposure. That is a challenge for them at Westminster and in Scotland, not for the Scottish MSPs. Westminster still has formidable responsibilities which impact directly on the lives of individuals, families and businesses in Scotland. It's for the Westminster MPs to demonstrate their significance.

One of the important things for the new Parliament was that it provided a completely clean sheet in new procedures for electing MSPs because of proportional representation. We could capture some of the high rhetoric of the new politics of Scotland by widening the interests, attracting a broader base and ensuring the complexity and differences in every part of Scotland were reflected in the new Parliament.

These were the aspirations, but the first hurdle was provided by the party political system itself. It was to be an equal opportunities parliament, so there was a major effort by the Labour Party to have gender balance. After the initial success of the 1999 election, the 2003 elections meant nearly 50 per cent of MSPs are women.

There were obvious difficulties in trying to achieve that. Under the party system, people have to join political parties to become candidates, but that is not everyone's preference. The Scottish Parliament list system held out the prospect of more independents and individual candidates, although it would still be a daunting task in vote-gathering and election costs.

The Labour Party devised a selection process which brought forward many new faces, but we were not trawling an entirely new pool of talent. Too many of those putting themselves forward were councillors, trade union officials and apparatchiks of one kind or another. At constituency level, many local parties opted for 'Buggins' turn' instead of looking for untried candidates with signs of promise.

At national level, the vetting process was supposed to be seeking 'the brightest and the best', clearing out dead wood and ending cronyism. Instead, the National Selection Board laid itself open to allegations that the Scottish leadership was more concerned with weeding out dissidents, removing awkward customers and ensuring a compliant Labour group in the Scottish Parliament. It was inevitable that the Scottish press would refer to the new intake as 'political clones' and named them 'Donald's Dollies', after the famous sheep.

Most of us had assumed that Westminster MPs would be approved automatically. We wanted the experience of a significant number from Westminster, but far fewer MPs chose to move back to Scotland than had been hoped.

It was surprising that those who failed the selection process included two Westminster MPs, Dennis Canavan and Ian Davidson; Mark Lazarowicz, the former leader of Edinburgh City Council (and now an MP); Isobel Lyndsey, who had been a valued member of the Scottish Constitutional Convention and had joined Labour from the SNP; Esther Robertson, a leading figure in the Campaign for a Scottish Assembly; Mary Picken, a highly regarded STUC official and spokesperson for Scottish Labour Action; and Susan Deacon – who appealed and later became the Scottish Health Minister!

Dennis Canavan proved a particularly costly omission. Dennis had created difficulties for the party and annoyed many of my colleagues with his strident views on a wide range of subjects, but he was a highly effective Labour constituency MP. To me, despite the antagonisms he had created, Dennis had managed to operate within the concept of the Labour Party as 'a broad church' and there should have been a more objective examination of his intentions.

It was curious, to say the least, that having been an MP for over a decade, he could continue to represent Labour at Westminster but was not good enough to represent Labour and his constituents at Holyrood. That inconsistency cost Labour the Falkirk West seat, which Dennis holds to this day as an Independent.

Donald Dewar was personally very hostile to him – which made Dennis's gesture of striding across the floor of the Parliament after being sworn in as MSP and shaking Donald's hand all the more breathtaking. It may have been meant in a spirit of reconciliation, but it was a classic piece of scene-stealing by Canavan, and Donald was startled and somewhat offended by it.

When I was First Minister after Donald's death, I got a call from the Chancellor of the Exchequer hinting that Dennis might want to return to the Labour fold. After discussions with him, and his further conversations with Gordon Brown, it was felt he was about to re-cross the floor, but he decided at the last minute he could not actually trust the party to agree that he would be accepted. He did not want to be put in the position of asking and being refused and, while he trusted the Chancellor and myself, he felt our assurances might be subverted by his opponents in the party.

For the first time in an election, the Scottish National Party were the main opposition. Post-1997, the Tories were dead in the water and the Liberal Democrats were a force, but only in specific areas. There was an understandable nervousness about the first election to be fought on Scottish soil about Scotland.

The 6 May 1999 election was the chance for the Nationalist 'big bang', when their wildest dreams might come true. For the first time we were having what amounted to a referendum on independence – because if Scots gave the SNP any kind of majority, they were starting the divorce procedure.

Our tactics amounted to what later came to be known as 'shock and awe'. That may seem crude, but the message had to be driven home that there were polarised positions about Scotland's future. The number one polling issue was that if the Nationalists won, it would mean separation and divorce from the United Kingdom.

Although I do not go as far as George Robertson's actual words that devolution would 'kill the SNP stone dead', I do believe devolution will eventually be the death of Scottish Nationalism in its present form.

Much of the SNP rhetoric creates unease among the Scottish people, who interpret much of what they say as a recipe for chaos, so the Nationalists are always going to try to distract the voters and distort their message to obscure their aims. Although they will not expose themselves in full frontal fashion, they seek ultimately to split Scotland from the United Kingdom, with a separate seat in the UN and separate membership of the EU. At different times, in an attempt to make this more attractive, they may disguise it as 'Independence in Europe' and more recently as 'fiscal autonomy', but we had to make the choice clear to Scottish voters: vote Labour and you stay in the United Kingdom – vote SNP and you leave the UK.

Gordon Brown and Douglas Alexander had set out the battle lines in a booklet *New Scotland, New Britain*, published by the John Smith Institute in the run-up to the election, with the theme: 'Better off together, worse off apart.'

They highlighted the stark, but deliberately understated, message of the SNP's election document that a simple majority, 65 seats, would be 'a mandate for independence negotiations'. They detailed the dire political and economic consequences for Scotland and the cost of setting up the apparatus of a wholly separate nation state, from a separate currency to embassies and consulates overseas.

Their most telling argument, which infuriated the Nationalists because of its truth, was the narrowness of identity politics and the way in which they would diminish us all. In particular, the issue of citizenship struck home, dividing cross-border Scottish families whose offspring resident in England would become 'children of Scots, but made foreigners in Scotland'.

Their booklet was the blueprint for the first Scottish Parliament election:

> The real battle in Scotland in May 1999 will be between those who put the politics of social justice first and those who practise the politics of national identity above and before anything else. Politics based on the expansive vision of social justice will defeat the narrow divisiveness of Nationalism.

It should not have been so surprising to commentators and opponents when Gordon Brown and Douglas Alexander took control of Scottish Labour's election campaign at the Delta House headquarters in Glasgow. As in the brilliantly successful UK election, Gordon was the master tactician and Douglas was appointed campaign director and ran the daily press conferences.

Ed Milliband, Gordon's special adviser at the Treasury, also came north with him, and John Rafferty, who became chief of staff to Donald Dewar in the First Minister's office, was the campaign's coordinator. It was thought inadvisable to have Scottish Secretary Helen Liddell too directly involved because of her official role as the link between Scotland and Downing Street, so the media were given to understand that she was attending to government responsibilities, i.e. 'running the country'.

Outsiders tried to make capital out of the fact that Donald Dewar and members of his team were sent on a tour of Scotland aboard a 'battle bus'. They failed to realise that this capitalised Donald's 'father of the nation' image and, by allowing voters to meet him personally, he was an undoubted electoral asset. Wherever he was, he relayed the public mood and concerns back to HQ and had a direct daily influence on the campaign.

The truth was that the Labour Party machine in Scotland, which had never been robust, was beginning to falter, as had just been shown by our poor performance in the European by-election in the north-east. The sharpness of attack provided by the reinforcements, along with greater resources for research and rebuttal, were badly needed.

Traditionally, Labour had been helped by the solidity of our vote, enduring through generations and across the classes in Scotland in a way it did not in the rest of Britain. The diffusion of the vote in a four-party context in Scotland, as opposed to three parties south of the border, had also been in our favour.

Over the years, the Labour Party in Scotland has been weakened by fragmentation and factionalism. Consequently, little thought has been given to the party's role and standing in Scotland and what influence the party can exert on Scottish affairs. The majority of Scots still share Labour's commitment to positive social change, but that instinct will not be satisfied until we have an invigorated and modernised party.

The logic of devolution should mean a more autonomous Labour Party in Scotland but it still lacks power over its own finances and internal affairs. Where is the Scottish Labour think tank, producing positive ideas and new policies? Where is the incisive communications machine?

An unexpected bonus for our campaign was that the SNP, under the usually astute Alex Salmond, managed to shoot itself in both feet. In the run-up to the election, Salmond described NATO bombing in the former Yugoslavia as 'unpardonable folly'. It was a typical knee-jerk attack on the UK Government, but also showed a lack of statesmanship and was a wild misinterpretation of public feeling. Electorally, it was 'unpardonable folly'.

Salmond and his team again miscalculated with their 'Penny for Scotland' proposal that Scots should reject the 1p in the pound tax cut in Gordon Brown's UK budget as a 'bribe' to Middle England and spend it on Scottish public services. This put the SNP at an obvious disadvantage as the only party planning to use the Parliament's tax-varying power and Scots did not accept Salmond's argument that it was merely a tax 'standstill'.

The problem for the Nationalists is that the views of those who speak for them range from a *Brigadoon/Braveheart* Celtic twilight to an old-fashioned left-of-Labour stance which wants Scotland to be like a pre-Gorbachev Russia. Seeking some up-to-date relevance, Salmond & Co. totally misread the situation on tax and public spending and suffered the humiliation of being forced to admit that there was a financial black hole in their plans for an independent Scotland.

Apart from the revelation of economic ineptitude, it has always been astonishing that a party which claims to be exclusively Scottish can be so consistently out of touch with the nation's mood. In desperation, the SNP decided take its campaign onto the streets, with the leadership using the language of the streets: 'Get the jaickets aff and get stuck in.'

The SNP also blamed the Scottish media, who had been more hostile to the Nationalists than ever before. The onslaught was so fierce that they produced their own newspaper, which proved an expensive flop. For once, I will defend the media and say it was absolutely right that they should have given the SNP a hard time, because the Nationalists were usually on the sidelines. Much of the media allowed the SNP to ebb and flow without any forensic analysis. Now, for the first time, they had to be examined as the potential opposition party in the new Parliament – and it was clear they were failing that test.

Scots had the right to know whether these were confused and sentimental separatists or whether they would take coherent policies to the Parliament. It was a crucial election for the credibility of Nationalism, and factors like the war and public finances undermined the pretence that they represented the instincts of the people of Scotland.

Apart from the independence debate, it was a reasonably quiet election with a 59 per cent poll. When Willie Hamilton was elected in Fife Central in the 1983 general election, the turn-out was 84 per cent, but in 2001 the vote in the same constituency dropped to only 54 per cent. In some Glasgow seats, the poll was nearly 40 per cent. I was disappointed by the turn-out in 1999, while recognising that it was not a reflection on the Scottish Parliament but was in line with a worldwide trend.

We had not realised the difficulties of the list system and had not given enough consideration to how we projected the complexities of the two-ballot system to the voters. This was particularly important for the Labour Party because by doing well in the first-past-the-post vote, as we always did, we would not gain too many list members.

We had not ensured that our supporters understood they should vote Labour *twice* and they did not see the point of my name being on the FPTP list for Fife Central, but also heading Labour's regional list for the second ballot. They reckoned, 'We'll support Henry on the first vote and anybody but Labour on the second ballot' – even though they did not know many of the names on the second ballot paper or what they stood for. With the appearance of the Scottish Socialist Party, the Greens and Independents, many voters did not exercise a positive choice and instead used their list vote for negative reasons.

The result was that we took 39 per cent of the first vote but only 34 per cent of the second, which gave us a total of 56 seats – 9 short of an overall majority. The SNP was second with 35 seats from 29 per cent and 27 per cent; the Tories crept in third with 18 seats from 16 per cent and 15 per cent; and the Liberal Democrats fourth with 17 seats from 14 per cent and 12 per cent. The minor parties and independents took only 3 per cent of the first vote but 11 per cent of the second vote, clearly showing the protest element. This gave the Green Party their first parliamentarian in Robin Harper and the SSP's Tommy Sheridan a regional seat. Dennis Canavan won the first-past-the-post vote in his constituency.

The Tories, a party grudging on devolution and opposed to electoral change, were saved from oblivion, but that is still not sufficient reason for them to be grateful. They continue to talk down devolution and have little regard for the electoral system that gave them a parliamentary voice. They have still to answer the basic question: 'What can the Conservative Party offer Scotland in the twenty-first century?' To date, apart from a couple of amusing individual Parliamentary turns, the answer is: 'Not a lot.'

The Scottish experience has confirmed my view that the list system is the poorest form of PR, because it becomes a Protesters' Charter and creates a two-tier parliament. Constituency MSPs have a localised link with those they represent, while list MSPs do not have the same constituency connection and often use their status to make mischief across a wide area. Whether MSPs accept it or not, 73 MSPs have direct constituency responsibilities while the remaining 56 are freelancing.

Coalition was the natural consequence of the new electoral system. We did not need an election to know that the result would inevitably mean a joint Labour–Liberal Democrat administration, since they were the only two parties with sufficient shared concerns, aspirations and policies.

I had never been involved in any form of power-sharing in my political life in local government or at Westminster. While those of us in the leaderships got on well enough (it would be hard to dislike the Scottish Lib Dem leader Jim Wallace), there were concerns at the rank-and-file level. Those who had fought them over the years knew that the Lib Dems were a diverse and sometimes eccentric lot who had subjected us to virulent attacks at local level. While we were constructing a solid coalition at the top, we knew that there was implacable hostility at ground level. Indeed, while the coalition talks were in progress between Donald Dewar and Jim Wallace, the newly elected Lib Dem MSP Donald Gorrie declared that he would not trust Labour any further than he could throw us.

Minority government had never been considered because that would have meant the Executive being at the mercy of the Parliament day in and day out, making government unstable and uncertain. Had we decided to go it alone, the first thing we would have had to do under the new settlement would have been to put Donald's ministerial team before the Parliament, and they might have been instantly rejected. The hope was that a formal arrangement would tie in some of the more recalcitrant Liberals and eliminate the danger of the Executive being ripped apart at any time. Experience has shown we were right to make that decision because even with the coalition, there have been times when it was difficult to muster a majority.

The coalition talks over four or five days were really about agreeing on a programme for Scotland. We could easily agree on 70–80 per cent of our policies, and the major differences were obviously on tuition fees and PR for local government. Liberal Democratic aspirations had to be accommodated and frequently the discussions became so acrimonious we needed civil service help to construct compromises that would be workable in practice. It was never plain sailing, but in the back of our minds we knew the whole of Scotland was watching and we had to make it a success.

The agreement on the abolition of up-front tuition fees had to be examined closely. There was a realisation that this was going to become a huge sticking point, which could have led to breakdown. It would mean that from the very inception of the Parliament we would have a policy in Scotland that was not then supported by the Labour Party and – as far as we knew then – would not be on the Labour Government's agenda in the UK. For the first time, devolution was going to come alive with a distinctive Scottish solution to a set of Scottish problems. Much of the discussion was not so much around the principle, as the nature of its implementation. What we attempted to do was to set it in the context of a longer look at higher education and student finances generally. On the Labour side, we did not have any other option but to agree and move onto the question of setting up a committee of inquiry.

Perhaps appropriately, the background to the talks was the shrieking of witches, 'ghosties and ghoulies and things that go bump in the night'. The reason was that we met in the former Lothian Council HQ at the corner of the High Street and George IV Bridge, which was to become the Parliament's administrative building, and the closes and courtyards around it were the venue for the Auld Edinburgh ghost tours.

I had my differences across the negotiating table with Ross Finnie because he was foremost in fighting the Lib Dem corner. We fought hard for what we wanted, but the Lib Dems had to fight even harder. Later, Ross Finnie was to become an excellent Minister for Environment and Rural Development, whose handling of the foot-and-mouth epidemic was exemplary when compared to the UK performance as a whole.

On their side, there was a fear of losing an important opportunity to make Liberal Democrats count. They were trying to gauge our commitment and there was natural and understandable suspicion on both sides. As the talks dragged on, certain sections of the media were obviously hoping for failure because that would make a better story.

No one should ever take credit away from Labour for the massive change in our loyalty to first-past-the-post elections. The Scottish Parliament did not have to have PR and it took the dominant party, who had formed a strong government at Westminster, to deliver it. It was a remarkable concession by Labour to permanently exclude itself from majority government in Scotland and create the conditions for coalition.

The Liberal Democrats had to be delighted because home rule had been their dream since the Gladstone era and this was their first whiff of power since the early part of the twentieth century, when the Liberals were in government in the UK. Ninety years later, the policy we had promoted was propelling them into ministerial office with the prospect of having their policies implemented.

That may be why Paddy Ashdown, the Lib Dems' UK leader, seemed more directly involved than Tony Blair, who took a more detached view. In Bute House, the First Minister's official residence in Edinburgh, which I was using as an overnight base during the talks, I was roused from my sleep in the early morning by a phone call. It was Paddy Ashdown looking for Donald Dewar and it was clear that he was using his Westminster friendship with Donald to make direct contact and seek to help reach a compromise.

By contrast, Tony Blair had sufficient faith in Donald and myself to leave us to get on with the negotiations. The Prime Minister was amongst the first to grasp the reality of devolution and recognise there would be issues on which our policies would have to differ. Others did not realise this, because Westminster MPs are predominantly centrists. On an issue like free personal care for the elderly, their worry was that Opposition members and some of their own colleagues would demand similar treatment for England and Wales. They had not expected policy differences and for many of them it was not part of the devolution deal to which they thought they had agreed. They could not adjust their thinking from a big Westminster majority and one-party control to understand how political life changes with coalition. They had to be reminded that the Lib Dems were now partners and that was what made the Scottish Government tick.

It was with a sense of history that the first Scottish Cabinet met in Bute House on 18 May 1999. I looked around the table and felt it was a good mix of experience and youth. There were three bright new women in

Wendy Alexander (Communities), Susan Deacon (Health) and Sarah Boyack (Transport); the Westminster and Government experience of Donald, myself (Enterprise and Lifelong Learning) and Sam Galbraith (Children and Education); Jack McConnell (Finance), who had been general secretary of the Scottish Labour Party; Tom McCabe (Parliament), who came with a good reputation from the tough arena of local government in Lanarkshire; Jim Wallace (Deputy Minister and Minister for Justice) and Ross Finnie (Rural Affairs) for the Lib Dems; and Lord Hardie, the Lord Advocate.

In the early days of the Parliament, Tom McCabe proved his worth by doing a tremendous job in a triple role for which there is no Westminster equivalent. As Parliament Minister, he combined Chief Whip, Leader of the House and party manager, and oversaw the new procedures and represented the interests of MSPs. He was a tough disciplinarian who did not suffer fools gladly and he gave a lot of sound advice.

One result of the coalition affected me personally. I went into the election as unofficial deputy to Donald Dewar and I had been Scottish Home Affairs Minister at Westminster. At the coalition talks, Donald simply announced that Jim Wallace would be Deputy First Minister and Minister for Justice (the equivalent of Home Affairs) in the Scottish Executive. Although it was no surprise, since I had become used to Donald's way of working, I had not even been consulted.

VIII

THAT Building

The national scandal that has surrounded the new Holyrood building has tainted our achievement, inflicted critical damage on the concept of devolution and brought our new Scottish Parliament into disrepute. The grotesque cost inflation and the day-by-day revelations in the Fraser Inquiry of irregularities, inefficiency and incompetence have created an atmosphere of shame instead of pride.

Given all that, my early warning to Donald Dewar and the Scottish Office team to 'ca' canny' on the new building may seem to have shown remarkable foresight. When I gave evidence before his inquiry, Lord Fraser actually described it as 'prescient'. In fact, it was plain common sense. With all that was involved in setting up the Parliament, I thought we had enough work to be getting on with. It was clear that the question of a permanent home would be time consuming and I did not see it as an overwhelmingly urgent priority.

This was to be no ordinary building project, because there was so much riding on it for the Scottish Parliament as a living and changing institution, but also as a worldwide icon and emblem of Scotland. I regarded it as daunting because so much rested on it. National prestige and pride demanded that we should use an architectural design that would express a historic nation in a modern way.

My memo of 11 June 1997 advocated minimum expenditure on the old Royal High School and 'making a virtue of that' while leaving open the possibility of the new Parliament deciding its own future. Paraphrasing my views, my private secretary added: 'The Minister also commented that, if the timescale and political costs had been more favourable, he would have preferred the bold option of a greenfield site.'

In 1999, we did not have the temporary home in the Church of Scotland's Assembly Hall on the Mound – which, by the way, was not a cheap option. We might have spent a similar amount on turning the RHS building into a temporary home, which would have also had the benefit of exposing its shortcomings as a permanent home for the Parliament. By the time we did settle on the Mound, the plans for the new building, under Donald's control, were virtually complete.

It really did not make any sense because I knew the parties and parliamentarians at Holyrood would want to make big changes, with the added finance that would have to go with that. I still believe that throughout the process we had neither the capacity nor competence at ministerial or civil servant level to select a site and design a new parliament building.

Written only five and a half weeks after we won the general election – we were hardly behind our desks at the Scottish Office – my memo is an indication of what I believed was the unnecessary rush for a new Scottish Parliament building. It did seem to me to be storing up trouble for the future of the Parliament and what was needed was breathing space and time to look at all the options. Even at that early stage (and even though there was then only one site to look at) it was obvious to me that we were taking on too much. And I believed that the new Parliament would have no sense of ownership of its own home because the MSPs who would be using it were not going to be involved in its creation.

People have asked why my memo was not followed up and why I did not press it further. The answer is straightforward: if the Secretary of State did not want something, it did not happen. At Westminster, the Secretary of State is a god who can involve their ministers and under-secretaries or not. In the UK Cabinet system, as we then were, the Secretary of State has ultimate authority on day-to-day policy.

I was no longer 'in the loop', presumably because of the attitude I had expressed in my memo. Donald Dewar had a way of working in which you might be involved in discussion, but he was still driving it. He would take decisions with civil servants, which were very difficult to shift later, even though he would listen to arguments.

I know the civil servants suggested that I should chair the selection panel for the designer competition, since I had taken part in preliminary consultations with the Royal Incorporation of Architects in Scotland and the Royal Fine Art Commission for Scotland. However, I heard nothing of that until after the panel had been chosen and publicly announced. Donald had assumed the chair and I simply got on with what I was doing, which was the more immediate priority of delivering devolution.

We were seeking consensus through the cross-party Consultative Steering Group, but there was no consensus on the Holyrood building and no consultation. There was no room for doubt that Donald Dewar had a very particular and personal interest in the project.

Even after devolution, Donald was very reluctant to give it up. I understood that, because he was seen as the 'father of the nation' and the custodian of everything to do with devolution. He simply found it very difficult to let go.

I urged him to release his grip on the building, because it would inevitably have to pass to the Scottish Parliamentary Corporate Body (SPCB), chaired by the Presiding Officer with representatives of the main parties. They could argue that they were presented with a problem-ridden site, a bad brief, an underestimated budget and could claim they were given 'mission impossible'. That does not mean that searching questions should not be asked about the role of the SPCB and the extent of their responsibility for the staggering escalation of the cost after they took over.

Nor did I think we had the capacity within the Scottish Office and, later, the Scottish Executive, for such a project. That is not a slight on the civil servants, but this was a unique undertaking. The evidence that has emerged in the Fraser Inquiry about senior civil servants being put in charge of the Holyrood contract without essential qualifications and experience has confirmed my doubts were justified.

There are now huge issues over the selection process, the framing of contracts, overseeing them, accountability and efficiency issues, value for money, sticking to a budget and a timescale, all of which need to be answered. It seems to me to be near-impossible for a building which was initially, if over-optimistically, budgeted at £50 million to become £200 million at the handover to the SPCB, and eventually over £400 million. Yet that is what has happened.

Early on, there were three positions:

- Do what Donald wanted, which was to decide everything and start building.
- Do nothing, get a temporary home and leave it to the newly elected MSPs.
- Work up some options to a level where they could be left for the final decisions to be taken by the Parliament with the message: we feel this is reasonable and sensible and we are passing it over to you.

Those of us on the Steering Group felt there were more important things to do and that it would be better to leave the new Parliament to pick the location and design and take it forward. The danger was that we would set in motion something that would run out of control. All the seeds of the problems were sown.

Donald's main concern was that the parliament would not be able to make decisions under the spotlight of the Scottish people and the press. There might have been counter-proposals that would delay the project by bogging it down in arguments, such as demands to site it in the west of Scotland or anywhere else. And there was always the possibility that MSPs might baulk at spending so much money on their new home and decide to spend it on other priorities. Or the Parliament would want to stamp its authority on the plans, which it did by doubling the space and developing its own specifications for a building that was already well advanced.

Even when Donald Dewar became First Minister, he found it hard to give up his 'ownership' of the new building even though it should have been left to the Parliamentary Bureau. We were responsible for the work of the Scottish Executive, but the Parliament should have been responsible for its own building. Tony Blair is responsible for the UK Government, but he is not responsible for the Palace of Westminster and all the other parliamentary buildings.

We had been the custodians of the preliminary stage of devolution; we had worked on it and were elected in 1997 with it as a central part of our manifesto; we had the right and responsibility to get on with devolution – but it just felt to me that the parliament building should be outwith that process. There was a case to be made for allowing the new parliamentarians, when elected, to influence and shape the building of which they would be the key players. Would they welcome us picking the site, investigating its possibilities, putting it out to tender and starting to build it, when they had not been allowed to have anything to do with it? It was a question of ownership and it just seemed to me to be storing up difficulties for the days ahead. I was also concerned that devolution was already such a huge challenge that we might be seen needlessly to be accelerating the process and not doing as thorough a job as we should.

The political parties did not feel they had any ownership of Scotland's new Parliament. After they became involved, far-reaching and expensive changes were made at too late a stage. It would have been better to widen the membership of the panel or allow the Consultative Steering Group, which included the leaders of all the political parties, to drive the project forward from its inception. Some may argue that is naive; but I would point out the entire report of the CSG on the parliamentary infrastructure was accepted virtually without change by the Scottish Parliament. From a political point of view, every time a Tory, Liberal or Nationalist jumped up in Parliament two years later to challenge decisions already made, it could have been pointed out that they had been involved from the start.

Outside Donald's office, the new Scottish Parliament building was not a pre-devolution priority. My official papers on the White Paper comment:

The happiest years? My first
year at Buckhaven High School
– the short back-and-sides
haircut was compulsory.

My grandfather Henry and mother
Mary at a Co-op function.

My grandparents (right) began the family tradition
of local service and shaped my future.

The author with his mother
Mary on a family holiday.

My grandfather Henry, father
Harry – who between them had 80
years' experience in the pits – and
my grandmother.

Three generations –
grandfather, father
and son.

My first wife Margaret (front) helping out Age
Concern in the constituency.

My grandfather (back row, third from left)
wore the East Fife jersey 50 years before me.

I was the youngest-ever player (back row, far left)
to play professionally for East Fife.

Wearing the Scotland jersey.

Early days at Bayview.

The Scotland jersey I never got to wear – promoting our Euro 2008
bid with Scotland manager Craig Brown.(© *Daily Record*)

Catching up on education –
graduating from Heriot-Watt
University in urban planning.

As the leader of Fife Regional
Council, with Dennis Canavan (left),
and Billy Connolly, who gave
fundraising performances for the
families of striking miners.

With fellow Fife MP Gordon
Brown – from the start and to this
day a friend of devolution.
(© *Daily Record*)

Closer to Europe – with Neil Kinnock, vice-
president of the European Commission, and
Scottish Secretary Helen Liddell.

Tony Blair in good form at the
2001 Scottish Labour
conference in Inverness.
(© *Daily Record*)

YES, YES . . . Scotland rises to the referendum
challenge. A triumph for Donald Dewar.
(© *Daily Record*)

Left: The first Scottish
Cabinet: Donald Dewar
and his coalition
ministers.

Below left: At the
dispatch box in
Parliament. Margaret
Curran and Alasdair
Morrison look on.
(© 2001 Scottish
Parliamentary
Corporate Body)

Below right: 'Team
McLeish': my Cabinet
meets at Bute House.
(© *Daily Record*)

The things a minister has to do! With the firefighters at Gullane training centre.

Inspecting a drugs haul with Strathclyde Chief Constable John Orr.

'Elizabeth II meets Henry I,' said the headline on the day of my inauguration as First Minister.

An audience with His Holiness Pope John Paul II – Cardinal Thomas Winning makes the introduction.

Scotland in the White House: a historic meeting in the
Oval Office with President George W. Bush.

Inset: Speaking on the steps of the Capitol during
America's Tartan Day celebration.

My wife Julie hosts a lunch with Mrs Mbeki during
the South African President's visit to Scotland.
(© The Scotsman Publications Limited)

At the early stages of drafting, the issue of the accommodation of the Parliament appears to have been given no prominence at all.

When the first draft of the White Paper was put to Scottish Office ministers towards the end of May 1997, it would appear that references were limited to an assumption that the Scottish Constitutional Convention's proposal for use of the former Old Royal High School would be adopted.

By 13 June, Donald was exercising personal control and instructed his officials to redraft the White Paper 'to reflect a decision not automatically to go for the old Royal High School as the site for the Parliament'.

The description of the old Royal High School building as 'a political shibboleth' has never been positively attributed to Donald Dewar but I am convinced he was the most likely person to have used such an archaic phrase. It is very easy to say that it was eliminated because of Donald's alleged view that the RHS building had become a Nationalist symbol. In the minds of many people it had become the focus of political controversy but more important was the inadequacy of the RHS building itself.

For decades, it had been assumed this would be the home of the new Scottish Parliament, but, like other ministers, I was firmly of the opinion that, on its own, it was not a runner. Although the site is attractive, it is a building with very limited architectural merit. It was a poor chamber for the Scottish Assembly envisaged in 1979, and 20 years later its inadequacies were even more obvious.

One option that was never discussed was the possibility of demolishing the RHS building as part of a much larger redevelopment on Calton Hill and along Regent Road towards Princes Street. I realise that may seem sacrilegious to some, but I fail to see why.

The RHS building was a constricted site which required an imaginative approach. Across the road from the RHS building is the 1920s art deco St Andrew's House, an impressive building in an important part of Edinburgh, with a magnificent view to the south and a hub of communications close by, with railway station, bus station and Princes Street literally a stone's throw away. It has ready-made office accommodation and below Calton Hill level there is room for the development of a full-size debating chamber and committee rooms.

It is easy, with the benefit of hindsight, to see that as more prestigious buildings became available at the General Post Office on the North Bridge corner, the space from Princes Street to Calton Hill had a great deal going for it. In terms of urban regeneration (which was my subject), there was a failure of imagination.

The area could have become a parliamentary campus, bringing

together Government, Parliament, civil service and politics close to the public throng at the heart of Edinburgh. It had the potential to become Scotland's Whitehall and still be at the heart of Edinburgh.

The merits of the site became lost in the political background. Also, there were the new options of a greenfield site at Leith, or utilising the existing Scotland Office at Victoria Quay with a completely new debating chamber alongside it, and Haymarket in central Edinburgh which emerged from a list of 30 possible sites supplied by the city. Leith had much to recommend it, especially with the incentive that we could have got the site for free because of the huge benefits for urban regeneration it would bring to the area. It was decided, however, the site did not have a sufficient sense of history and tradition and was not central enough.

Official papers for June 1997 also show that Donald dismissed Victoria Quay and the redevelopment of St Andrew's House 'at the outset'.

Then in December came the revelation that Holyrood was the front-runner. The site was added by Donald and officials on 8 December, less than a month after I had been briefed to announce that consultants would be commissioned for design feasibility studies into alternative sites. A letter had arrived on 3 October from DM Hall, chartered surveyors for Scottish and Newcastle plc, who owned the Holyrood site, and it was minuted that Holyrood:

> . . . contrary to previous expectations had just become available to
> a timescale that it was thought would permit a Parliament
> building to be built by 2001.

From then on, everything was done in a rush. Donald said he favoured Holyrood 'on policy grounds', explaining the new building 'would provide a practical working home for the Scottish Parliament as well as a symbol of the new system of government, and [he hoped] a building of some architectural worth, which would be a statement of confidence in the new constitutional arrangements'. He was enormously attracted by the setting at Holyrood and the juxtaposition of the Palace and the park. The decision to proceed with Holyrood was announced on 9 January.

A 'design' versus 'designer' competition was discussed. Months earlier, Donald had announced that the design would be subject to competition and there would be an element of public consultation. He preferred a designer competition because it would be quicker, give more client control and 'would provide greater assurance that the selected designer would be competent and well resourced'.

I believe that romanticism and the link with Catalonia, itself recently devolved within the Spanish state, played a big part in the selection of

Enric Miralles as the architect. After picking the designer and the site, the debate, which was already limited, became even more so.

My hope is that Lord Fraser's inquiry into the reasons for the spiralling cost of the Parliament building will not further damage devolution or detract from its historic achievement. While it is important to establish these facts, the search for the truth should be greater than a search for scapegoats, and it cannot be allowed to override the consideration that Scotland's Parliament needs a home of which we can all be proud.

Instead, it can provide insights for the future spending of hundreds of millions of pounds on capital projects. The Scottish Government and the Parliament will continue to approve public sector projects, none of which may be on the scale of the Parliament building, but the lessons of Holyrood can still be applied to them.

In the rush to deliver Holyrood, important questions of capacity and competence were brushed aside. Did we have the capacity within the ministerial team and the civil service to give this unique and complex project the expertise and close oversight it needed? Did we have the necessary qualifications, management savvy and insights to deal with all the things it would throw up? Should we strengthen the team?

In my experience, the civil servants in Edinburgh do an excellent job and are among the best in Britain, which means the world. That did not prevent my feeling that we should have brought in outside expertise. Nobody is building parliaments. There are many supermarkets and office blocks but, apart from Berlin, there are no new national assembly buildings to use as a yardstick. Although we did look at some large public projects elsewhere in Europe, it was not done in any detailed manner, which would have allowed lessons to be learnt. It seemed advisable to take more advice and assistance from the UK civil service, even if there might have been some parochial objections in Scotland.

There were other factors at work to do with competitiveness, cost control, value for money and efficiency. If we look at these properly, we may avoid making the same mistakes in the management of big public projects in the future.

I, for one, believe all of the heartache, recrimination and anxiety, and the search for scapegoats, will be forgotten in the longer term. We will end up with one of the most ambitious and exciting buildings in the world, an architectural achievement on a world heritage site in Scotland's historic capital that will be a modern statement of a historic nation making a new beginning in the twenty-first century. It may not be Miralles's original design, but it will still be all of these things.

IX

A Shaky Start

I knew the Scottish Parliament meant coalition and taking the Lib Dems into the Executive. I was unofficial deputy to Donald Dewar (although that was not something he ever took too seriously) and I had been Home Affairs Minister for the two years since the 1997 election.

Although there was no discussion between Donald and myself, I heard almost incidentally that Jim Wallace had become Deputy First Minister and Justice Minister. The discussions with Jim Wallace were private and I was excluded from them. It was not so much the outcome as the manner in which it was done that bothered me.

I had been thinking of becoming Minister for Finance, but I believed, and still do, that Minister for Enterprise and Lifelong Learning was far more important. Enterprise Minister allowed the opportunity for imagination, innovation and the ability to influence Scotland's future.

Donald did not view the post of Finance Minister too highly either, because it was more managerial, and he gave it to Jack McConnell. The Finance Minister could not negotiate the block grant, which was set by the Barnett formula, and without a revenue-raising role, his main task would be modernising government in Scotland.

Having said that, there were significant increases in public spending under a very ambitious Chancellor of the Exchequer and UK Labour Government. After consolidating for the first two years, which caused anxiety in the party, the savings went into providing Scotland with the biggest boost to public spending in the post-Second World War period. Amidst all his other considerations, Chancellor Gordon Brown ensured that finance was not a problem for the new Scottish Parliament. In fact, since devolution the problem for the Scottish Executive appears to have been spending money, not the lack of it – as successive under-spends have shown.

In a future Scotland, this does raise an important question: how much influence will we have over the block grant? There are real concerns about a Westminster-inspired reassessment of financial needs in Scotland and, as in other regions and provinces throughout Europe, whether there will be a serious debate about the raising of further revenues – whether by the use of the 3p in the pound tax-varying power, which I do not think can happen until we have substantial devolution throughout the whole of the United Kingdom; a more imaginative use of the power, such as the US-style voter approval of specific spending proposals; or whether we should look at other forms of revenue-raising like sales taxes or tourist taxes. None of these are on any party agenda but they should always be matters for debate as devolution matures and Scotland faces new challenges.

Again, this refers back to my abiding concern about the stability of the constitutional settlement. The sovereignty of Westminster is absolute and the Scottish Parliament and its powers can be abolished with a one-line clause in a House of Commons Bill. Most other devolved governments and regions in Europe have constitutions with built-in safeguards – not conceived as handed-down devolution, but in those countries a sharing of power with all that means.

Financially, the Scottish Parliament has been fortunate to start life with a New Labour Government committed to a huge increase in public spending; a Chancellor of the Exchequer who lives, breathes and thinks Scotland; and the block grant Barnett formula, which has stood the test of time and has been fair to Scotland. There is nothing in writing, no binding legal agreement, no constitutional guarantee for any or all of that.

We have seen in the first few years of devolution that some, often English Labour MPs, feel a sense of grievance when they compare the treatment of their regions to the contribution Scotland receives from UK funds and they have been making noises about revisiting the Barnett formula.

Others – including, I regret to say, Scottish MPs – instinctively do not like devolution. They seize on the annual Government Expenditure and Revenue in Scotland (GERS) report as proof that Scotland is somehow 'sponging' off the rest of the UK. Misleading headlines in our own newspapers, such as 'Scotland makes a net gain of billions from Treasury coffers', perpetuate this distortion of the truth.

The GERS report for 2001–2 shows that State spending in Scotland totalled £39.4 billion while £31.4 billion was raised in tax and national insurance, which is interpreted as an £8 billion 'subsidy' to Scotland. That misinterpretation ignores the fact that Scotland's needs are being assessed and met as part of a strong and stable United Kingdom during a period of higher spending on public services in the UK as a whole. Nor does anyone make such a surplus-or-deficit calculation for the needier regions of England – nor, for that matter, London.

While I hope the plus factors of a Labour Government, a sympathetic Chancellor and the block grant all continue for many years to come, that cannot be guaranteed. Without any formal constitutional safeguards, should we in Scotland seek to consolidate the basis on which devolution has been applied? Or should we just wait and see what changes may be inflicted on us?

This should be a wake-up call to make sure the settlement is not undermined at some time in the future. Every party in Scotland that wants an enduring settlement has to recognise that there are no safeguards, and unless or until there is devolution in England we will have an asymmetrical settlement. It should be a cause for concern that, if devolution falls into the wrong hands, there could be problems.

Public expenditure could be one of the areas where a future Tory government might cut back and provoke a public outcry in Scotland. That could revive our worst memories of the Thatcher–Major era, with the additional explosive element of undoing devolution completely or by degrees. It is important that these matters are not lost to debate, even though they may provide grist to the Nationalist mill. By not facing them and failing to put in place the necessary guarantees for devolution, we would be providing the conditions for Nationalist feeling to flare up.

No matter what judgements are made about devolution and the problems we have experienced, it has to be acknowledged that just two years and two weeks after Labour won power in 1997 we were sitting around the table as the Scottish Cabinet. The philosophy we all shared was to make it work.

There had been talk of a 'shadow year' but that did not make much sense. In view of the ferocious attitude of the media and the opponents of devolution, we would have been bedevilled by criticism for being a pointless institution, and the full assumption of devolved powers was brought forward by seven months to start from the Scottish Parliament election.

The morning of 1 July 1999 brought a day that could not go wrong. The ceremony had to live in the national memory, mark a moment in history and reflect the importance of what we were doing. We had decided it had to be dignified but also a day of enjoyment, so there was pomp, pageantry and the State procession up the Royal Mile; but there was also the fly-past with vapour trails creating a St Andrew's Cross in the clear blue sky over Edinburgh, Concorde provided by British Airways as a special tribute to Scotland, pop music and fireworks at night.

Her Majesty the Queen contributed to all that in the way only she can. The most experienced monarch of the modern era, with 50 years of involvement in State affairs, she is one of the shrewdest politicians I have ever met and she was very well aware of the constitutional implications. She is strongly committed to Scotland and has a much firmer grasp of politics and the future than many people realise.

Those who think devolution is only about modernity and shaking up an outdated constitution are wrong. The Queen's presence and the way she was received by the Scottish people showed it is about strengthening the integrity of the United Kingdom, while recognising its great diversity.

All the ingredients of Scottishness had to be on display, enshrining everything that makes us proud to be Scots but in such a way as to show Scotland as a nation in the twenty-first century. The single moment that will live in the memory of everyone who was there was the voice of Sheena Wellington performing 'A Man's A Man For A' That', one of the most haunting and defiant songs ever written and redolent with Scotland's socialism and collectivism. It is the Marseillaise of humanity as well as a positive statement about the future of mankind. It is not just because I am a Burns fanatic that I believe a single verse of that song captures, as the words of no other poet can, the doctrine of the dignity of man. As performed unaccompanied by Sheena Wellington, it was uplifting but it avoided the sentimental and maudlin Scottishness of which we can be guilty. There was a strong Donald Dewar influence in that.

It would be a pity for Scotland to lose the magic of that day. We must not forget that its promise and potential are still within our grasp.

Very quickly, it became clear that the Constitutional Convention's hopes of a more consensus-based, less confrontational parliament would not be realised. Donald Dewar memorably described our steep learning curve as more like 'political abseiling'.

It was a tough transition for anybody who was at home at Westminster, where most of the political ground rules had been settled over the years. At Westminster, the Prime Minister and his Cabinet dominate Parliament and exercise control through a system of checks and balances. The Scottish Parliament was designed so that there were no comfortable control mechanisms and issues can have a different outcome from those which ministers may want. A private member's bill can be thrust to the fore and – again, unlike Westminster – can intrude on the Executive's programme. It is a more open and democratic, but less certain, way of doing things and we had to get used to that.

The Labour–Lib Dem coalition was not always united. We were being asked to forget enmity, mistrust, hostility and differences that had built up over decades of the run-of-the-mill politics in Scotland and agree on a joint programme of legislation and administration in which they would be members of the Cabinet.

The obvious benefit for the Liberal Democrats was that this was their opportunity to be in government, their first experience of responsibility and their first chance to implement some of their policies. However, while Jim Wallace and Ross Finnie were very easy to deal with, they had very little control over their backbenchers. It was a new occurrence for Labour ministers to have to depend for a majority on MSPs of another party who were less experienced in discipline. Not only were there differences between ourselves and the Lib Dems but also between the Lib Dems and their own leadership. Indeed, during the coalition talks one of the more recalcitrant Lib Dem MSPs, Donald Gorrie, said he would not trust Labour any further than he could throw us (a feeling, I have to say, that was reciprocated by many on our side). And this was the party on whom we had to depend for a united front!

Although the Scottish Parliamentary Labour Party is more disciplined, new MSPs often felt threatened or influenced by competing parties, lobbies and interests, and wavered when asked to toe the party line. This was far removed from Westminster, where, in 14 years, I had never voted against the party whip.

Nobody at Westminster had taken this on board and we constantly had to remind Westminster and Downing Street that the political facts of life had changed in Scotland.

Devolution had to be more than merely transferring responsibility for certain powers from London to Edinburgh, more than merely managing services like education, health, transport, housing and the justice system – important though these are – and more than competently handling a budget that is now £26 billion. It also had to excite and enthuse Scots and give them a glimpse through the door that was opening up with devolution.

Donald Dewar had to get the show on the road, get the Parliament established and the Executive working. At that point, making the difference might not have been that important. When I took over, I felt we should at least be able to handle public services effectively. I then wanted to define what we meant by 'the difference' and realising Scotland's potential.

As Minister for Enterprise and First Minister, tuition fees and free personal care, the European Nations Cup and the Ryder Cup bid were all ways in which I sought to make a statement about how we would do things in the future, working with the people of Scotland. I make no apologies to anyone for that.

Politicians are criticised for building up expectations. The danger now is that a lot of the real promise of Scottish devolution could be lost if constraints and pressures are forcing the politicians merely to become managers of services. Westminster would be happy with that, even some

Scottish ministers and MSPs would be happy with that and the Nationalists would certainly be happy because down that route lies discontent.

Looking back on some of the more controversial issues which focused a harsh spotlight on the Parliament and Executive and cast us all in a bad light, there were clearly things that could have been handled better. That happened because of inexperience and over-enthusiasm but also there were many times when the media made mischief with no good cause.

• The issuing of medals to MSPs to commemorate the State opening was farcical and an unmitigated public relations disaster for the new Parliament. The first I knew of this was when I read about it in the *Daily Record* and it was complete news to me. I believe they were produced, but I have not got one and have never seen one. I can think of nothing more ludicrous than politicians patting themselves on the back and awarding themselves a medal for being in Parliament on a particular day. Also, I know too many Scots who went to war for their country and did not get medals.

Whose stupid idea was it? I still do not know. In some strange way, it became a black mark against the Scottish Executive, although it was the responsibility of the Parliamentary Bureau. This inability of the public and media to distinguish between Parliament and Executive, blaming each for the other's mistakes and treating them as one, was to become a familiar pattern.

• There is no discussion about Westminster expenses and holidays, yet when the package of salaries, office expenses and holidays for MSPs was made public, there was a media furore. Why is the Scottish media not discussing MPs' expenses and holidays? Could it be a case of out of sight, out of mind? No information is given at Westminster about secretarial or travel expenses and it is a product of history that these are regarded as private matters between the MP, the Parliament and the Inland Revenue.

By comparison, the payment for MSPs is not unreasonable; their holidays reflect Scottish holidays for the benefit of those with families and they actually have less time off than their counterparts at Westminster.

The Scottish Parliament has chosen to be transparent about a host of things that are not transparent at Westminster and this gives the Scottish media the opportunity to investigate and comment. That is as it should be – but they also dramatise, distort and discredit when they so wish.

Much of this is driven by the wish to portray Scotland's Parliament as somehow inferior and like a glorified form of local government. Much of the opprobrium that was previously heaped on local government has now passed to the Scottish Parliament.

• Fox hunting dominated the Parliament at a time when our people wanted to see us getting on with things that more directly affected them. It may have been politically correct but the timing so early in the life of the Parliament was poor. I agree with the sentiment that hounds ripping foxes apart is uncivilised, but fox hunting is not extensive in Scotland and is well down on the list of the public's priorities. Mike Watson's bill in the Scottish Parliament was not a subject of hot debate among the people I represented in Fife Central, Glenrothes or Methil. It was simply more ammunition for the critics who sought to portray the Scottish Parliament as an irrelevance.

• The repeal of Section 28 was an unfinished piece of business at Westminster. I voted against the Tories when they introduced the ban on the 'promotion' of homosexuality in schools in the Local Government Act of 1988, so my credentials were sound.

It continued to cause controversy over the next decade and was a long-standing target for anti-discrimination campaigners, although no one was ever prosecuted under the legislation. Anti-discrimination was one of the Labour promises in the 1997 general election victory.

Nonetheless, I and a number of other Scottish Cabinet colleagues were surprised when the abolition of Section 28 was announced as a priority of the Scottish Executive by our colleague Wendy Alexander during a speech at Glasgow University.

Once again, my concern was that it was the wrong issue at the wrong time so early in the life of the new Parliament. Despite all the substantial reasons why we should remove discrimination against gays and lesbians, there were a number of other considerations.

It was a deeply divisive issue which would be difficult to get through the parliament against a considerable body of public opinion. It was not an issue of real importance to the vast majority in Scotland. In the early years, we always had to be conscious of the powerful detractors of devolution in Westminster and the media – not to appease them, but to be aware of the damage they could do.

As a liberal-thinking person, I had no wish to undermine the move for abolition – my caution was neither a statement of opinion nor in any way in favour of perpetuating prejudice. But a formidable head of steam had built up and it was hard to operate as the issue generated opposition from the Roman Catholic Church, the popular press and key individuals, led by Brian Souter of the Stagecoach bus group. It was another wrong priority which became a major distraction.

I felt justifiably angry and disappointed, as someone who supported the removal of discrimination and who had voted against Section 28, that I should become one of the three 'Big Macs' who were pilloried by liberal sections of the Scottish media. There could be no rational discussion of the politics of the matter and anyone even advising caution was labelled a homophobe. It was especially galling that this opinion was fuelled by leaks and briefings by other members of the Scottish Cabinet.

Jack McConnell, Tom McCabe and myself were not opposed to the change in principle, nor the thinking behind it. We simply believed that at that time, so soon after devolution, it was bad judgement, bad timing and bad politics. That became obvious with the public onslaught that followed, a petition with one million signatures and mass-circulation papers like the *Daily Record* giving us an extremely difficult time. Most people quickly lost sight of the substance, and the issue became a discussion of how out of touch the Scottish Parliament was and how we wanted to ride roughshod over the public majority.

It seemed to me that, while the Executive could have given a broad commitment, we could have handled it better. Unknown to the First Minister, I even had a secret meeting with Brian Souter, the Stagecoach bus tycoon who had led and funded the 'Keep the Clause' campaign. I got on well with him in my capacity as Minister for Enterprise and we met at his Perthshire estate before his anti-legislation rally in Glasgow. I made it clear to him that I supported the removal of Section 28 but I was concerned about the timing, the bitterness that was being created and the damage that was being done to the Parliament. To be fair to Souter, we had a reasonable discussion in which he explained that he felt very strongly about the issue and the fact that the Executive was not listening to the people. That made him more determined and he declared publicly that he was going to see it through to the bitter end.

That still bothers me. It was not about the merits of the argument, but so early in the devolution process the public perception already was that we as a parliament were arrogant and insensitive and did not care about the opinions of ordinary Scottish people.

I tried to explain it was not a case of 'We have the power, so we will do it.' The meeting served a purpose, because I did not want to lose him as a major entrepreneur and controller of a large sector of Scotland's transport.

In politics, timing can override and obscure the importance of the principle. What we three 'Big Macs' feared actually happened and it had a political cost. The Scottish Parliament by-election in Ayr became a referendum on Section 28 and Labour came third, giving the Tories their only Scottish Parliament seat on a first-past-the-post basis.

Another undesirable side effect was the damage it did to our dealings with Cardinal Thomas Winning, whom I respected hugely as an old-fashioned socialist and a leader of men and women. He had often felt snubbed by Donald Dewar, although I believe this was more a product of the west of Scotland ethos than any political disagreement. The public clash over Section 28 further soured the relationship and resulted in

Cardinal Winning's denunciation of the Parliament as 'an utter failure'.

● The Scottish Qualifications Authority (SQA) debacle threw up an extraordinarily difficult situation in which administrative chaos put at risk the futures of many young Scots. It was a dramatic example of how, when quango management goes wrong, it can affect life chances.

The SQA is an awards organisation for which I was technically responsible at the time, but Sam Galbraith's education department had day-to-day oversight and he took responsibility. From the start the question was: how can you make bodies like that accountable?

We still need a serious debate about quangos and public agencies. I would rather see them removed or brought directly into the Executive's departments, but Donald Dewar did not think that was practicable. Departmental ministers may be responsible for various quangos, but the dilemma is how much hands-on control they can have without being accused of meddling. When things go wrong, the Minister takes the flak for something over which he does not have day-to-day control and which is left to checks and counter-checks through the civil service.

We had to completely reorganise the SQA and ensure the shambles could not happen again. It is interesting that over the last two years England has experienced similar failures by examination boards and had not learned lessons from north of the border.

We had inherited the SQA and, both in the Scottish Office days and under the Scottish Executive, it may have been moving towards that kind of meltdown for some time, unbeknown to us. It was also an example of how such matters should not be handled. In Scotland, there is no distance between politicians and the public, and that immediacy demands sensitivity to their concerns. Insensitive comments made by some of my colleagues made the Executive appear patronising and dismissive of parents who were justifiably worried about their children's futures.

All these issues showed a lack of political sense. Even if they were worthy, there was no thought for how they would be perceived by the electors and taxpayers nor what the media response would be. Before any of them were put forward, some thought should have been given to what the issues would do to the credibility of the Parliament. As Aneurin Bevan said: 'Socialism is the language of priorities.'

When John Reid took over as the post-devolution Secretary of State for Scotland in May 1999, it was clear that the role had been greatly diminished and the powers of the office were much reduced. John was not the kind of person who would easily accept this shrunken status.

From day one, it was clear to me (and I am sure it was even more forcibly clear to Donald Dewar) that the changed nature of the relationship between London and Edinburgh would be disputed. It was also clear that this Scottish Secretary would be taking a much more aggressive, but typically well-informed, view of his new responsibilities.

John Reid is a formidable politician with a sharp intellect. The so-called 'Turf Wars' were the inevitable result of an office with declining interest being filled by a larger-than-life personality.

I was given an account of 'Devo Day' when the new Scottish Secretary moved into Dover House with his personal private secretary and fellow-Lanarkshire MP Frank Roy. They discovered they had been left with 40 staff, only 4 of them secretarial and the rest porters and cleaners. Stripped of the trappings of power and without assistance as basic as the daily cuttings service, they read it as a very clear message that the power now lay with Donald Dewar and Edinburgh.

Sitting at either end of the large conference table in the Scottish Secretary's office overlooking Horse Guards Parade, they started going through the Scotland Act and the memoranda about their reserved powers, civil servants and facilities. The report I was given says all that was heard was the rustle of paper, interrupted by cries of '**** me, have you seen page 16!' and the response would be, 'Wait till you get to page 26 – it gets even worse.'

When Donald phoned from Edinburgh, supposedly to wish the new incumbent well, John Reid told him: 'If you hear an echo, it's because this bloody place is empty. It's like the *Marie Celeste*. You've left us with bugger all.'

Although the position of Scottish Secretary was still a Cabinet post of importance to the UK and Scotland, it was obvious that it would be what he could make of it. Some of the aggravation was due to thoughtless oversight in the confusion about civil service responsibilities. For instance, when John Reid flew to Edinburgh airport, there was no official car for him because the Scotland Office (as it was now known) had assumed it would be provided and the Scottish Executive's civil servants in Edinburgh were waiting to be asked. John's remarkably tolerant reaction was, 'It's no big deal – just tell me which number of bus to get.'

Politics are about power and it was totally understandable that a Secretary of State, who was combative by nature and intellectually very robust, should fight his corner. Donald Dewar, surprisingly, was not keen to mix it with the new Scottish Secretary, for no other reason than it was not Donald's nature.

I saw things differently and was concerned that, while no one could take issue with the Secretary of State testing the boundaries of his new remit, there were press briefings that were designed to downgrade the Scottish Executive, and early disagreements that suggested to me this was going to be a difficult period. Typical was the question of who would handle the unemployment figures in Scotland. While unemployment remained the reserve of Westminster, I felt there should have been more sharing of the responsibility. On that issue, as on others, we in Scotland would be blamed if the employment situation worsened and would have to face questions in the Scottish Parliament about what we were going to do to bring the figures down. John Reid made it clear that we were not to be allowed to comment officially and I felt that Donald should be making a strong case for the Scottish Executive. As so often happens, it became a behind-the-scenes skirmish with media briefing and counter-briefing. I felt the First Minister should have responded privately to the Secretary of State but this did not happen.

I remember being in Glasgow, where I was based as Minister for Enterprise, and being given a polite but firm dressing-down for briefing against the Secretary of State. I tried to express to Donald that there was a great deal going on behind the scenes and, whilst there was the expected to-ing and fro-ing of personality politics, he should be taking a more robust stance. That was not his view and my role then became one of trying to fight Donald's corner for him, but with more discretion.

This was not Donald's type of politics. He could be tough and quite ruthless, but the bigger stage at Westminster was more suited to him. Post-devolution politics in Scotland are more 'in your face' with aggressive opposition, media and (yes!) colleagues. Issues flash around Scotland, impact and evaporate, and the cut-and-thrust is much rougher. The politics become more personal, often brutal, and few prisoners are taken. Donald Dewar was not comfortable with any of that.

It was felt that most of the issues on which we were skirmishing with the Scotland Office were not too important in the scheme of things. The Secretary of State was trying to re-establish an authority that, in actual fact, no longer existed. He was trying to use certain things reserved to Westminster to make a point about influence but, as far as the settlement was concerned, that had no real effect.

Relations were soured unnecessarily and the publicity that was generated gave the impression that devolution was not as robust as it might be. It should not be a battle between Scotland and Westminster – Edinburgh versus London; MPs versus MSPs – fought by different players at different levels.

We were warned very early on that the head of the Scottish Executive would have to be First Minister, not Prime Minister of Scotland; the Parliament must have a Presiding Officer, not Speaker; and it wouldn't be a Lab-Lib Government, but an Executive. It amazed me that the weekly Scottish Cabinet meeting in Bute House, Edinburgh, had to be scheduled to avoid the meeting our Permanent Secretary had with the other UK permanent secretaries, held in London. In unofficial briefings, one UK minister dismissed the new administration in Edinburgh as 'the Ramblers' Association Scottish Executive'.

The impression being created by a powerful and vocal group at Westminster was that we were to be an Executive that administered and managed but would not be of real political significance.

X

Minister for Scotland's Future

My approach to my new job as Minister for Enterprise and Lifelong Learning was to acknowledge the fundamental importance of enterprise and learning for the future of our country. This is a time of dramatic worldwide change with fierce and intensifying competition in innovation, information technology, telecommunications and other rapidly emerging twenty-first-century industries. My travels and my instincts suggested that many small countries and regions of the world have embraced these changes more effectively and enthusiastically than we are doing in Scotland – and with greater urgency.

There can be no doubt that the key to success in the future is human capital and the development of the knowledge society which is based on the skills and abilities of our people. It is not just a case of 'education, education, education' but also a new concept of learning throughout life and a ruthless focus on providing opportunities.

In taking on the job of Minister for Enterprise and Lifelong Learning, I realised that the past had become too important in Scotland. History, sentiment and nostalgia all have their place, but the great industries that put Scotland in the forefront of the Industrial Revolution and made us a hub of the Empire have all but faded from the scene. Scotland's famous shipbuilding, coal-mining, steel-making and heavy engineering industries have all declined; indeed, deep mining has disappeared entirely. As each of these traditional industries collapsed amid closures and job losses, there was sadness and real hurt in many communities. It is no consolation to people losing their livelihoods to know it is part of a greater economic picture; but for political and business leaders there comes a point when it makes no sense to struggle on a little longer with a factory or an industry that will inevitably die. Far better to manage that transition, help communities to change and innovate, and individuals to transfer their undoubted work ethic into other areas.

There is a dead weight of complacency in Scotland that says we have always done well enough and we do not need to make radical changes. If you are prisoners of the past, you cannot take a positive view of the future. My task was to combat that failure of vision and the reluctance to acknowledge that these cherished industries would not have a place in Scotland's industrial renaissance.

We can march and demonstrate about the loss of jobs and we can back the workers in protests. In the longer term, though, we have to understand that the global economic game is tough and uncompromising. Take just one of these declining industries, for example textile manufacturing – if Scotland does not get into high-value end products like Harris tweed, cashmere and technical textiles, there will be no textile sector left. Too few people in industry and government have the insight to see that we have to play to our strengths and focus on the areas in which we can compete in international markets.

There is also a psychological problem: the well-paid manual jobs of the past were regarded by most Scots as 'real' jobs, 'serious' jobs. I sensed it was very difficult for them to understand the importance of the new world of financial services, tourism, electronics and telecommunications at the heart of the knowledge society. A change of attitude was needed to accept that light industry and sophisticated jobs would be the new basis for our prosperity.

There was also an astonishing lack of understanding in some official and government circles of what would be needed in terms of national effort and commitment to attract these new jobs. Not only changes in attitude and mindset were required, but also the mobilisation of our public and private resources to allow us to compete in a market without frontiers. That is why the opportunities provided by devolution are so significant.

In the transition from the old order to the new economy, we have to acknowledge that we have been heavily dependent on direct investment from overseas. That has been important and we have done reasonably well from it but in the process we have not given enough support to indigenous economic activity, including business formation, entrepreneurship and competitiveness.

Around the world, there are examples of smart and successful countries, regions and states which have taken steps to assess their own economic situation, understand global change and appreciate the dramatic and accelerating pace of change in information technology and communications. They learned quickly from the experiences of others but, more importantly, translated that into realising their own potential.

That is the message I wanted to take to all parts of Scotland, no matter how remote they might seem. In the age of global communication, especially the Internet, it is salutary to know that people in Japan or California or Australia can with the click of a mouse book a bed and breakfast in the Outer Hebrides.

Devolution provides Scotland with the ability to control one of the key levers of the information or knowledge society: learning and education, in all its forms from pre-school to college and university. We have a very impressive education base which, while not as good as many people think, is capable of maintaining Scotland as a world-ranking knowledge society.

As Minister for Enterprise and Lifelong Learning, I also wanted a closer relationship between private and public sectors. For the first time, regional government gave us an opportunity to work closely with those companies, entrepreneurs and industrialists who matter. It was a chance to create the conditions for a national partnership.

One of the pressures of the job was to manage the consequences of decline and the effects of the world market. Sometimes, global or UK employers would sack or impose redundancies on workers who had shown commitment and the willingness to adapt. The unions and the media would rightly play up the human dimension, but behind the headlines was the harsh truth of international competition. We had to find new opportunities and move on.

Success can only be won in the future because of decisions we take today. Linked to devolution was the feeling that all the significant Treasury, fiscal, economic and regulatory machinery remained at Westminster. It is felt that in some way this is a disadvantage but far too often it is merely an excuse not to address our own problems.

Too often in our blame culture we are seeking to find scapegoats when we should be looking for ways to tackle problems which should be our responsibility.

Devolution links us with the United Kingdom and its market, but my thinking was that we had to be more open to the world. Scandinavia, Finland, Ireland, Singapore and individual states in America provide us with models of successful indigenous economic growth.

We must adopt a more collective view as political thinkers engage with industrialists and others to get to grips with this new economic order. In politics, because we are in office for four or five years, we tend to think in terms of short timescales, but the nation's perspective has to be for the longer term.

It was also obvious that the social composition of the workforce was changing with as many women as men in work. This creates implications for families and communities and raises the fraught question of Scots adjusting to a new, flexible and family-oriented order in which the male wage packet is no longer as dominant as it once was.

The e-revolution means further dramatic change in the workplace, at home and in lifestyles. In the scheme of things, our industrial history has been based on a progression from land to labour to capital to skills and now to knowledge and information. For the first time, present and future jobs depend on us building a knowledge society in our country. What that situation should be screaming at us is the message that our pre-eminent requirement is the quality of our people, and that learning is the key.

I visited Silicon Valley in California on an official trip to speak to some of the major players in this global revolution. They told me that international regulations placed so many limits on the investment incentives and subsidies they could be offered in different countries. More and more, their major decisions on overseas expansion are taken on the quality of a country's 'human capital' and its business environment. They also want the assurance that there are enough people in that country's business community, in parliament and government who understand their problems. In Scotland, we are not yet at that point.

Government should be open to outside wisdom in a way we never have been in Scotland. Politicians should be big enough to accept that we do not have all the answers and we need the input that the private sector is always willing to give.

The private sector also has to change its deep-seated attitudes. The dependency culture is still too evident in Scotland and when there is a problem, the first question is always 'what is the Government going to do about it?' – wanting the Government to do everything is a powerful constraint on Scotland's progress.

The CBI, the Institute of Directors, the Federation of Small Businesses and other business organisations represent the interests of their members, but their input into the thinking on the future of Scotland is limited. They clearly have a valuable contribution to make but have either assumed or been granted a limited role. It is no longer enough for such bodies (and that includes the STUC and unions) to be partisan and only seek to be protective. These business organisations may be regional arms of UK bodies but they, too, should be more devolved and their thinking should be more distinctively Scottish. They should be telling government in Scotland what needs to be done and government should have an open door at all times.

It worries me that since I left office major companies with plans that are crucial to Scotland are saying that they have problems in getting access to the Scottish Executive. Scotland needs the best of thinking and the best of experience.

However, none of that will help if it is not linked to a vision of what our country should be in the twenty-first century, with the confidence and competitiveness to pursue these ambitions. In the course of time, we can rest assured that other parts of the UK will be as competitive as they need to be. That is already happening in Europe and North America.

Despite some improvements in Scotland – within the UK economy where interest rates, inflation and unemployment are at a historic low and employment levels are at their highest for 40 years – there are areas in which we are not improving relative to the rest of the UK and that has to be a considerable worry. We have been key beneficiaries when the UK Government has been redistributing wealth from the centre with aid and subsidies to reduce inequalities of wealth, employment and growth between regions. Now, we have to turn ourselves into a competitive nation, less concerned about redistribution from the UK to Scotland and more concerned with what we can do for ourselves. Scotland's mindset has to change; we have to stop looking south and do more on our own initiative within Europe and internationally.

The idea of competitive regions is a new phenomenon in Europe. We have to anticipate that international and European regulation means that nation states cannot do what they have done in the past. There is a powerful movement in Europe away from redistribution, towards competitiveness. In Scotland, it will not be a question of what devolution has given us but what we do with its powers.

We have seen how inward investment can turn sour on us. International markets collapse and foreign companies have to retrench or find it more advantageous to invest elsewhere. Motorola and Hyundai were only the largest examples of a trend that bit deep into our electronics sector.

The lack of a national outcry at the loss of 3,000 jobs at Motorola astonished me – there was more outrage and many more acres of newspaper coverage over something like the loss of 50 jobs at a shipyard or textiles factory. This brought into sharp focus the question of what were 'real' jobs in the minds of Scots. Was it also a passive acceptance that this was a global company and that is what you have to expect?

Scotland needs to do a great deal more in generating new businesses and encouraging growth. The formation and support of small businesses is vital and would go some way towards reducing Scotland's dependence for employment on the public services, international industries and redistribution from London. Yet our entrepreneurship compares unfavourably with other countries; our record of small business creation is one of the lowest in the UK and one of the worst in Europe.

Governments cannot legislate to change attitudes or to set up new businesses; they can only educate, encourage, support and provide leadership.

The Scottish character will have to change from the 'we know our place' and 'let the Government do it all' mentality to a more confident, upwardly mobile, risk-taking attitude. Successful countries are very different from us. In the 'can do' culture of the US, it is not a disgrace to fail or go bankrupt because they know that to succeed you have to try. There, it is the business that fails, not the human being. Here, it is the individual who is held up to ridicule. Those who are successful are not given the credit for their success.

The Nationalists claim you need to be an independent country to be successful, but experience in the wider world shows there are successful countries, regions and autonomous provinces who can boast success. It is not the constitutional description that matters but the energy and concentration, the realisation that the world is changing – and, above all, the leadership they are given that matters. At the present time, I do not see that kind of direction in Scotland.

PART III

First Minister

XI

Death of a Statesman

Donald Dewar's health deteriorated dramatically in the months after the opening of the Scottish Parliament. The sheer pace and pressure of work, the heavy responsibilities of the high offices he held, the great events in which he played a leading role and the hard grind of delivering devolution (not to mention an endearingly chaotic lifestyle) would have tested a lesser man.

They finally took their toll on Donald and it was noticeable that he easily became breathless and was struggling walking through airports. Early in 2000, he had a heart valve replacement in what appeared to be a routine (but serious for a man of 63) operation. Everyone urged him to take time to recover and not to come back too early, but he was soon fretting at home and involved in government affairs during what should have been his recuperation. The early return to work was the essential Donald; he did not work to live, he lived to work.

It was natural that during Donald's illness Jim Wallace became Acting First Minister. I admit it was sometimes frustrating to be minding the Labour shop and looking after the party's interests in the coalition government without recognition, but at that time there was no official position as Deputy Leader of the Scottish Labour Party.

Donald seemed to make a good recovery and at the Cabinet meeting on Tuesday, 10 October 2000, he looked well. He was a man of mood swings but he was sharp-witted and in good humour. I last saw him alive just before lunch when I left for an appointment in Glasgow. On the way back late that afternoon, the call came from Sam Galbraith to tell me that Donald had been taken into hospital again. He sounded very apprehensive and worried, with a note of shock in his voice. It was an unprotected line and Sam was very guarded, saying with heavy emphasis: 'It's very, very serious.'

When I asked, rather foolishly in retrospect, 'What do you mean, Sam?', he replied, 'Just be prepared. It's very, very serious.' Although we did not know it until some time later, Donald had suffered a sudden and massive brain haemorrhage.

By the time I got home to St Andrews, it was clear to me what Sam had meant. While I had not been Donald's close friend or confidant, I felt a deep sense of loss on a number of levels. I thought of the remarkable legacy he had left to his country, his unmistakable achievement in creating the Scottish Parliament and everything we had been through together.

My wife Julie was crying, remembering the immensely warm and witty speech he made at our wedding in 1998. The reception had been held at the Old Course Hotel in St Andrews, and Donald's speech was, as usual, funny and wide-ranging enough to encompass what was a disparate gathering of guests. Also as usual, a friend had to help him as he struggled with his buttonhole!

I recalled Donald having to buy an overcoat because he didn't own one when he had to visit Scandinavia to see devolution in practice; how the civil servants always made sure there was a box of biscuits on the table in his room at Dover House in Whitehall (at times he seemed more intent on emptying the box than listening to the discussion); and the possibly apocryphal story of the police reporting a break-in at his office, which had been left in a complete mess, only to find that was how Donald had left it himself.

I remembered how much Donald loved sport and had a great knowledge of the subject, which drew us together in our off-duty moments. He was a man of culture, widely regarded for his great interest in the arts and his collection of Scottish literature. I was also sad because after his divorce, despite his many friends, he seemed a solitary figure and I often thought he was a very lonely man.

Donald was a politician of stature and I believe he missed Westminster, where he felt at home and had a sense of security. Like me, he found the step back home to Scotland much bigger than he anticipated.

But there were sadder thoughts, too. It may come as a surprise to many people, especially the media, but politicians are human and have feelings. Donald may have seemed thick-skinned but he was often bemused and baffled by his detractors, who were unnecessarily vindictive. He was a sensitive man who could be wounded by the way he was presented in the media. As someone who had given so much of his life to public service, he could not understand why he was subjected to personal ridicule. He was particularly hurt by a cruel cartoon of him carrying his head under his arm; and when he came back from illness went out of his way to give the media a special photoshoot on the steep grassy slope outside the

Assembly Hall. But despite promising not to take any photographs until he was ready, one Scottish newspaper published the shot of him taking an ungainly fall.

I also recalled a taxi driver telling me with some disgust how he had Labour MSPs in his cab, openly being disloyal to Donald without caring who overheard.

Nor could Donald understand the conduct of an erstwhile assistant of his, Tim Luckhurst, who was for a short and undistinguished period the editor of *The Scotsman*. Earning a living as a freelance journalist, Luckhurst mercilessly criticised his former employer while his byline used his connection with Donald to enhance his credibility. Because of such let-downs, Donald did have some moments of deep depression.

I felt that fate had dealt cruelly with Donald. His image for most of his career had been rather grim and dour, but he had a great sense of fun and his humanity had come to be recognised. On his return to Scotland he had become a much-loved leader and was regarded with fondness as the 'father of the nation'. No one deserved it more, but he did not live long enough to enjoy the warmth of that national regard.

That was a long night, dominated by calls from Chancellor Gordon Brown, Scottish Secretary John Reid, the Prime Minister's office, political colleagues and journalists. It was clear from these phone calls that the senior people in government had received the same information I had. While the most important thing was to honour Donald, there was also concern about the interregnum and the handover. This was not politics, it was the business of government and the need to do what was appropriate to maintain continuity.

The overnight press and broadcast programmes the next day were as gloomy as they could possibly be, but everything had to wait until Donald's children had been to the hospital. An informal meeting of the Scottish Cabinet was held to take stock and, because of my seniority and experience, I was again looking after Labour's interests and went to the hospital to be of what help I could.

Appropriately for Donald, the funeral was a unique blend of State occasion and warm-hearted send-off by the people he served, in the city where he was born and which he loved. What made it impressive was the high turn-out of ordinary people, which reflected his public service, his high profile and his contribution to Scotland. But there was something more: sheer affection for 'Big Donald'. He had struck a chord in the hearts of ordinary Scots that no other politician could touch. Many people are remembered for what they do, but few are remembered for what they are and Donald is remembered for being himself.

At a sombre reception after the funeral, Julie and I met with Tony and Cherie Blair and Anjie Hunter. As usual, the Prime Minister was supportive, but he did ask us if we were prepared for what should happen next.

Anjie, with whom I had worked for many years as part of the Blair team, gave Julie a piece of advice which, in the light of subsequent events, was very far-seeing: 'Never read the newspapers. Tony and Cherie don't – that's how they survive.'

I can do no better than recall the tribute I paid to Donald in the Scottish Parliament, the institution that will always be his memorial:

> When Donald Dewar walked into this Parliament 15 months ago, as First Minister of the first Scottish Parliament, he spoke not only as the architect of Scottish devolution, but as the advocate for what had shaped his lifetime of service – social justice.
>
> In an age of cynicism about politicians, to the people of Scotland Donald was never 'one of them'; he was always 'one of us'. He had no pretence and no pomposity. He was a man of the people and was close to the people – a man whom people felt they knew before they met him. There was no title of which he was prouder than the one he shared with every one of us: Member of the Scottish Parliament. Donald Dewar was a man who sought that position for what he could do, not for what he could be.
>
> Donald also had faith in his nation and he truly embraced the soul of Scotland. Let us remind ourselves of the brilliant and moving speech that he made at the opening of Parliament last July:
>
>> *This is about more than our politics and our laws. This is about who we are, how we carry ourselves. In the quiet moments today, we might hear some echoes of the past.*
>>
>> *The shout of the welder in the din of the great Clyde shipyards; the speak of the Mearns, with its soul in the land; the discourse of the Enlightenment, when Edinburgh and Glasgow were a light held to the intellectual life of Europe; the wild cry of the Great Pipes; and back to the distant cries of Bruce and Wallace.*
>>
>> *The past is part of us. But today there is a new voice in the land, the voice of a democratic Parliament. A voice to shape Scotland, a voice for the future.*

I concluded: 'Donald Dewar – 1937 to 2000 – now takes his special place in the list of Scotland's favourite sons. Donald the person, the politician and the patriot gave us a unique record of public service and his greatest achievement was devolution – a great life and a great legacy.'

As we were still mourning the loss of Donald, the nation's business had to continue and the Scotland Act laid down that a new First Minister had to be elected within just 28 days. That meant a short, sharp election for the Labour leadership in Scotland and, by definition, the office of First Minister. There was not a great deal of campaigning, because the objective was simple. The majority of Cabinet colleagues were supporters and it was a question of getting in touch with the electoral college, which was a small constituency comprising the Scottish party executive and MSPs.

I had never coveted the Leader's job, yet here I was fighting for it because of a tragic misfortune. It was not something I had ruled out but, given Donald's age and apparent fitness, it was not a consideration that arose in the short term. Indeed, I had thought that if Donald carried on for another five or ten years, the more able of my younger colleagues would have gained experience and matured sufficiently to compete for the top job in Scottish politics. I know that was also Donald's feeling.

In that sense, two obvious candidates for the future were Wendy Alexander and Angus MacKay – both intelligent and visionary and each in their different way with an enormous contribution to make to Scottish government and to Scotland. Wendy was difficult to deal with, but I admire her talent and I believe that if she had stood against Jack McConnell for the leadership, she would have had a good chance of winning. The leadership election after Donald's death was something no one had expected or wanted, and I was very ill-prepared, both mentally and politically. Curiously, because of my lack of confidence earlier in life and because of my attitude of always doing things on my own, I may have been a bit naive.

While I had done reasonably well in politics over many years, I was never the plotting, conspiratorial type who is immersed in the details of politics day in and day out. Throughout my career, I had worked hard and made the most of my opportunities, but I was not beholden to anyone or any clique.

Unlike others, I was not fired up by minutiae and intrigue and was not into the cronyism which is a major factor in Scottish Labour politics. I was not from Lanarkshire or the west of Scotland and had not been involved in continually wooing MSPs. Nor did I have a wide circle of friends and people working on my behalf. There was no calling in of favours from the past. All of that made me vulnerable.

It was a time for taking stock and when I looked back over my life I was conscious of having settled so often for second place. I went to Leeds United at the age of 15 as one of the most talented youngsters in Scottish football but came home soon afterwards. I played for the Scotland Under-18 side but never made full international. At university, I was top in every year and won a scholarship but did not get a first because I messed up my final engineering paper by writing so much that it was virtually unreadable. Following the 1987 general election, I was on the front bench after only two years in the Commons but never made any progress in the Shadow Cabinet elections.

I had all of these thoughts, but I knew this was the opportunity I could not give up. I had served my constituency and country at different levels – there is no more passionate Scot; and I had a developing vision of where my country needed to go at the start of the twenty-first century. I had greatly enjoyed the enterprise portfolio, dealing as it does with industry, business, the economy and jobs. It also included my major passion – learning. I was committed to giving it the profile it deserved in twenty-first-century Scotland.

There had been talk that I might be unopposed, but I never believed that. I knew that Jack McConnell, well connected and well versed in party manoeuvring from his days as Scottish General Secretary, was holding meetings with political allies at the Iron and Steel Trades Confederation office in Motherwell.

With only three days between Donald's funeral on Wednesday, 18 October and the vote on Saturday, 21 October, Jack was quickly off his mark on the Thursday, sending e-mails to every MSP and a press release to all the major media outlets before embarking on a campaign tour across Scotland. Tactically, this gave me the advantage of getting the lunchtime news headlines with my own announcement and producing my own vision in a more considered fashion. In fact, there was broad agreement on our aims – creating a dynamic Scottish economy, full employment and social justice. But the differences were significant.

In order to show that he was a moderniser with a radical agenda, Jack's aides let it be known there would be drastic changes in the Scottish Cabinet, and Communities Minister Wendy Alexander, Health Minister Susan Deacon and Education Minister Sam Galbraith would be among those to be replaced. There were also clear indications that Jack did not support the 'new politics' and would be less consensual in his dealings with those who had been our opponents in the past.

Unbeknown to me, there was in existence in SNP circles a dossier which could have been embarrassing during my campaign: a list of 'nice' things I had said about their party leader John Swinney! At the same time, the Nationalists were seeking to portray me as 'Whitehall's man'! Meanwhile, I was reassuring Labour backbenchers that I would stand up for Scotland within the UK and, as always, be an implacable opponent of the separatists.

People knew me as a hard worker; I had the experience; I had significant support from trade-union colleagues; I had been campaign organiser for the UK and Scottish elections; I would provide the continuity that was needed. Enough people clearly felt I had earned the leadership on my own record.

Although there were only 81 votes at stake among the party executive and MSPs, it was important to show that I had wider support in Scotland. I made a point of visiting the office of the *Daily Record*, Scotland's largest-selling newspaper, where I outlined my programme to Peter Cox, who was in his first week as editor. I learned later the *Record* had two possible front-page layouts: 'It Has To Be Henry' and 'Jack's The Lad'. Although 'Jack's The Lad' had a better tabloid ring to it, they made a political judgement and went with 'It Has To Be Henry'.

The same morning, the *Good Morning Scotland* programme reported that all the Scottish Cabinet ministers, bar Jack McConnell, would vote for me. I was confident of winning and, because of the limited constituency, I was not surprised that I won by 8 votes: 44–36. The surprise was my opponent's obvious, almost disbelieving, shock that he had lost.

However, after the result was announced, Jack McConnell pledged loyalty and declared, 'I don't think anyone wants to see ministers in the Cabinet campaigning in opposition.' I thought the campaign was over but for some it never ended. There were briefings that the party was now seriously divided with 'simmering enmities', and one quote was: 'Henry looks like a lame duck. This is the worst of all worlds for Labour.'

Nor had I any idea of what lay ahead of me as First Minister. I had not appreciated the magnitude of the job, the mental and physical demands and the intense and obsessive attention of a media with an attack mentality. In the early encounters at First Minister's Questions and the activities in the parliament chamber, I did not do myself justice or reflect my own ability and vision for Scotland. There were continual off-the-record and anonymous media briefings, which could only have come from members of the Scottish Executive who were intent on undermining what we were trying to do. These are not excuses, simply a statement of the unnecessary pressures that are created in the feverish atmosphere of the Scottish Parliament.

Since devolution, Scotland's politicians have been in the front line and under closer scrutiny than at Westminster. The more senior you were, the more likely you were to be the subject of personal viciousness and backstabbing, often fuelled by the anti-devolution sentiment among Westminster MPs.

Certain sections of the Scottish media had decided that the Scottish Parliament was not a serious policy-making forum, so for them it became a personality forum. They certainly gave no credit to our scale of achievement over such a short time, nor did they make any allowances for the number of MSPs and ministers who were new to politics at that level.

Those of us who are in public life must expect criticism and scepticism but should not have to cope with corrosive cynicism and destructive negativism. I always said I was interested in outcomes, not outcries.

Scotland is a small country and, unfortunately, these faults are magnified in a tight-knit political and media community. Small irrelevancies became magnified into huge problems for the Government. What was a minor issue at the start of the week could, with the help of a few mischief-makers on the Mound, become a crisis that filled every newspaper by Thursday and disappear by the following weekend.

In many ways, the Scottish press reflects the worst excesses of our national character – our determination to find fault and our grudging refusal to give credit for success. When it becomes a media game, it is not pleasant to be the prey. If the press is playing these games to increase circulation figures, it does not seem to have worked.

The diary for my first day in office as First Minister reads:

> *Friday, 27 October 2000:*
> 7.45 a.m. Bute House, Edinburgh, BBC interview
> 12.30 p.m. Audience with the Queen at the Palace of Holyroodhouse
> 2 p.m. Swearing in of new First Minister at Court of Session, receive Great Seal of Scotland
> 8 p.m. Speech at fundraising event, Prestonpans Labour Club

Despite what the broadcasters may think, the engagements were listed in the order of timing, not the order of priority!

The *Daily Record* headline read 'Elizabeth II meets Henry I'. I had met the Queen formally and informally on a number of occasions, but my appreciation of her grew enormously during my year as First Minister. It is easy in matters of politics and society, especially Scottish, to look over the history from 1603 and the Union of the Crowns and have some doubts and criticisms about what happened centuries ago. More important to remember is that Her Majesty is Queen of the United Kingdom, with a particular interest in Scottish affairs. Each time she came to Scotland for audiences and ceremonial occasions, I always found her very concerned and well informed about Scotland and Scottish politics. She was committed to the constitutional changes and expressed her hope that the Scottish Parliament and Executive would grow in strength. She also talked very movingly about Donald and her regard for him. She was very shocked that her First Minister had died so suddenly; she wanted to know the details of what had happened and asked about his family.

She is the most experienced 'politician' in the world. In her 50 years on the throne, she has been everywhere and met everyone. In Scotland, she discussed very frankly her concerns about where the constitutional settlement was going and what was happening in devolution.

Months later, Julie and I had the enormous privilege of being invited to Balmoral and stayed overnight with the Royal Family. It was one of the most enjoyable evenings I have ever spent in my life.

After a private meeting with the Queen and socialising with Prince Philip, Sophie, Countess of Wessex, and Prince Edward, I was sitting between Her Majesty and Sophie at the dinner table when my pager went off during the second course. It should not have happened because I thought I had turned it off. I was naturally horrified. It was the night Scotland played a final World Cup qualifying game against Belgium in Brussels and I had organised someone to page me with the score. I cannot put into print what was going through my mind as Her Majesty stopped the conversation and asked: 'What is that?' I replied: 'Ma'am, it is my pager' and I could only apologise. I decided to tell her the full story about the Scottish football match and she immediately said: 'Philip, we need to get the scores!' The Duke of Edinburgh had a word with one of the servants who returned a few minutes later and said: 'Ma'am, there is good and bad news. The good news is England won. The bad news is Scotland lost.' The Queen said: 'Well, that's a pity.' In view of our team's form, it was not wholly surprising. We got on with the meal and did not allow the football news to spoil what was a very pleasant evening.

The Queen was at her most relaxed and informal, extraordinarily good company, very open and warm and instructive. I never needed reminding that devolution meant the country was being viewed differently, but the Queen and her family are keen to be involved in Scotland in a way they had never been when Scotland was merely a department of state in a Westminster government.

My meetings with Princess Anne and Prince Charles opened my eyes to the grossly distorted images that are presented in the media. At one rugby international at Murrayfield with the Princess Royal in her capacity as president of the Scottish Rugby Union, Princess Anne's husband made a very shrewd observation, delivered with feeling to my wife: 'Remember, your life with the press is short-lived but for the Royal Family it is a life sentence.'

My first task was to reshuffle the Scottish Cabinet, giving Wendy Alexander my old job as Enterprise Minister to make use of her encyclopaedic grasp of the subject; moving Jack McConnell (an ex-teacher) from Finance to Education and bringing in the able Angus MacKay as Finance Minister.

Jack would be in charge of the formidable task of negotiating a teachers' pay and conditions package on the back of the far-reaching McCrone Report. He would also have to sort out the SQA exam-results fiasco, which had been a tragedy for so many of our young people and had understandably become a preoccupation of the Parliament. I felt it was important that Jack undertook both these challenges and also ensured that we continued to reform education, one of the key areas of increased investment. It was also felt that Jack should have more to occupy him than was the case in Finance.

Angus MacKay had quickly proved himself to be one of the most impressive politicians of his generation. His strong intellect, unflappable disposition and ability to focus makes him one of the best talents available to Scotland. I am sure his 2003 election defeat in the Edinburgh South constituency is only a temporary setback and he is destined for higher office in the future.

Because of my football background, the Cabinet was dubbed 'Team McLeish' by the media. This was, to say the least, ironic – since a few of them showed precious little team spirit. Being new to national politics and to government, the doctrine of joint Cabinet responsibility meant nothing to some ministers. There was a faction that continued to plot and were never off the phone to lobby journalists, leaking things that had not been discussed, trying to bounce the Executive into making decisions by headline, undermining me and their other colleagues and simply stirring up trouble for the sake of it.

Immediately, we found ourselves in the midst of a typical Scottish Executive 'crisis', created from nothing and with no real significance. A BBC journalist latched onto the fact that Tom McCabe had spoken several times during a media briefing about the 'Scottish Government'. There were phone calls from Whitehall – mainly from the office of the Scottish Secretary John Reid, who had previously (and wrongly) declared: 'There is no flexibility in the devolution settlement.'

There were snide personal attacks on myself, alleging that I was showing worrying signs of self-aggrandisement, which were damaging only weeks ahead of a UK general election. Worst of all was the abuse from Scottish MPs and ministers who variously described the Scottish Executive as 'The White Heather Club', and its members as 'thick' and 'fools'.

At the same time as the media said our backbench MSPs were feeling 'bruised', we were together at a party in the Holyrood Hotel and they were happily, perhaps defiantly, singing 'Stand By Your Man'.

When the Westminster lobby journalists tried to embroil the Prime Minister, a Downing Street official was quoted as saying there was no question of a name change. I spoke to Tony Blair and he was not in the least bothered by the phrase 'Scottish Government' and blamed the Scottish media for stirring up another pointless row. When I said that in terms of devolved responsibilities we were a Scottish Government, he simply said, 'Fine', and Alastair Campbell issued a statement reflecting the Prime Minister's relaxed attitude. Behind the scenes, the most 'hands-off' person in the UK Government about devolution was the Prime Minister.

After three days, I ended the fuss by declaring in the Scottish Parliament: 'We *are* a Government.' Some people read a great deal of significance into my use of 'a' and not 'the' – but it was noticeable that a year later Jack McConnell was speaking of his 'Government' and no one appeared to be scandalised.

Since then, the loss of a full-time Secretary of State for Scotland within the British Government has caused no problem whatsoever. In fact, it is a sign of the strength of devolution and was bound to happen. We have not fully realised the effect of devolution on the future of our politics and the way we are governed. Relations between Westminster and Edinburgh, and between the UK and the English regions, will have to change.

Naturally, we could well have done without the bad publicity and stupid blunders of the early days of the Scottish Parliament. We did not like it any better than the knockers in the Westminster Parliament. What we did, but what they did not do, was to put it in perspective.

They were only looking for ways to diminish and denigrate the Scottish Parliament. Their ignorance of devolution was shown when they completely missed more meaningful matters that showed the development of a strong Scottish Parliament. The real point is that we did not set up devolution merely to administer in Edinburgh and apply London-made policies and Westminster instructions.

I did not mind taking the flak for trying to create a vision of Scotland worldwide and in Europe, but I did not expect personal animosity for trying to do as much as possible with our devolved government. A rift is always a better story than a united front, and what would be a raging crisis in the Scottish media was usually a mere hiccup, dealt with in a few minutes at First Minister's Questions.

XII

'A Confident, Competitive and Compassionate Scotland'

Some of the thinking I had developed as Enterprise Minister, which had built on my experience of Westminster, local government and my own life, could now be realised. The basic questions I wanted to bring to the job of First Minister were: what kind of country do we want Scotland to be and how can the Executive and the Parliament help us get there?

In the first phase of the project, Donald had got the Parliament up and working, and we could now consolidate his achievement. For the credibility of the new Parliament and Executive, there now had to be a wider vision and a view of Scotland that was beyond managing and delivering services, improving the governance of Scotland and the effective spending of nearly £20 billion. It was up to us as practical politicians to harness the new momentum and develop some of these bigger themes.

The second phase of devolution, in my mind, was to be more concerned with Scotland's role on the world stage, coping with global changes and challenges and creating a competitive country. I was in no doubt that to be successful, Scotland would have to change in a very dramatic way. At my first press conference, at the launch of my new Cabinet and in my first television interview on BBC's *Newsnight*, it was important to me to define these issues, not necessarily to set me apart from my predecessor but to illustrate how I was determined to move Scotland forward in a much more ambitious way.

From the start, I said I wanted a much stronger commitment to the needs of older people in Scotland. Population changes in our country were not being taken seriously and we had to be careful about two considerations: the declining workforce and our expanding older population.

I was very interested in developing the idea of free personal care, which would not solve all the problems of the elderly but would be a statement of a country that was compassionate. Of course, this posed an immediate and obvious problem because it built on the Sutherland Commission's report which had been rejected by the Westminster Government. However, in my view it could and should be developed in Scotland because its recommendations made so much sense and were so relevant to a very substantial number of Scots.

On my first day, I also talked about the need to be ambitious, to look at reordering the priorities of government and announced that we were embarking on a major policy review – which was more colourfully described in tabloid language as 'dump the crap'.

I touched on the sensitive issue of the reduction of the number of Scottish MPs at Westminster, which, under a strict application of the Scotland Act, would result in an automatic reduction of the number of seats in the Scottish Parliament. I had been very unhappy with the inclusion of this clause in the Scotland Act and was keen to signal my position at the earliest stage. Such a reduction might have made sense in the context of London opinion about the 'West Lothian Question'. To me, it made no sense in terms of the practical politics of a new parliamentary institution whose MSPs would be understandably angry. It was my first opportunity to bring the politics of common sense to the fore.

To be fair to Donald Dewar, when I discussed this issue with him during the passage of the Scotland Act at Westminster, he was not enthusiastic about the clause but No. 10 was insistent that this should be part of the settlement.

I took the first chance I had as First Minister to establish some distance from those in London who seemed to think that the Scottish Parliament and Executive were wholly owned subsidiaries of Westminster. That had to change and MSPs had to be able to determine on behalf of Scots what was to happen in Scotland.

There would always be tension and I was not unhappy about that. I believed it was time for Scotland to be looking at our role in the United Kingdom, in Europe and internationally. Later, I was to sum up our hallmark aims for Scotland as confidence, compassion and competitiveness. Around all of these early statements was a real determination on my part that devolution must make a difference.

I also wanted to disabuse some at Westminster, including Scottish MPs, of their apparent belief that devolution had been a grudging concession: not one well thought out; not one that would be able to adapt and change in the future; not one that was designed to give our nation new opportunities in a settlement that was going to be part of wider progress in the UK towards some kind of devolved federalism.

It was clear to me, as someone intimately involved with the Scotland Act, that there were many positive supporters but few people had any concept of where devolution was taking Scotland – not down the path of narrow nationalism, which enthuses some and repels many, but towards more ambitious changes for our country. I am not talking about separation but a bolder agenda in which devolution could be used as a platform to tackle long-standing problems and realise our country's potential.

I kept in mind the historic declaration in the Scotland Act: 'There *shall* be a Scottish Parliament.' Despite the certainty of that statement, there is a worrying uncertainty behind it. Strictly speaking, any future Westminster Government could abolish the Scottish Parliament with a majority of one in the House of Commons – although, obviously, that would create a constitutional crisis of unthinkable proportions.

More worrying is that a later government might alter the relationship between the two parliaments, rewrite the devolved and reserved powers or change the financial arrangements in the Barnett formula and block grant. They might even impose further restrictions on our ability to build alliances and new relationships worldwide. The lack of constitutional safeguards means all of that could be possible.

While having had so much support from the Prime Minister and the Chancellor of the Exchequer throughout devolution, especially as First Minister, it was my declaration of intent that the new settlement could achieve great things – but for that to happen we needed a much broader and bolder vision. I saw nothing wrong in letting people know that there was a new First Minister in Scotland and that I was prepared to be more aggressive on Scotland's behalf, not irresponsibly but certainly more progressively.

In the new political landscape of the United Kingdom, we could go ahead with this more ambitious agenda. It was for the rest of the UK to decide whether they could benefit from similar thinking through more regionalism or devolved federalism. UK-wide change would be significant for Scotland because the more we moved ahead alone, the more we might be vulnerable. And, although we in Scotland believe we are special, other regions of the UK believe they are just as special . . .

My fear, which shows signs of being realised now, was that the mere delivery of services and spending of a handed-down budget (both of which had previously been done with reasonable competence at Westminster) would not be enough to justify devolution. Devolution had to be about much more than that. To be meaningful, it had also to be about pride, our position in the world, gaining more autonomy over our own affairs and using to best effect the enthusiasm that had been released. My worry was that enthusiasm about devolution would wane, criticism would grow and many people would be asking what was the point of constitutional change.

The entire project would lose its lustre if we had constant criticism, sniping and instability. I believed the way to counter that was by being seen to tackle the deep-seated problems of our country, improving everyday lives and making ordinary Scots feel better about their country. Recent surveys underscore this with the finding that two-thirds of Scots do not believe the Parliament has made any difference to their lives.

I also wanted to see Scotland as we were in the Enlightenment in the eighteenth century: a nation of learning and ideas, tackling the big modern issues in a way big national governments cannot. We are well placed to become one of the world's learning centres, with excellent universities and some of the best further education colleges: in Scotland, 50 per cent of 17–24 year olds are in higher education, compared to 39 per cent in England.

One of the biggest modern problems is the ageing population. We welcome the fact that people are living longer, but we do not take enough account of their quality of life. While that section of the population is growing, the population of working age is rapidly declining and the ratio of workers to dependants is worsening.

We have Europe's highest percentage of teenage pregnancies, some of the worst levels of alcoholism and drug abuse, some of the worst figures for violence and domestic abuse and an unenviable record for religious bigotry and intolerance. Who do we blame for all that? We need to think about it and come up with answers. If we have to look at Scandinavian countries or elsewhere in Europe for the solutions to these problems, we should be free to do so.

As well as tackling the problems of social and economic transition, we also have to tackle the growing issue of poverty. With one in six Scots officially defined as below the poverty line, we need a welfare agenda, but the key is the success of our economy and the creation of wealth.

The long-term solution to all of these problems lies in a dynamic and vibrant economy, but we are still a long way from achieving that – and one of the reasons is that politicians are not concentrating on our core problems.

In November 2003, *The Economist* reported:

> An unexpected ray of economic sunshine broke across Scotland with a survey showing the order books of local businesses swelling faster than at any time in the past three years. It seemed like great news . . . Since the creation of the Scottish Parliament in 1999, a near stagnant economy has dashed once rosy expectations of prosperity. But actually the news is not that good and it looks

increasingly as if local politicians are the problem, not the solution.

The survey, a purchasing managers' index by the Royal Bank of Scotland, showed that the current upturn, caused mainly by the American economy picking up, is actually bigger everywhere else in Britain. So Scotland, where the economy has grown by only 14.5 per cent since 1955 compared with 23 per cent in Britain, is still lagging behind.

It added: 'Given the national reputation for canniness, drive and thrift, Scots still ought to be doing a lot better.'

The Economist pointed out that much of this reputation was earned abroad, rather than at home, by the generations of Scots who emigrated and created or ran great commercial and industrial empires. Our bright young people still want to leave Scotland – a recent MORI poll found that a third of 17–25 year olds would emigrate given the chance.

The Economist also pointed out that public spending in Scotland consumes almost 10 per cent more of the Scottish economy than the UK generally and is fast approaching 50 per cent of GDP. One result is that the business birth rate in 2002, at 28 per 10,000 Scots, is well below the British rate of 37 per 10,000 of population, and self-employment is similarly low.

Meanwhile, poverty levels in Scotland have increased while the figures for the rest of the UK have improved since Labour came to power. The annual survey by the New Policy Institute of the Joseph Rowntree Foundation found that the number of individuals living below the poverty line in Britain had fallen, but remained stubbornly high in Scotland because of poor health and high unemployment.

In Scotland, the number of people with incomes below the poverty line (most commonly defined as 60 per cent of median household income) rose from 21.5 per cent to 23.5 per cent. This was despite Labour's anti-poverty programme – the national minimum wage, child tax credit, Sure Start, pension tax credit, working families' tax credit and disabled person's tax credit – which reduced the all-Britain figure from 25 to 23 per cent and the proportion of children in low-income households from 34 per cent to 30 per cent.

The article remarked that the number of premature deaths in Scotland was markedly higher than the rest of the UK, at 353 per 100,000 of population against the UK average of 260 per 100,000. The mortality rate in Scotland was 16 per cent above the UK average and 7 of the 10 worst UK local authorities for male life expectancy were in Scotland, as were 4 of the 5 worst local authority areas for female life expectancy. The rate of teenage pregnancy in Scotland is the highest in Europe. Five year olds in

Scotland have twice as many missing, decayed or filled teeth as in parts of England.

These problems cannot be solved overnight but it is not enough just to aspire to reach the same levels as the rest of Britain. We are falling behind other small and smart countries, regions of Europe and states in North America.

People may be forgiven for thinking that I was not involved in government at Westminster and in the Scottish Executive. I admit that in the concentration on devolution and the distractions of the new Parliament, we were not sufficiently awake to many of these issues. These real problems have now become more urgent.

The Nationalists argue that we need still more investment and help from the UK Government. But why is it that throughout the United Kingdom other regions are improving while Scotland's relative position is getting worse? Why are our more shameful figures not coming down as they are in Wales and other regions? Is it something the UK Government is not doing effectively in Scotland – or, with 20 per cent extra public expenditure per head, could it be something the Scottish Executive is not doing? Instead of always looking for the safety net and blaming the UK Government, we should first be looking at ourselves.

My main theme was 'Scotland as a state of mind'. Linked to the setting up of a new parliament, we could use the spirit of devolution to open up a new era for our country. Thinking along these lines led inevitably to questions about the relationship with Westminster and Scotland's role in the United Kingdom.

There was a view that 'putting Scotland first' was to appease nationalism and in some way to undermine the unity and integrity of the UK. That was an understandable view because Labour is a UK party and a UK Government while the Scottish National Party is narrow in perspective, with moribund policies, and is virulently anti-Labour.

However, I felt Labour in Scotland must always be the party that promotes Scotland's interests without in any way weakening our commitment to the UK – and certainly not pursuing the small-minded 'we need someone to blame' agenda of the Nationalists.

I saw no contradiction in that view, but many people refused to accept it. For two decades, the SNP had cast its shadow and, too often, the debate in Labour circles was how to counteract it. The less complicated, much more positive and genuine way forward – which, to some, might look like small 'n' nationalism – was for Scotland to make a statement about our aspirations for our own future within the UK. I knew this would be construed as distancing ourselves from Westminster and playing the Nationalist game, but that could not be further from the truth.

The debate had been distorted by Nationalism and now had to be re-focused on facing up to the real meaning of devolution. There really had not been any deep thinking over the previous decade about what would follow the Scotland Act and the setting-up of the Parliament in Edinburgh. Westminster, including Scottish MPs, thought it was a task completed. For them, the journey had ended – but for myself it had only begun.

It became a key issue for me: who sets the agenda and who decides the policies? The media, interest groups, think tanks, Westminster and political parties all have their ideas, and we could be knocked off course by things that arrived with breathtaking speed and were blown up into so-called crises but disappeared just as quickly.

Part of the mission was not only to change the governance of Scotland but also to change how government was perceived by Scotland. It was important to make speeches, discuss ideas, define the difference between the Scottish Parliament and Westminster and pose questions about how far we wanted to go with devolution and how to use the powers we had.

The media want things to report, but there is a constituency of interests that really does not want innovation, change or new policies. One of the difficulties as I write is that the Scottish Government is becalmed. The Executive does not get credit for the unannounced things it does day in and day out, things involving education, health, transport, housing, social justice and law and order – but it is not moving devolution forward. In that apparent vacuum, you find the credibility of the Parliament being undermined.

I began to see that doing things differently was going to be very difficult because of these conflicting interests. I had to steer a careful course between the SNP, who wanted to tear up the settlement and move to independence, and those at Westminster who wanted us to continue to manage and improve services as the word 'Executive' suggests, but not to do any original thinking.

Also, instead of pandering to nationalism, it was actually dealing with the Nationalist threat. If we were standing up for Scotland and finding distinctively Scottish answers, how could they claim to have a monopoly on 'Scottishness'? How could they criticise us for not being 'patriotic'?

Because Labour had not been encouraged to think about these things, we were accused of being nationalists or fellow-travellers. My internationalism and my experience of other countries informed what I was doing and thinking. Perhaps we in Scotland, by history and constitutional constraints, were not supposed to think for ourselves. As someone who believes strongly in the United Kingdom and who has seen how devolution has developed in Europe and the US, I also believe that the UK will only be strong in the future if it pursues devolved government throughout Britain with some urgency and commitment.

Scotland is a different country from England or Wales or Northern Ireland with different needs and attitudes. I saw no reason why we should not have different answers to similar problems. Other people saw this as creating difficulties with Westminster and testing the boundaries, but I saw it as implementing the spirit of devolution.

We had been elected on a promise to find Scottish solutions to Scottish problems. I needed no other justification for going our own way, irrespective of UK policy, on a number of important governmental issues:

FISHING: Strong views are held by the fishing community, but there was no escaping the cold fact that too many fishermen were hunting for too few fish. Ninety per cent of the British fishing industry is Scottish, so we had every right to be looking at the industry's future and we earmarked £25 million for the decommissioning of boats to reduce capacity. The industry did not like it because they wanted a tie-up scheme, which would see them being subsidised to have boats lying idle at the quaysides, which did not make economic sense or address the basic problem. The United Kingdom Government was not giving financial help and it was not looking at decommissioning down south.

We were defeated in the Scottish Parliament because, despite the coalition, some Liberal Democrats would not support the Executive and, more specifically, their own colleague Ross Finnie, who was Fisheries Minister. The deal had to be rescued and after some harsh words with the Liberal Democrats we won the vote the following week. I recognised the nature of politics in Scotland was now 'in your face' and individual MSPs could be under enormous, and often unreasonable, pressures, but 14 years at Westminster had taught me the need for discipline.

When we lost the vote, I drove to Inverness for the Scottish Labour Party conference and stopped at Pitlochry for a fish supper. Given the political price and the millions we were giving to the fishermen, I reflected that the lady behind the counter had no idea she was serving me the most expensive fish supper ever!

FOOT-AND-MOUTH: The outbreak of foot-and-mouth disease was a difficult time for the country, causing devastation and real hardship in rural areas. There have been lasting consequences for the future and many personal tragedies. What got us through was the extraordinary way Scotland dealt with the catastrophe compared with England. The National Farmers' Union of Scotland took the lead in showing how to deal with the crisis. In particular, I could only admire the remarkable sacrifices made by those in the Dumfries and Galloway region, where the farming community and the local authorities demonstrated great solidarity and consideration for the greater good. Again, it highlighted how we could do things differently in Scotland and achieve better results.

Throughout the crisis, I had constant meetings with the NFU and representatives of Dumfries and Galloway. There was impressive unity of purpose, whereas in England there were competing interests and serious differences over policy. Whether or not to vaccinate cattle became a major controversy in England, but it was never an issue in Scotland. From the start, the unanimous view in Scotland was that vaccination would be a backward step. Apart from being a distraction from the immediate task of eradicating foot-and-mouth, it would become an enormous threat to future exports.

When I imparted the Scottish decision to both the Prime Minister and his Minister for Agriculture, Fisheries and Food, Nick Brown, there was something of a wobble in Whitehall, where they were thinking very seriously about the vaccination of the national herd. I made clear to Nick Brown that we would definitely not be vaccinating in Scotland, no matter what they did in England. When I spoke to him late on a Friday night, I got the impression there was a difference of opinion between No. 10 and the Department of Environment, Food and Rural Affairs, and Nick said I should inform the Prime Minister.

Although it was not my place to say so, I made it clear I did not think they should vaccinate in England. Tony Blair welcomed Scotland's good sense and praised the way the outbreak had been handled north of the border. We may have played some part in firming up opinion in Whitehall because the issue disappeared. This was how I imagined devolution working, at times advising the UK Government of Scottish practice and policy and showing how it could be better than London's.

Meanwhile, we had to get on with the task of rebuilding the fragile economy in those rural areas where agriculture and tourism had been so badly affected. There has been recovery, but the spectre of burning pyres of cattle is still deep in the consciousness of the community.

TEACHERS' PAY: As a consequence of my own experience, I have always been a supporter of the highest possible quality of teaching. In May 2000, the Independent Committee of Inquiry led by Professor Gavin McCrone reported on teachers' pay, conditions of service and promotion structures, and ways to ensure professional, committed and flexible teachers for all children in Scotland. It led to a landmark agreement on creating 'a teaching profession for the twenty-first century'.

Significant pay increases would be matched by far-reaching changes in the way teachers worked. This immediately led to claims of pressure being exerted on the Westminster Government for a better deal in England, with teachers' unions using Scotland as a lever for higher pay.

It was a good deal for teachers in Scotland, but it was in the country's interest because learning lay at the heart of the strategy for successful individuals, communities and the economy. I had always borne in mind a 1988 editorial in *Business Week* which said, in a remarkably visionary view for a business magazine at that time, that school teachers should be paid the same as hospital consultants. That might be wishful thinking but the main point remains: that we do not yet value teachers and education in the way we should.

The responsibility carried by a teacher standing in front of 30 children in a primary class is about more than merely instilling information; the teacher often becomes family adviser, social worker, protector and the person to set standards. It was right for the Scottish Parliament to set its own higher value on the teaching profession.

The McCrone award was more than just footing the bill for a pay increase; it was a statement of how my administration regarded education in Scotland in the twenty-first century.

FREE PERSONAL CARE FOR THE ELDERLY: This issue provided a fascinating new insight into how policy in Scotland can emerge and how political parties and civil society can make an impact. When I expressed my interest in its introduction, it caused waves, especially in my own party. There was little support for it within the Scottish Parliamentary Labour Party, partly because Donald Dewar had been strongly opposed to it, and the Scottish Health Minister Susan Deacon was not supportive.

The Sutherland Commission report had been comprehensively rubbished and dismissed by the UK Government and I felt there had not been a proper debate in Scotland. I knew Sir Stewart Sutherland, the principal of Edinburgh University, was angry and bitter at the way he and his Royal Commission had been treated by the UK Government after producing a report which would have broken new ground in helping some of the most deserving and vulnerable people in our society.

The development of the policy within the Scottish Executive was certainly not a textbook example of government at work. It was messy and bedevilled by leaks from those in the Cabinet who were opposed to it, and it was no surprise that one headline described it as 'Making Policy on the Hoof' – I am not sure it was even that sophisticated!

My position was strengthened quite remarkably by the support of other political parties, including the Liberal Democrats, and by special interest groups the length and breadth of the country, who represented not only older people. Despite my internal difficulties in the Executive and the Labour Party and a significant misunderstanding about what free personal care entailed, this created a natural majority in the Parliament. The measure went through its various stages, helped by important work done by two working groups that were set up – and also my own absolute unwillingness to bow to the growing pressures from Westminster and Scottish MPs.

The discussions with UK ministers were difficult and there was simply no way to bridge the divide between us. I had a lively dinner in London with the Health Secretary Alan Milburn. Ironically, he had been my junior on Health when I was No. 2 to Harriet Harman, so we had a close friendship and I admired his outstanding ability, which I believe could take him to the top. However, at our dinner on the South Bank there was a lot of 'pit language' and there was no smoothing over our differences. Alan was adamant that he and the other UK ministers would not support the policy, not least because of the budget cost of £1 billion in England and Wales. We decided to enjoy the rest of dinner and we parted amiably. It had been important that the meeting took place so that no one could be in any doubt about our positions.

A subsequent meeting with Work and Pensions Secretary Alistair Darling was in a similar vein as far as ministerial and party positions were concerned. It will inevitably become a theme throughout devolution that a policy created north of the border will engage interest groups in England, who will then demand parity. With devolution, it is constitutionally within our powers to go our own way on such matters. There was no acrimony, but no movement on either side.

Due to the complexities of the healthcare and social security systems, we would be saving the social security budget about £25 million in benefits already paid by the UK Government to elderly people in Scotland. Although this was an untested area, in my view it should have been possible for the Westminster Government to provide that £25 million to help in financing free personal care. This met with an absolutely firm refusal.

If other legal complications had been examined, there might have been further protracted dialogue with the UK Government but it was clear they would not be worth pursuing at that particular time. In practice, it would have meant exhaustive departmental and ministerial discussions, identifying doubtful areas and disputed powers that would then have proceeded to endless discussions. Informal one-to-one discussions between ministers over dinner may be one way of resolving inter-governmental problems without jumping through legal and constitutional hoops, but we need to acknowledge this informal method did not work to Scotland's benefit in this situation. I cannot foresee a Scottish Labour First Minister having a private tête-à-tête over the dinner table with a Conservative counterpart in London. We have to find better and more formal ways of resolving potential problems at ministerial level.

On care of the elderly, the obvious question of finance loomed large. Much of the debate was influenced by those who demanded how on earth we could find the money to pay for it and the more cynical view taken by those at Westminster who claimed that the settlement must be overgenerous: 'If you have the money, then we must be giving you too much.'

What surprised and shocked me was the old-fashioned thinking behind these views. Not only can things be different in Scotland but we can also have different priorities and different spending commitments. By being more effective and efficient on spending, money can be found for new priorities. If that were not the case, the Executive would do nothing new, especially when the public purse strings may have to be tightened.

We found the money by being prudent and looking for savings. We had to change the mindset at every level of government so it was understood that merely because money had been spent in a certain way for decades, it did not have to be the permanent pattern. Under the block grant, the Scottish Executive has to work with a fixed amount of money but it also has the responsibility to constantly review its priorities. If a case can be made for more creative spending, ministers must have the courage and common sense to release the resources. We found £25 million for the fishing industry, £800 million for the teachers and £125 million for free personal care.

It is true that the cost of free personal care will rise, but I believed – and still do – that Scotland wanted to deal with the iniquities and inconsistencies of the old system. Why should an elderly person's well-being depend on an inter-departmental argument over payment? What was the difference between an NHS bath and a social services bath? If care qualified as medical or nursing attendance, it was free. Yet if the same person had a debilitating condition, no less harsh in its impact but not classified as 'medical', such as those with dementia who need constant attention and physical care, it had to be paid for by the individual or the family. In what should be a totally integrated healthcare approach, this made no sense and created cruel anomalies.

For reasons they will have to justify, cynics at Westminster and in my own party had lightly dismissed the humane recommendations of a distinguished expert group. All the political parties in Scotland, with the exception of Labour, supported the Sutherland Report and so did overwhelming public opinion. So who was out of step?

I was the First Minister of Scotland doing what most of Scotland wanted. What was the fault in that?

The media seemed very keen to suggest my wife was involved in promoting the policy. Certainly, as one of Scotland's foremost experts on care of the elderly, she was interested and gave me enthusiastic encouragement. As a key professional in that area, she felt, along with the rest of Scotland, that it was an important step to take.

That was as far as her influence went, because I felt it was far more than a personal policy. It was a statement on behalf of a compassionate Scotland, a society that has yet to address the consequences of our increasingly ageing population. The growing number of frail and elderly, who are benefiting from new drugs, advances in medical science and technology and huge improvements in facilities, will stretch our thinking and our resources as a caring community.

Another major concern for society must be how these financial costs will be shared between private and public, between citizen and government. The free personal care question opened up that debate and for the first time some serious consideration was given to the anomalies and iniquities of the present and the pressures of the future.

Virtually unnoticed, it also focused attention on the well-tried Barnett formula, plus benefits of rising public investment from Westminster and the protection of a formidable Scottish Chancellor. There are no written guarantees that we will have these in the long-term future.

Instead of giving us credit for using the powers given to us by devolution to create a specifically Scottish policy to help the elderly, the political and media comment consisted to a large extent of alarmist rubbish. I was accused of creating a 'constitutional nightmare' and there were laughable predictions of a flood of wealthy pensioners crossing the border to protect their savings, a boom in nursing homes in the Scottish Borders and 'a queue of cars at Gretna as the English middle class rush north with granny in the back'.

All of that was forgotten when free care for the elderly in Scotland was finally introduced on 1 July 2002, eight months after I left office. It was universally welcomed and no one dared to repeat the attacks. I must say I was alarmed when my successor announced a three-month delay in its implementation while the new administration examined methods of limiting future rises in the cost. The usual 'ally' of the First Minister was anonymously quoted as saying: 'It was definitely looked at, but there was no wriggle-room. Free personal care had majority support in the Parliament and all the criteria were laid down in statute. It would have been politically very difficult to change it.'

For the sake of Scotland's older people, I can only say I am very glad we did not leave any 'wriggle-room'.

It seemed important to me to have a policy review to look creatively at what we were doing right across all the Executive's activities. It was also an attempt to look at the psychology of government and the things that could be scrapped. We had inherited a great number of policies developed over the years at Westminster. If we were able to implement new policies like free personal care, it should not be beyond us to review all our policies and create new opportunities.

The First Minister should always be looking for some definition of what the nation represents, what its population wants it to be and what kind of government its people want presiding over them. Not change for the sake of change but to lead a forward-thinking Executive that should never take anything for granted.

The essence of the policy review was to modernise our approach across the spectrum of government and in particular the notion espoused by the Prime Minister that more of our public investment has to be linked to more reform and modernisation.

For too long and too often in Scotland we have turned a blind eye to inefficiency and ineffectiveness in the delivery of public services. This must change. Apart from the reform issue, we need to ensure that any investment of public money is made wisely.

This is especially critical in the context of the Scottish Parliament, where the block grant formula defines how much investment we will have. Reformulating our priorities becomes difficult and, because most of these public service priorities were set for us in London, it is not something that we have been good at north of the border.

There is also a traditionalist view that because we have been spending money on a particular service or in a particular way, it has to continue indefinitely. It should be obvious that we must be continually reviewing not only why we are spending money but what we are actually doing with it and for whom.

This requires a degree of focus, thoroughness and determination that is lacking among civil servants and ministers, but that lack is particularly noticeable at local government level. In local government there is a massive disconnect between spending money and raising it, because it only raises 12 per cent of its budgets through council tax.

The spending review was meant to create a new awareness about spending other people's money and to introduce a new urgency into our ways of operating. Once on the treadmill of government, you are subject to competing demands and the pressure of a wide variety of reasonable needs. You attempt to do as much as possible and often that conflicts with the notion that literally every penny should be scrutinised in terms of the impact it achieves.

The result is a considerable waste at every level and in every form of government. It is the nature of the culture of government in Scotland and there has to be a major change in our thinking, especially when we consider that the massive increase in investments we experienced between 1999 and now may not happen again. That is why, when people said we could not find new money for new projects, my response was that we could, because we had a new way of thinking.

In addition, I was keen to build up good systems for constantly monitoring long-established policies; hammering out and assessing the implications of policy fields in which there was considerable change; and dealing with new policy fields like technology, telecommunications and e-business. We also have to embrace some of the extremely complex and challenging issues like our ageing population and declining workforce and the consequences for pensions, social services and the economy.

Improving our capacity for policy-making should automatically mean that civil servants and ministers consult a wider range of interest groups, think tanks, experts in business and industry and have a much more interactive relationship with those in the Scottish community who can contribute. Government in Scotland does not have a monopoly on wisdom but is too often unwilling to step outside its own confines.

I also wanted us not to be content with bench-marking against the rest of the UK. Sadly, in many areas we are not as innovative as the Westminster Government (and even some English local authorities), but in the twenty-first century we should be setting our standards against the wider world. That involves using statistics and criteria provided by the UN, the World Bank, IMF, OECD and the European Union, and being more aware of what other parts of the world are achieving.

It is easy to spend money, but – as the present Scottish administration is demonstrating – much more difficult to deliver. Spending money does not guarantee outcomes and much of our public investment is a scatter-gun approach.

The public are now more discerning, have higher expectations and are less accepting of failure. What is missing is a clear focus on what we are trying to achieve.

A great deal of spending on education and the health service is not focused. In particular, we found we were spending vast amounts of money on health, not getting much public benefit but receiving continuing media criticism. It is a high-priority area and it eats up finance because of massive expectation, ever more expensive technology and a huge salary bill. Investing more in healthcare does not achieve overnight results, and the hope is that by buying new technology, building more modern facilities and improving morale among the workforce you will achieve better results. Most of the health service works far removed from the centre and finds change difficult. And where there are always recognised improvements, ministers are not always good at communicating and explaining.

Since we will not always have increases in public investment through

UK government funding, in Scotland we will need to think of new ways of getting the private sector involved and new partnership methods of creating more investment.

The Scottish Parliament is in a similar situation to local government, in that all the money spent in Scotland is a tranche of UK tax expenditure. Ultimately, there should be more freedom for the Scottish Parliament and Scottish Executive to innovate in terms of finance. This could mean new ways of looking at the tax-varying power and new forms of public-value partnerships with the involvement of both private and public capital.

Midway through the first fixed four-year term of the Scottish Parliament, I sought to re-state the core aims, beliefs and values of my administration as: 'A confident, competitive and compassionate Scotland'.

I wanted Scotland to feel confident in its future, its constitutional relations and, above all, confident in its own capacities; competitive in taking tough decisions for the long term, spending money wisely and building an economy to compete in global markets; and to be a fair, caring and tolerant nation in which everybody matters.

The message of my speech on 20 August 2001 at Glasgow University was the new realism in Scotland's government: what matters is what works.

I wanted it clearly understood that in any conflict between pragmatism and ideology, pragmatism would always prevail without sacrifice of principle. The examples I gave were the public–private partnership to renew Glasgow's schools and the new PPP hospital in East Kilbride, which was at the time ready to open.

There was also a firm warning that the interests of consumers would be put before those of producers. Even the best of the traditional public services could lose sight of their main goal – to serve the public – and often did. So in the Scottish NHS we had swept away the internal market and set out a programme of change, including 300 one-stop clinics, organised around patients' need and for patients' convenience. A tough decision about Trunk Road Maintenance Contracts had clear consequences for the producers but delivered substantial savings for use elsewhere.

Across Scottish life, there was an untidy legacy of quangos, left over from the bygone age of pre-devolution Scotland. Scrutiny showed that a third of them no longer needed to exist and another third were in need of fundamental review. This became known as the 'bonfire of the quangos', but as far as I can see, over two years later, it has yet to be lit.

I hoped the speech would sum up the considerable achievement of delivering devolution and the benefits that were beginning to flow from it, as well as communicating a longer-term view that devolution or regional government gave us the chance not to be shackled by the past or by the baggage carried by political parties.

In Scotland, we now had the chance to put ideas before ideology and to be consensual rather than adversarial. Outwith the overheated hothouse atmosphere of politics we could look at things that matter most directly to ordinary people and make them work, irrespective of party divides. A lot of political opposition is ritualistic and I was sending a signal that I was prepared to be pragmatic and work with others to achieve the best results. The slogan 'what matters is what works' encapsulated a whole new way of thinking in Scottish government.

Making speeches was to be increasingly important. Scotland is very traditional, at times not at all forward-thinking, and had in the previous years been very much dependent on Westminster and Whitehall. Civil servants, some special advisers and the media seemed largely uninterested in thinking creatively and were more interested in personalities and problems and the daily ebb-and-flow of life on the Mound in Edinburgh. Our new Parliament should have been generating more original ideas and debate, taking stock and challenging the Executive. Instead, the short-lived appeal of the cut-and-thrust in the chamber seemed to be more important to MSPs.

It was no wonder that the Scottish electorate was becoming disconnected from what was supposedly being done on their behalf. In this atmosphere of cynicism, mistrust and lack of confidence, and in the light of the media's lack of interest in explaining government to the people, I felt it was an important part of my job to air the ideas and issues that did not make the headlines.

Scotland is no different from Westminster in that Question Time in Parliament and the skirmishes across the floor are more important for image and public interest than policy discussions. For me, the weekly First Minister's Questions slot posed a dilemma.

Formal addresses such as the statement on the death of Donald Dewar, the welcome to President Mbeki and speeches in debate were no problem. To this day, I am at a loss to explain what I was doing in my early days at the lectern in First Minister's Questions. I look back with some puzzlement because, despite having been a minister in a similar situation both at Holyrood and Westminster, I was strangely ill-prepared when I succeeded Donald Dewar. I had not given enough thought to the tactics of Question Time and I had not realised the significance of that 20 minutes every week.

When I went into the chamber, I had spent too much time in briefings and not enough in thinking of the broader arguments. We spent most of the day going over every conceivable question that might be asked, thinking about every issue, preparing ready responses. The effect was that the preparation was too thorough. Instead of giving concise and crisp, but adequate, responses, I had so much material that every reply became a speech. I had always been a person for statistics and detail but that was not what was required in that arena. Too often, I tried for dramatic overkill rather than a modest, businesslike and effective riposte. In fact, I think I took First Minister's Questions far more seriously than it merited – and I was my own worst enemy. When I was good, that was what was expected of a First Minister; when I was bad, I was awful.

What made it more inexcusable was that my difficulties had nothing to do with the other party leaders because the performance of the Opposition was lamentable. They were always predictable and our prediction of what they were going to say was rarely wrong; they were often personal in their attacks, which made them look petty; and, of course, they were always partisan.

I now realise that First Minister's Questions is little more than a TV game show, giving the other party leaders a weekly audience they are unlikely to get otherwise. I should have settled for a workmanlike 20 minutes, never being concerned with what the Opposition tried to throw at me, taking the chance to highlight the issues I wanted and contrasting our growing list of achievements with the lack of constructive ideas from them.

XIII

Scotland in the World

With a new wider vision, we could see Scotland in the worldwide context and I wanted to seize the momentum offered by devolution. We are now at the point where being international, interconnected and interdependent are the paths to success in the twenty-first century.

I was conscious that those with a limited outlook could construe any go-it-alone Scottish initiative in international affairs as incipient nationalism. That was why it was difficult to explain publicly: a great deal of what happened in my year as First Minister was less than transparent and a lot of it was done in code. It may have looked incremental and fragmented, but there were good reasons why I did not present it for what it was – part of a bigger idea of the future of our country.

That low-key approach to what was an ambitious plan for Scotland was conditioned by the likely reaction from Westminster and Whitehall, which was at its most difficult in relation to Europe. I believed we had to be prominent in Europe but this was 'forbidden territory' as far as Westminster was concerned at this early stage in devolution. Change in our relations with Europe and the world was possible, but we had to ensure this was not misconstrued or distorted by those opposed to devolution. By taking one significant step away from Westminster we could help Scotland exploit the opportunities of the future – but it had to be done quietly and without fuss.

To promote Scottish tourism and industry, we had to strengthen existing international links and alliances and establish new ones. We also had to acknowledge that it was important for a country like Scotland to learn from the rest of the world. This could only be done by changing our national attitudes and understanding the significance of globalisation. We also had to look afresh at the international dimension of Scottish Enterprise and our export wing, Scottish Development International, as well as UK organisations such as the British Council and the British Tourist Authority. We also needed to establish our own events strategy and capability to attract prestigious occasions.

An important role for the First Minister is to raise Scotland's profile in the world and this meant being host to important and distinguished foreign visitors. These included a day in Scotland for the vice-president of China, Hu Jintao, now president and head of state, who visited the Royal Botanical Gardens and was guest of honour at a banquet in the Great Hall of Edinburgh Castle; President Mbeki of South Africa participated in a financial services lunch at the Palace of Holyroodhouse chaired by the Prince of Wales; and a number of heads of important regions within the European Union, including President Pujol of Catalonia. These visits were an indication of the status that devolution has given Scotland but, more importantly, these initial visits had to be followed up to build on the goodwill in terms of economic, social and cultural benefits. China is a good example. I met the Chinese Education Minister in Edinburgh and Kunming, western China, and also met the president and head of state. This country, with its population of 1.4 billion, will be a world leader and economy in the twenty-first century. A vital area of interest for us.

On the vexed question of tourism, which had suffered such severe setbacks in recent years, we had undertaken a very significant review of policy. The industry does reasonably well but could be doing so much better. It is a major employer, earning £3 billion per year, sells our country abroad and, by its very nature, improves the quality of life throughout Scotland.

Despite the huge income it earns for the nation, the Government put in tiny resources of £25 million to finance the Scottish Tourist Board and its various agencies worldwide. It was obvious that we had to increase the budget, while making sure the industry gave us value for the extra money.

It was a difficult time because the tourist figures for Scotland had been declining over the years. There is a distinct lack of ambition and we do not show confidence in what we are selling, despite Scotland's outstanding qualities as a country to visit. A huge amount of goodwill is created by our history, our culture, our products, the natural beauty of our country and the Scottish emigrants and their families in every part of the world.

I did not think it would be hard to reorganise and build a bigger picture for our tourist industry. However, there are many conflicts, many different opinions about the best way forward and too many people in the industry had become complacent – allowing Scotland's image to sell itself may have been good enough in the past but nowadays there is far keener competition for the tourist dollar, yen or euro.

The Scottish Tourist Board had to become more sophisticated and focused but there were personal clashes within the industry and its institutions, and divisions between the central organisation and area tourist boards. The major cities were always very keen to look after their own interests and saw themselves in competition with each other. Edinburgh and Glasgow could benefit from a 'twin city' approach, complementing each other in so many different ways, but they largely remain rivals. The same could be said of local tourist boards all over Scotland, which are fragmented and cling to their local identities. Tourism should be about selling Scotland, using Edinburgh and Glasgow as gateways, and forging partnerships to open up all of Scotland to visitors.

We attempted to develop the additional concept of Scotland as a niche player using our genealogy, our historic sites, our scenery and the universal appeal of our culture. For instance, having lived in St Andrews, I know the singular worldwide appeal of a visit to the 'home of golf'. It was all new thinking for the tourist industry, which had been underselling Scotland in spite of our unique advantages.

Here again, we came up against resistance in London to Scotland doing things for itself. Questions were asked about why we should be making the effort to market ourselves when there is the British Tourist Authority. There is a great deal of discontent within the Scottish tourist industry about not being able to do things abroad in our own way, with our own special product. That issue has yet to be settled.

As First Minister, I was continually looking to Scotland's role within the UK, and Europe, as well as its role as part of a world that is increasingly interconnected and interdependent. Global finance, trade, investment and the electronic revolution know no frontiers and it seemed inevitable that Scotland should become more active in developing relationships and alliances, without necessarily relying on the UK or Westminster for initiatives or permission.

However, foreign affairs and Europe were reserved matters and I had a sense of having less room to manoeuvre on the international front than in any other area. European and international relations were regarded as a litmus test of whether we were abiding by the spirit and small print of the devolution settlement. Post-devolution, there were people in Whitehall waiting for us to move in that direction so they could put us back in our box.

During that period, it was a help to have Robin Cook as Foreign Secretary. Our personal relations were good and, as a pro-devolution Scot, he was able to provide encouragement and defend what we were doing to those in London who were critical or downright hostile.

As Minister for Enterprise, I had travelled widely and was responsible for developing technology agreements with Maryland, Virginia and California. That kind of activity did not create problems, but there were difficulties over international visits, hosting international dignitaries and delegations in Scotland and moves to become directly involved in Europe.

I felt it important to play a part in a strong 'Europe of the regions' and undertake activities in Scotland's interests, which would not necessarily be served by the UK. In particular, a continuing dilemma was the question of representing Scotland in Europe. Who should lead United Kingdom delegations on agriculture and fishing? How best could Scotland contribute to UK policy on European matters? How could our Parliament participate in and scrutinise legislation emanating from Europe? How could Scotland be given more of a foothold, building closer links with regions, autonomous provinces and states in an increasingly integrated Europe?

The new regionalism was an issue of growing importance to Scotland. We should be thinking 20 or 30 years ahead to when there will be a powerful regionalism in Europe and a potentially different United Kingdom with federal devolution.

Interestingly, while we are now talking about a new constitution for Europe, many of our problems in the devolved setting stem from not having a constitution in the UK. As with the Scotland Act and our financial powers, there are few safeguards for Scotland in Europe. That may not be an issue as long as we have a Labour Government with personalities largely sympathetic to Scotland and devolution, but all that could change with a different UK Government. Under a strict interpretation, Scotland has a very limited role, but even that could be circumscribed by a change in personalities, policies or government at Westminster. Currently, there is peaceful co-existence between a Labour–Lib Dem Government in Scotland and a Labour Government at Westminster, but a change in the complexion of the government in either place could create constitutional chaos.

Tartan Day had been established by the Senate to mark 6 April as a day for the celebration of Scotland in the USA. Initiated by Senate Leader Trent Lott, himself of Scottish descent, it builds on the past, enormous goodwill, shared experience, shared language, shared culture and a huge Scottish-American population. This had been caught up in a great deal of sentiment and nationalism operating in the US, but to me this was just the narrow opening of what could be a window of opportunity for Scotland. I thought it should be extended to at least a week of opportunities.

Our visit to the US in April 2001 gave me the opportunity to start this process seriously. With much more pre-planning, we were able to showcase Scotland's world-class resources – universities, industries, science and technology, and, of course, the natural beauty and endless attractions of our country.

During discussions in Washington, it was disappointing to discover that there were two representatives of the Northern Ireland Assembly working from the British Embassy, but no Scots. There and then, I raised this omission with the ambassador Sir Christopher Meyer, who was most sympathetic and helpful. Instead of regarding a special Scottish presence as an outrageous idea, he saw it as his task to enrich the UK's representation by adding the diversity of Scotland, Wales and Northern Ireland. Scotland's representative Susan Stewart is now at the heart of our embassy, with the rank of First Secretary.

The Foreign Office were concerned about the ambassador's attitude, but it is now a reality. The significance of this was that it broke the mould and held out the prospect of a Scottish presence in other key British embassies around the world.

As part of our visit, we combined with Brian Souter of Stagecoach in launching his new open-top bus service for tourists in New York – another Scottish entrepreneur and a little bit of Scotland at the heart of one of the world's greatest cities. Among the receptions and private occasions with the business and media community was a meeting with the Secretary of State for Technology of Virginia, with whom we had signed an agreement. Virginia, one of the most advanced states in the world, had recognised the importance of technology by creating a special Cabinet post, and it seemed to me this was something from which we needed to learn. Our Cabinet had been based on the traditional Westminster model, when instead it should have reflected the new priorities of the electronic age rather than replicating what existed in the mid-twentieth century.

The highlights of the US visit were two meetings which had not been scheduled when we left Scotland – one was with President George W. Bush and the other with Sean Connery. It is hard to say which was more impressive!

The meeting at the White House was an opportunity to show Scotland on the world stage, but back home the news was received with a remarkable degree of cynicism and sour grapes. The attitude was: 'What on earth is the First Minister of Scotland up to?' It was typical of the small-minded thinking of those who were still wedded to the Westminster-led style of government we had left behind. Their 'know your place' posture was a very Scottish trait – disappointing and, in the longer term, damaging.

They could not see that it was Scotland at the White House, in the person of the First Minister. Some people are so restricted in their thinking and so narrow in their vision that they cannot understand how this was in the interests of Scotland and was giving an added status to our new Government and Parliament.

On the way into the White House, we passed through several security checks and at the last the secret service agent asked my private secretary from Edinburgh if he was carrying his gun with him. We told him a gun wasn't standard equipment for us but it was a telling reminder of the state of alertness and the fact that we were in a culture with 300 million guns, one for each citizen.

The meeting with George W. Bush was fascinating but I could be forgiven for being slightly self-indulgent. In my youth I had looked at the White House from afar, read the biographies of great presidents and later studied US politics in detail; now, unexpectedly, here I was sitting in the Oval Office with the President, his national security adviser Condoleeza Rice and chief of staff Andrew Card.

Having arrived in the US with no meeting planned, we were scheduled to have ten minutes with the President (again, something which caused snide comments in Scotland) but the meeting lasted half an hour. George W. Bush showed a very informed interest in Scotland and this was not simply the result of some presidential briefing for the occasion. Ours was a country he had visited more than almost any other because of his father's links with the oil industry, and as a teenager he had spent holidays in Scotland. All the more significant, since it is well known the President did not travel widely before he entered the White House.

As well as his familiarity with Scotland, he talked about the problems of State he was dealing with that day. A US spy plane had been shot down over China, which explained the presence of his security adviser, and America's biggest-ever tax cut was on the floor of Congress; he had dispatched his vice-president Dick Cheney to make sure there were no slip-ups. Over a mug of coffee, President Bush could not have been more relaxed and he made it plain that he would have talked longer but for the somewhat intimidating presence of Condoleeza Rice, who insisted several times, 'Mr President, we really have to go.'

Before he left, his final comment showed his intense dislike of the media. Bush is under constant attack from most of the media but he makes no concessions to his critics. He told me: 'I'm on my way to meet the editors of every newspaper in the USA and sit down to lunch with 1,500 of them. I can't think of anything I'd less like to do with my lunchtime.'

As I left, I reflected that this was a first for Scotland. With the exception of the Prime Minister, at that time probably no one else in government in the UK had sat down in the Oval Office with the President.

155

Part of the Tartan Day celebration was the presentation to Sean Connery of the William Wallace Award on the steps of Capitol. It was a spectacular ceremony with a magnificent setting, looking from the Congress building along the famous mall to the Lincoln Memorial and the Washington Monument, flanked by the National Aerospace Museum and the Smithsonian, two of the most impressive buildings in the capital.

After our speeches, we walked through Congress and had lunch with Senator Trent Lott, the Senate majority leader, and his wife. It was well-deserved recognition by the Scottish-American community of an outstanding Scot and I took the opportunity to follow it up with a meeting with Sean Connery in the embassy.

I already had a strong relationship with his agent James Barron, another American with Scottish forefathers, and we had been discussing the possibility of Connery becoming active in helping Scotland develop its worldwide contacts. It was very easy to talk with Connery, who is wise, unassuming and down to earth. It helped that we were both ex-players with a shared passion for football and, from our previous meeting, we were able to resume reminiscences about his days with Bonnyrigg Rose in the junior league in the Lothians.

During our discussions, I could not help thinking what an underused asset this man was to our country. There was no disguising the fact that Sean Connery was no friend of Labour, having espoused Nationalism and the Scottish National Party. Although it was never openly referred to, he was clearly disappointed at being snubbed by Donald Dewar over his knighthood. Had the matter been raised, there was no explanation I could have given, other than that at that time there were some in the Executive who could neither forgive nor forget his Nationalist ties – even after the important role he played in helping the referendum campaign. Above all, there can never be any doubt about Connery's great affection for his country.

Most of my colleagues were unaware of my discussions with Sean Connery and his agent, but in putting an international jigsaw together, I thought it was important to get him involved on a non-political basis with what the Executive was trying to do for Scotland.

It was not going to be easy, as I found out, because Sean Connery found it very difficult to accommodate the idea of being on one hand a Scottish Nationalist and supporter of the SNP, and on the other working with a Labour–Lib Dem Government. Within the SNP, it might have been felt that he was 'selling out'. This was nonsense, since his love for his country is so genuine and so obvious – but it was understandable that he should have reservations because of the way he had been treated and his dislike for Labour's policies.

My task was to convince him that we could do business together for

Scotland's good. I impressed on him the need to promote Scotland in the changing world and the good he could do in supporting our strategy for attracting international events, making the most of Scotland's assets and also in the development of creative industries, including film and theatre.

The meeting was not immediately productive but step-by-step we were building a relationship. I was unconcerned about the party political considerations: there was a clear distinction between what Sean Connery did for the SNP and what he could do for Scotland. I was merely interested in having one of Scotland's greatest living icons, with worldwide recognition, helping to promote our country.

After my resignation as First Minister, I kept in close touch with James Barron and, during a family holiday, spent time in California with the Barron family. We talked a great deal about Scotland, during which I impressed on him my desire to have Sean Connery working for Scotland. In turn, he had arranged for me to address the San Francisco Scottish club. On a foggy night, over 60 expatriates and Scottish descendants turned out, a reminder to me of the potential of the Scottish diaspora – a global network, waiting to be used for the good of their home country. They certainly made the most of our greatest export and the evening closed with the distribution of large whiskies ('large' being the equivalent of a half pint) and one of the best specimens of the greasy Scotch mutton pie, made by a local Scottish baker, that I have ever sampled.

After my departure from office, Sean Connery continued to be keen to make himself available and become an unofficial ambassador for Scotland. However, in a front-page story under the headline 'Shnubbed', the *Daily Record* reported that while Connery could work easily with me, he could not say the same about my successor as First Minister, Jack McConnell. He had felt my door was always open to him and his calls would always be returned, but the Scottish Executive's door had now slammed shut.

Apart from being a waste of a true Scot, who is the embodiment of a national asset, there were other practical consequences. With money set aside in the Scottish budget for a Scottish film studio, the project could have gone ahead with Sir Sean as the figurehead and motivator. While he wanted it in his native Edinburgh, the Executive wanted it in Glasgow and others in the Parliament were lobbying for Inverness, so the project fell apart. No one saw the irony of a country without a single film studio, squabbling about three – and ending up with none.

Golf's Ryder Cup was last held in Scotland at Muirfield in 1973 and I felt that after 30 years it should return. In this, of all sports, our credentials go before us. The home of golf, with some of the most famous, challenging and beautiful courses in the world, was more than qualified to put in a world-class bid.

We saw the significance of staging major sporting and cultural events as matters of national prestige, pride and (it should not be underestimated) prosperity. The Ryder Cup attracts the third largest television audience of all the global sporting events, after the Olympic Games and the World Cup. Bringing it to Scotland would be a major boost for the strategy I was trying to create.

This was about far more than golf and sport in general. Hosting sports and other international events would create massive TV advertising for Scotland reaching a worldwide audience, attracting visitors and generating tourist income for years to come. The perfect example of this was Australia, whose image had been transformed as a result of hosting a successful Olympics. That has been maintained with spectacular New Year fireworks and the recent Rugby World Cup, which both served to boost its reputation as a 'fun' destination, along with highly effective marketing by the national and state governments.

We decided to support a bid for the 2008 competition (which became 2009 because of the postponement in 2001 after 11 September) at a Scottish course. This had to be made to the Ryder Cup committee, whose secretary was a Scot, Sandy Jones, from Lanarkshire. The early indications were that England, Portugal, Wales and Scotland would be in the frame. As discussions proceeded and presentations were made, it became quite clear that it was coming down to Scotland and Wales.

However, from our very first dinner with the Ryder Cup representatives in Edinburgh through to our final presentation at Stirling Castle, I was very uneasy about the process. It was clear to me that, for reasons that were never apparent, the front-runner was Wales. There were all kinds of informal comments in the newspapers about deals being stitched up between the Ryder Cup committee and the Welsh, who were pressing the claims of the recently built course at Celtic Manor.

The Professional Golfers' Association let it be known that they favoured the Scottish bid, which included the championship courses at Loch Lomond, Carnoustie and Turnberry, but their first preference was for the magnificent new course at Gleneagles, designed by Jack Nicklaus. However, it was reported that Celtic Manor's selection 'had been decreed since May', a full four months before the decision was announced.

Telecoms multi-millionaire Sir Terry Matthews had spent over £60 million on creating the Celtic Manor Resort and, although he was only a background figure in the bidding process, he had made it clear that he would do whatever it took to win. Told that it would cost over £10 million to stage the match, he commented: 'It's just pocket money. The value to Celtic Manor and Wales is incalculable, and I am going to do it regardless of what it costs or how long it takes.'

The host country has to provide the hotels, infrastructure,

communications and policing – all the absolutely essential support for a huge international event. There was no doubt in my mind that Scotland had shown we could deliver on all fronts, but there were serious doubts as to whether Wales could meet these criteria and there were some questions about the championship quality of the course at Celtic Manor.

As time progressed, we seemed to get into a difficult and confusing set of circumstances in which the competition was being conducted on two levels. We could not pin down what was happening between the Ryder Cup committee and Celtic Manor, but there was enough evidence to suggest that all was not well.

The final presentation of what Scotland had to offer was made at a dinner at Stirling Castle, and we made sure it was a wonderful evening of which Scotland could be immensely proud. It brought together some of the best golf courses in the world with the best support services and a unique video presentation, hosted by sports presenter Dougie Donnelly, which included Colin Montgomerie, Jackie Stewart, Sir Alex Ferguson and Sean Connery. Sam Torrance, the victorious Ryder Cup captain, had also been an enthusiastic supporter.

Jackie Stewart is another internationally renowned Scot who for years has been keen to help his country. We had talks about ways in which he could promote Scotland, but, sadly, the Scottish Executive has let that initiative go cold. At the last minute, I phoned Sir Alex at Old Trafford (unfortunately on the weekend when Manchester United had just lost to Celtic at home in a friendly) and asked him if he would come to Stirling and help promote his country. Without hesitation, he said he would be absolutely delighted to be 'on the team'.

The final decision was made by a very small group of people but what happened before then was quite dramatic. I had a call at about 2 a.m. from Sandy Jones, who was at a golfing event at Gleneagles, and it was as close as he could get to saying it did not look as if Scotland was going to make it. He asked what the implications would be and I told him that we wouldn't go quietly.

I said I wanted to know the reasons why the decision may have swayed in Celtic Manor's favour over a Scottish bid that was second to none. I would be bitterly angry and would want to express that and explain it publicly.

I showed my indignation with frankly harsh comments and we had a no-holds-barred conversation in which some strong language was used. Sandy was very sympathetic, but there were others who were less so. I told him: 'Put it this way: Celtic Manor may have won 2009, but I don't want Scotland to lose.'

The result was that, for the first time in their history, the committee were forced to name two future venues at the same time: Wales for the

2009 competition and Scotland as hosts for the Ryder Cup match in 2013. We had lost in the short term, but Scotland had won in the long term. The Irish will host the 2005 Ryder Cup and already they are beginning to experience the enormous benefits which Scotland can look forward to enjoying.

The decision caused a rift between the Professional Golfers' Association and the PGA European Tour, both of which have representatives on the committee and share the revenues when the competition is held in Europe. The understanding has always been that the two bodies would take turns choosing the venue. With the PGA seemingly in charge of the 2009 choice, everyone expected Scotland to get the tournament. When the Welsh bid was successful, the *Guardian's* much-respected golf correspondent Alistair Tait commented:

> If yesterday's Ryder Cup announcement signalled anything, it is that the Ryder Cup is up for sale to the highest bidder. If you have the money, then you can buy golf's most prized asset and the Celtic Manor owner Terry Matthews has the deepest pockets in the game right now.

The bid had been a baptism of fire; international events promotion is a hard ball game and not for the fainthearted. Although we could never exactly pin down what was happening, we had the impression we were losing from day one. I had to try to exercise some political leadership and speak up on behalf of our country to make it clear we were not going to be happy with that outcome.

The whole experience opened my eyes to the need for experience and expertise in situations where background shenanigans can be more influential than the public bidding.

A logical next step was to bid for another great sporting event: the 2008 finals of football's European Nations Cup. Apart from my passion for the game, it seemed a fitting recognition of the country that had given so much to the game and whose supporters were acclaimed as the best in the world. However, I was initially dismayed and surprised by the lack of interest and enthusiasm from a wide cross section of Scottish life, including the Scottish Football Association.

We were well provided with stadia and I believed we could meet the FIFA and EUFA requirement for six or eight top-class grounds. We would have had Hampden, Murrayfield, Ibrox, Parkhead, Pittodrie in Aberdeen, the two main club grounds in Edinburgh and Dundee, and, possibly, Rugby Park in Kilmarnock. The moaners and whingers cast up that a number of these stadia would need improvement, but that was by no means insurmountable. When the Dutch and Belgians combined to present the finals in 2000, they put up temporary seating that met all the standards and was later removed. We could do better than that.

The necessary ground improvements might have cost £70 million, not necessarily from public funds but mixed public–private finance, and would have created first-class facilities for community use. The spin-off would have been hundreds of millions of pounds in income and, again, an incalculable boost for Scotland's international image.

The reality was that we might not win with the first bid (Austria made three bids before they won) and for a large number of my colleagues the fear of first-time failure was a reason to give up without trying.

The rest of the story is now history. There was not a great deal of support from certain ministers within the Scottish Executive and, after I departed, the distinct lack of enthusiasm was made obvious. I believe they would have been happy to abandon the project but could not be seen to do so publicly. There was a distorted assessment of the costs and Scotland's capacity, which in my view translates as a lack of confidence and a failure of courage.

A joint bid with Ireland was mooted and, although Prime Minister Bertie Ahern was committed and encouraging, it was quite obvious that they could not provide the stadia. One of the stadiums, the so-called 'Bertie's Bowl', had not yet been built and the other was the headquarters of the Gaelic Football Association, which would not release it for soccer. The move was designed to weaken our chances, since our bid was tainted by the publicity for Ireland's problems and Scotland's unwillingness to go it alone.

I was not surprised our bid failed; just more surprised by the miserable way it happened. When the announcement was made, we should have said very positively it was only our first attempt and it would be followed by a second try for 2012 and a third for 2016, if need be.

My staff were now beginning to be alert to what we were trying to do on the world stage and one suggested we should try to host the MTV annual European music awards. This, too, had a huge global audience but this time of young people. It would give us an entry into a mass culture which carries status and immense spending power. It was also part of our ambition for Scotland to be at the forefront in the creative industries and the MTV Europe Awards would provide a world stage; there is no way of quantifying the effect of the rest of the world looking at Scotland in such a new light.

One of the last things I did in office was to write the letter inviting the MTV organisers to consider Scotland and when the awards event was held at Leith in 2003 it fulfilled every expectation.

We had made bids for three events and won two; we were starting to build up an events strategy and an events team with growing experience. But what was needed was more outside expertise – to be fair to civil servants, working in a government department cannot possibly prepare them for this highly competitive and often unpredictable field.

Day in and day out, the Scottish Government should be looking for such opportunities. If we have the courage and the confidence in our own assets, the amount we invest will be more than offset by the earnings. The more bids we make, the more we will win.

What ultimately proved to be an important visit to Scotland had a disastrous start. Unbeknown to myself and Cabinet colleagues, the Taoiseach Bertie Ahern was to pay a visit to a Roman Catholic pilgrimage centre, the grotto at Carfin in Lanarkshire, to unveil a memorial to the Irish community who had fled the potato famine in the mid-nineteenth century and settled in Scotland. A regular Celtic FC supporter who made frequent visits to games at Parkhead, he would also attend an Old Firm game on the same day.

Not knowing that these arrangements had been made, we were even more surprised when a political and sectarian storm blew up, triggered by concerns raised by the local MP Frank Roy. Roy, who was also PPS to the Scottish Secretary John Reid, had claimed there was a public order and security risk in having the Carfin event immediately after the Rangers v. Celtic football match, which had been a flashpoint in the past. He appeared to think that rival gangs of fans from both clubs would converge on Carfin and use the presence of the Taoiseach to demonstrate their respective loyalties.

In what was an embarrassment for Scotland and an apparent rebuff to the Taoiseach, the Carfin ceremony had to be abandoned on that day, to be restaged later. Not surprisingly, the media were eager to find someone to blame but in this case it was not the Scottish Executive. There had been no consultation whatsoever and the whole affair had been badly handled.

It was ridiculous to think that the head of another country could visit Scotland in such a private way to perform a public ceremony, or for those making the arrangements not to think it was appropriate to involve the Scottish Parliament and the Executive. It was bad for Scotland because it looked chaotic in its organisation and gave the appearance of an important occasion being subject to sectarianism – the worst possible image for Scotland.

While it is not the government's role to involve itself in every visit, it would have been courteous to inform us, especially since Carfin is in the constituency of the then Education Secretary and now First Minister, Jack McConnell.

I was determined the Taoiseach should make an official visit to Scotland and immediately extended a formal invitation which resulted in a successful lunch on 20 June 2001 (with Mr Ahern paying his respects to Cardinal Winning, who had died on 18 June) followed by the Carfin ceremony in the evening.

The fear of sectarian violence was pure fabrication which made no sense because there was no reason to believe there was any threat to public order. The thinking behind the whole affair was outdated because the entire Scottish community would wish to pay tribute to the tremendous contribution made to our country by Irish immigrants and their descendants.

Perhaps appropriately, the spiritual surroundings of Carfin grotto saw a fitting end to another minor spat which had greatly excited the Scottish media. During the UK general election campaign, after a media conference in the Scottish Labour HQ, I made a rather unfortunate comment about Scottish Secretary John Reid. A dormant microphone that had somehow become active picked me up describing him as 'a patronising bastard'.

Politics being what they are and comrades being what they are, my most enjoyable memory of the evening at Carfin was walking arm-in-arm with Dr Reid, both of us grinning broadly – showing the world that we might be somewhat aggressive and slightly abusive, but we could still shake hands and make up.

I was always very conscious of the need to maintain good relations with the religious communities in Scotland and to make sure that old wounds were not reopened. I am not a member of any organised church but have always tried to implement my grandfather's Christian values through practical politics. Although congregations are declining and the church may not be as important as it once was in Scottish history, there is still a role for religion in the governance of Scotland. The churches still have a powerful influence in our society in relation to moral and community issues, an influence which is far too often dismissed in society and especially in politics.

It was against that background that I saw the bruising dispute over Section 28, when the Roman Catholic Church and evangelicals, with key individuals amassing more than a million signatures, and Scotland's most powerful tabloid, ranged against the Executive. That was something I did not think needed to happen and was certainly something to be avoided in the future.

It was essential to build bridges and keep them in good repair and, to this end, I engaged with the Church of Scotland, the Roman Catholic Church through the late Cardinal Thomas Winning, and other faith groups. Although we disagreed on many things and His Eminence was solid in his beliefs, we had similar working-class backgrounds and we quickly formed a reasonable relationship.

As devolution was developing, there were frequent meetings with the Moderator of the General Assembly of the Church of Scotland and the Cardinal at the official residence at Bute House. Between them and the all-faith groups, including minority faiths and the large Muslim community in Scotland, they represented large numbers of Scots whose interests should be considered. This was especially important after 11 September when people were wrongly linking all of Islam with terrorism. I met with Muslim leaders to reassure them and announce protective measures.

I responded with enthusiasm to an invitation to go to Rome with the Cardinal and the Secretary of State John Reid for the 400th anniversary celebrations of Scots College and a memorable meeting with Pope John Paul II.

Despite his infirmity, it was obvious we were in the presence of one of the most significant figures of modern times and a leader with passion, commitment and humanity. When he received representations about the great global issues like hunger and poverty, he listened before responding fluently and knowledgeably in half a dozen languages. He was particularly at ease with the young people and appeared to enjoy what must have been a taxing occasion; whatever his critics may say, to me it was invigorating and inspiring.

When John Reid and I were presented, I gave him the best wishes of the people of Scotland and thanked him for the honour he did to our nation and our new Parliament by receiving us. I did not realise at the time that it was a small piece of history because it was the first time that the head of a Scottish government had met the Pope since the Reformation.

It also meant something to the Roman Catholic Church in Scotland and the Glasgow archdiocesan newspaper *Flourish* wrote of a new feeling of mutual acceptance and a real sense of reconciliation.

I had lunch with Cardinal Winning at his Glasgow residence, when he cooked a very tasty spaghetti bolognese and we talked about football – and, of course, wider issues affecting Scotland. Shortly before his death, I was touched when he remembered that my personal assistant Joan Serafini had been disappointed by my visit to the Vatican. The only strong Roman Catholic in my team, she had asked for a souvenir but it was forgotten in the flurry of activity. Cardinal Winning arranged for Joan's mother to receive a special set of rosary beads, blessed by His Holiness the Pope, which were delivered just before his untimely death. It was a simple and thoughtful gesture, typical of the man.

Scotland's direct links with Europe and the rest of the world are increasingly important as globalisation gathers pace. It seemed odd to me that, apart from a service operating to Scandinavia, there was not a more direct ferry route from Scotland to Europe. The benefits were obvious for trade, tourism and reinforcing our links with the heart of the EU and its fast-growing market.

Early discussions with Superfast Ferries, a subsidiary of the Greek conglomerate Attica Enterprises, for a service from Rosyth on the Forth to a European port were very positive. However, things became complicated when clearances from the EU were required, support was needed from the Scottish institutions and the DTI in London became involved. The project became bogged down in bureaucracy and, although I could move my own officials, we were also dealing with London and Brussels. I had urgent discussions with Chancellor Gordon Brown, one of the two local MPs for Rosyth, and Helen Liddell, who was now Secretary of State for Scotland, and was assured that the problems were being resolved.

Superfast Ferries, who had been selected as the preferred bidder from 42 expressions of interest, are a fast-moving, innovative and enterprising company who have grown tenfold in just ten years. They had ultra-modern car-passenger ferries on order for the Rosyth link, but these could be used on any of their other routes, from the Aegean and Adriatic to the Baltic. They were also being wooed to provide a rival service from elsewhere in the UK to continental Europe.

The crunch came at a breakfast meeting at the Balmoral Hotel, Edinburgh, with president and managing director Alexander Panagopulos. He is charming and courteous, but also a dynamic businessman, and he did not mince his words. He could not believe that a development with so many advantages for Scotland, and an important commercial opportunity for him, was being dealt with in such a dilatory fashion. While he appreciated our hard work, he had a business to run and he virtually gave me an ultimatum: if the outstanding issues were not solved within the next few days, Superfast would sail away over the horizon.

I knew that in a hostile and ever-changing economic environment, in which most ferry operators in Greece and elsewhere have struggled, Attica Enterprises had survived and grown by being flexible, aggressive and not afraid to drop unprofitable activities.

When I got back to St Andrew's House, I read the riot act to my own officials, who, to be fair, were already doing their level best. Thankfully, the matters were resolved and the project went ahead on schedule with financial assistance of £12 million towards infrastructure work at the port of Rosyth and funding from the European Union under the PACT Programme (Pilot Action for Combined Transport).

At stake had been the first daily direct service linking Scotland to the European continent; until then, the only way to travel to the Continent was by a combination of a long drive south and then a ferry crossing. As Mr Panagopulos pointed out, Superfast were the first to offer what is a national service to the Scottish economy, creating a totally new market and establishing new patterns for trade and tourism: 'Like Greece, being on the geographical periphery of Europe, Scotland's economy has a lot to gain from a direct daily link to its European partners.'

I was relieved, but worried whether or not we had the capacity and expertise to deal with these big issues which need focus, speed of action and the ability to cut through the layers of red tape and obfuscation that still strangle initiative and investment in our country. Scotland has the potential, but international companies and potential investors have a wide choice of opportunities. Government has to deal with them in a way that shows Scotland is a good place to do business.

XIV

Unruly Partners

Coalition government is now a fixed part of the political furniture in Scotland. There is still a great deal of resentment about this within the Labour Party in the Scottish Parliament and the rank-and-file membership. This was partly because very few people understood proportional representation – very much a European way of electing, although Liberal Democrat party policy – and very few understood the inevitable consequences of Labour adopting PR for the Scottish Parliament. It was also partly because in the Labour Party there is significant dislike of the Lib Dems and what they stand for. While these feelings never really became a serious problem, they were always just beneath the surface.

The Scottish coalition government is built very much around the relationship between First Minister and Deputy First Minister. I found the Scottish Liberal Democrat leader Jim Wallace an excellent colleague to work with; as usual in politics, there were more issues that united the parties than divided them but we often disguise that fact and create controversy where none exists.

However, there were differences on a number of things: PR for local government, drugs policy and law and order issues. As Scottish Home Affairs Minister in the Blair Government I had built a reputation for taking a hard and uncompromising line on drugs, especially in relation to dealers, but also in opposing the decriminalisation of cannabis. As First Minister, there were still clear differences and I think as a consequence the coalition was not as focused nor as tough on the drugs issue as we might have been. I freely admit there is a wide range of views on drugs, but it seemed to me that Labour's policy was being diluted because of Lib Dem thinking and Lib Dem backbenchers.

For Lib Dems, the application of human rights meant the rights of individuals, especially offenders, were in conflict with a much more punitive approach to crime and antisocial behaviour. The Lib Dems were less tough on crime than we wanted to be and their over-concern for offenders' rights often ran against the grain of popular feeling in Scotland.

As policy in some of these areas became blurred, the Lib Dems (especially their backbenchers) would argue privately that they were winning on these issues.

On proportional representation, we established a committee to consider changes in local government. It did not meet often. To be fair to the Lib Dems, their strategy was that they were not going to force this issue in the first four years of the Labour–Lib Dem coalition. This was wise, because there was no particular appetite for it within Labour and it could have jeopardised the fragile goodwill that had been built up on the backbenches and between the leaderships of both parties. They also thought, as I did, that a great deal more debate and consideration needed to take place before legislation on local government PR could be introduced.

Dealing with Jim Wallace was straightforward. He is a firm and honest politician – more than can be said for some of his backbenchers, who clearly hated Labour and found it very difficult to accept the discipline of a coalition. They gave Jim Wallace and his ministerial colleagues a hard time when they were standing up for a coalition deal that was new territory for everyone.

The most obvious example of Lib Dem unruliness was during the fishing debate when we were putting through a significant sum of money for decommissioning. We lost the vote and Tom McCabe, in his role as our business manager and fixer, was absolutely furious – as I was – that the Lib Dems had failed to deliver on our agreement. What we were proposing was a good deal because it was obvious to everyone that there was overcapacity in the fishing industry. We accepted there were difficulties for some of the Lib Dem members and Tavish Scott, their junior minister who represented Shetland, was under enormous and unfair pressure to break ranks. I was sad to lose Tavish Scott from the Executive: he was an excellent performer, a good minister and has the presentational skills that are increasingly necessary in politics. In any case, the reversal was temporary because the following week we made sure with our Lib Dem colleagues that the vote was won.

Jim Wallace's absolute trustworthiness was demonstrated to me on one of the tours we made together around Scotland. In a Chinese restaurant in Inverness, with a few of our advisers present, I became violently ill and collapsed. I was taken back to the hotel and after a series of tests was diagnosed with exhaustion. The point is that this was never made public – something I am convinced would not have happened if some other ministers had been present. I must say that dealing with Jim Wallace was easier than dealing with some of my Labour colleagues and our conversations were always secure. There was a degree of trust and honour in Jim that I did not experience from some in my own party.

Sometimes, my own Labour colleagues imposed more of a strain within the Cabinet than the Lib Dems. On an official visit to Japan, I was residing in the British Embassy when I received a phone call from my wife Julie, rather upset at the fact that a suspicious package about to be delivered to our home in St Andrews had been intercepted by the Special Branch and had caused a major security scare. It was sent for analysis. The police regarded it as very suspicious because it was addressed to me personally, was marked 'top priority' and was badly wrapped with layers of adhesive tape.

Later in the day, I phoned the police and they confirmed it had been a letter from Jack McConnell back in Edinburgh, in which he was again demanding a special adviser and saying he was tired of waiting. The letter had first been sent internally within St Andrew's House, but his concern about my civil servants meant he retrieved it, reopened it, repackaged it and sent it to my home.

I phoned from Tokyo and got him on his mobile at a Celtic game being played in Europe. What I had to say must have made his evening less enjoyable.

Before the first coalition, there was talk of Labour, as the largest party, forming a minority government. The idea is superficially attractive but does not stand up to examination. In the Scottish Parliament, we need stability and security in the considerable number of votes that take place. In the present mindset, victory on policy issues is everything and a go-it-alone government that cannot command an overall majority would be in constant difficulty.

No one should take away from the Lib Dems their success in coalition; they got more out of the first four years of the Scottish Parliament than any other party. What struck me in dealing with them was that they are the only party in the last 100 years who were consistently in favour of home rule and federalism. So the achievement of devolution was their policy, only later embraced by Labour.

Some people have suggested that a Labour–Lib Dem coalition may not be the only permutation for a Scottish government. In the short term, in the present adversarial politics and the yawning gap between the parties, it is highly unlikely that Labour could ever form a coalition with the Scottish National Party or the Conservatives. The nature of Scottish politics and of these parties would have to change dramatically for that ever to happen.

What is a possibility in the medium- to long-term is for the Greens or environmentally minded parties to link with Labour to create a working majority. And there is always the potential for the changing face of Scottish politics and the changing moods and needs of the electorate to take us to the point when other parties might form a coalition which does not include Labour.

We must not think along tramlines, as we tend to do in politics. Because of Labour's dominance in Scotland, it is assumed they will always be partners in any coalition. Any or all of the parties could attempt to form a coalition after a future election, especially with lower turnouts and the growth of single-issue and minority-interest parties. That is why, despite criticism, I was very keen to continue Donald Dewar's work in coalition politics. I felt it was in the interests of Scotland for coalition to work and in the interests of the Parliament to have stability. There were irritations in having the Lib Dems as partners but it was better to have them at this early stage in the Parliament. Over the next decade, the make-up of the Parliament may change, reflecting a completely different Scottish electorate.

One of the most important issues for Scotland is the future of Europe and our role in it. Europe, comprising 15 member states, soon to be 25, has had difficulty in facing up to what has been described as the 'new regionalism', whether it be devolved government in the UK, the autonomous regions of Spain or the federalism of Austria and Germany. While Scotland is obviously a nation, the reality is that we are a region for European and UK purposes. As a result, there is enormous sensitivity in Whitehall in relation to anything Scotland does in Europe.

For far too many people in the UK and Scotland, devolution was perceived as a uniquely Scotland/UK phenomenon. In reality, it is happening throughout the world and there are a number of outstanding examples in Europe. Unfortunately for Scotland, we have lost a great deal by not developing a wider view of devolution and I was aware of our need to build an alliance and be part of this new regionalism in Europe. Despite the Whitehall sensitivity, I wanted to move this debate on and take advantage of any opportunities that presented themselves. Just such an opportunity came when Scotland was invited to become a signatory to a major agreement, called the Flanders Initiative. I was glad, and somewhat surprised, that even at this early stage of devolution our Parliament and Government were being viewed by European regions as among the strongest, along with Catalonia and Bavaria.

Although there was nothing dramatic about the Flanders Initiative, the symbolism was vital. It allowed us to become an integral part of the new regional thinking in Europe. At the signing ceremony in Brussels, I felt Scotland's First Minister was in the midst of regions and nations that were proud of what they had achieved, ambitious in their view of the future and expected to play an increasingly important role in Europe, especially on social and economic policies. It was not quite a 'Europe of the regions' but a definite step on that path.

What gave the Flanders agreement added sensitivity was that it was signed during the UK general election campaign in 2001. The timing of the signing of the agreement was not in our control and I was apprehensive that the wrong interpretation might have been damaging during the election. My tactic was always to push out the boundaries of devolution but to be careful how it was promoted and projected within the UK and within Scotland. A lot of what I had to do was in code or deliberately underplayed.

Our officials had cleared the way with Whitehall, but it was fortunate for us that the Foreign Secretary was the ever-helpful Robin Cook, a fervent supporter of devolution. I phoned Robin to explain what I was doing, not to seek his approval but to bring him up to date in case of any adverse publicity. He very much welcomed my call and I assured him that we were not even going to issue a press statement.

In the heat of the election campaign, the enemies of devolution would have portrayed Scotland's move in Europe as a step too far and an attempt to undermine the UK. The Conservatives in particular, with little understanding of devolution and their anti-Europe attitude, would have used the Flanders Initiative to make mischief.

I saw the agreement as the opening of a new chapter for Scotland in Europe without undermining the United Kingdom. It recognised, as other countries had, that the regions of Europe have a practical role in building economic, social and cultural links. It also illustrated that we need not be constrained in developing our European thinking because of Whitehall, the press, the Conservatives and the genuine lack of public understanding that this was commonplace in Europe. Scotland's signing of the Flanders agreement sent a strong message to the UK that there is more to devolution than merely conceding powers, setting up elections and building parliaments. We were becoming more involved in the Council of Ministers' discussions on agriculture and fishing, the development of Scotland House in Brussels, bilateral discussions with heads of other regional governments and the ongoing discussions with the Foreign Office. As our Parliament matures and the other regions exert themselves, it would be wrong not to want Scotland to share in the advantages that will flow.

In a way, we were only revisiting old alliances and old trade links between Scotland and the Continent. There is nothing that can, or should, hold us back from Europe.

The devolution story is punctuated by personalities and Robin Cook is one of the prominent Scots who have been helpful in resolving problems and making devolution work.

I always had a great respect for Robin, not always shared by my colleagues. Early in my career at Westminster, Robin was doing particularly well in the Shadow Cabinet elections, but one year he tumbled down the list and was perplexed. When he asked me in a rhetorical way why that happened, my comment was: 'You're well respected but not well liked.' I think he was taken aback, but it was meant as a compliment rather than a criticism.

Robin Cook has always been an assiduous worker and a formidable and forensic debater, as was shown by the Scott inquiry, but he was often prickly and difficult in his relations with others. He is not someone who suffers fools gladly and his definition of fools is quite extensive.

In a curious way, I sympathised with him. In the aftermath of my resignation, he sent me a very moving and supportive letter. In it, he outlined some of his own difficulties in the days of his marriage break-up and expressed his solidarity and fellow-feeling.

I think Robin has been a loner in politics and he has achieved so much on his own without a wide circle of friends or a personal clique. Like me, he is from the east coast and I do not think he had a great affinity or affiliation with the clannishness of Scottish politics; and, horror of horrors, he was a successful councillor before becoming an MP – something our more elitist colleagues regarded with disdain. I recognised these characteristics in myself.

Robin has always enjoyed Westminster and the cut-and-thrust of the Commons, where he is at his best. Recent developments like his departure to the backbenches – which has weakened the Labour Government – and his strong support for more integration with Europe could change that. It is not clear what path his career will take. Is it within the realms of possibility that at some time in the future Scotland might benefit from Robin Cook leaving Westminster and figuring more prominently in Scottish politics?

This may be wishful thinking but it does highlight a wider problem that has to be tackled. At present, politicians are obsessed with status and any elected post outside Westminster is unreasonably characterised as second class. This is very much at odds with Europe, where elected politicians move through the different levels of Brussels, national, regional and local government.

My political career has been enriched by serving at three of those levels, something no other current politician in Scotland can match. When I was a minister in the Scottish Office team at Westminster and when I was First Minister, because I was also a former council leader I was able to defend local government against unreasonable attacks from civil servants and other ministers who felt local government was populated by poor-quality representatives. The Scottish Parliament has been subjected to jibes about being a 'White Heather Club' and other inferences that it is substandard. I have also heard it said openly that MEPs contribute absolutely nothing.

One result is that as these images become imprinted in the public mind they will also become imprinted in the minds of possible candidates. It is vital for the future of our democracy that we improve the quality of representation by attracting a greater diversity of candidates. With these images, we will not be able to persuade people of the right calibre to serve in the Scottish Parliament or on councils with budgets of hundreds of millions of pounds. A growing pattern in many local authorities is that far too many unelected officers run the council and decide what it will do; democracy must reclaim control back from officials.

All of these institutions will change and it is likely that the European and Scottish parliaments will grow in importance while the Westminster Parliament will lose powers to both.

While some institutions will gain powers over the next few years at the expense of others, each will remain important in representing the people, spending taxpayers' money and influencing every aspect of our lives. The quality of public service can only be improved by more flexibility and movement by people of talent and experience within the levels of government.

XV

Officegate

Things appeared to be going well; in its first year, my administration had already had some significant achievements and had started to improve the lives of Scots, not least the elderly; Scotland was beginning to play a role on the international stage; we had made a good start to creating the 'confident, competitive and compassionate Scotland'.

I had no idea that a political time bomb had been ticking away in my constituency for years – and was about to explode.

In April 2001, a disgruntled local man in Glenrothes involved in a legal wrangle over the feudal title of his retirement cottage told the *Mail on Sunday* that the law firm Digby Brown had been paying £4,000 a year for the sub-let of rooms in my constituency office. The facts were that Digby Brown provided legal services to many of my constituents, specialising in helping union members with employment, health and safety matters. The money for the rent between November 1998 and June 2001 was paid into a constituency office fund and not into any personal account; not a penny of it was used for anything other than support for the Fife Central constituency. If there had been a mistake, it had been an honest one.

Most important of all – as was to be proved by rigorous parliamentary, police and Inland Revenue investigations – I was entirely innocent of any wrongdoing. Even my political adversaries did not question my honesty and, as one of my harshest media critics, *The Scotsman* newspaper, admitted in an editorial, there had been 'no benefit' to me.

When I was newly elected to Westminster in 1987, I decided to establish a constituency office as a contact point, something that had not been done by my predecessor in Fife Central. Because of inexperience and my desire to provide a first-class service, I rented a modern, conveniently located office in Hanover Court in the Civic

Square in Glenrothes. I soon realised it was too large and too expensive but was unable to strike a deal to take the ground floor only. The easy solution was to sub-let the upper floor and everything flowed from that.

On 3 April 2001, the day after I became aware through the press that the sub-lets might present an irregularity, the leases were registered with the appropriate parliamentary authorities in Edinburgh and London. The Edinburgh authorities were very pleased that I had responded so quickly to clarify the position and had registered with the Scottish Parliament that I had leased part of my office from 1987.

However, opponents smelled blood and the matter was raised in the House of Commons by the Tory MP Dominic Grieve, then Shadow Secretary of State for Scotland. I also started to discuss with the Westminster authorities the paying back of any monies they felt I owed them. The House of Commons rules are vague, but, on a strict interpretation, I had breached them. After inquiries by the Fees Office and the Parliamentary Commissioner for Standards lasting several months and a personal payment of £9,000, they wrote to say that the matter had been resolved to their satisfaction.

In my mind, I felt I had done nothing morally wrong and perhaps that is why I did not tackle this issue vigorously enough. It was a Westminster matter and, as First Minister of Scotland, I had kept it too much to myself and did not seek advice. I was still an MP and MSP and was anxious to keep the two parliamentary institutions separate. Also, the UK general election was looming and I knew Labour's opponents would seize on any excuse to embarrass the Government.

I also failed to take the early advice offered by an editorial in the *Daily Record*: 'Tell it all. And tell it fast.' By not putting all the facts in the public domain from the earliest stage – and not even when I paid back more than was strictly necessary – I allowed my critics to create the impression there was something sinister afoot.

Although the process was handled badly, I was anxious to clear up the problems and move on. The House of Commons had no records prior to 1994–5 and they could only deal with sitting members (I ceased to be a MP after June 2001), but I nevertheless insisted that I should repay the money claimed right back to 1987. They had no way of verifying the amount and I did not have the records, but I saw no point in any legal action or negotiation of any kind. I worked out the total sum at £9,000, covering the Digby Brown let, and sent it off. There are former colleagues in the Commons who do not appear to have done as much.

That did not stop the relentless build-up of a grotesquely exaggerated campaign that became a witch hunt. Over the next six months, the media and opposition parties created a crescendo of abuse, innuendo, half-truths and distortions designed to create a crisis and denigrate me and everyone connected with me.

As the campaign escalated, the smears became wilder and more ridiculous: my constituency office became 'a secret cash cow'; I was described as 'a shifty-looking dry-mouthed politician squirming, twitching and contorting his features'; there were unsubstantiated allegations of 'a blizzard of irregularities and inconsistencies' and 'incredible and blatant misuse of public money'; one mind-boggling article in a newspaper that should have known better even calculated the amount of money involved could buy 1,440 bottles of malt whisky!

In all of this there were few facts and a great deal of fiction: categorical denials of dishonesty were ignored. More accurate was the comment in *The Guardian*: 'Taken on their own, the things which make up the Officegate row seem trivial. But Mr McLeish and his spin doctors have been caught in U-turns, retractions and obfuscations. They have failed to close the issue down.'

The disproportionate response astonished neutral observers as it spiralled out of control. There were a number of reasons why what had begun as a minor fuss became a furore and then a feeding frenzy. From its very beginning, the coverage of the Parliament had shifted very quickly from policies to personalities. Some sections of the press hated Labour, still opposed devolution, disliked the Parliament and scorned Scotland: the new Scottish politics are 'in your face' and often callous.

Because you cannot win in situations like that, I had decided to take a vow of silence. I did not have a bottomless pit of money with which I could engage lawyers to counter some of the outrageous libels which were being perpetrated, nor did I have any intention of dragging the office of First Minister through the courts. In any case, the nature of the press being what it is, it is not necessary for them to prove you have done something wrong – merely to create the impression that you have.

After I had satisfied the House of Commons and the Scottish Parliament authorities, the matter seemed closed. However, in October my announcement of the settlement, with an apology for the errors made, only gave the affair a new lease of life and unleashed a new onslaught. Matters were made worse when the case was reported to Fife Police for what proved to be a completely pointless and wasteful investigation.

'Officegate' dominated First Minister's Questions as Opposition leaders returned to the attack. On 1 November 2001, I was outraged when the SNP's John Swinney quoted ministerial standards of constitutional and personal conduct and questioned whether the Digby

Brown office even existed. I explained, yet again, that the sub-letting had been dealt with over the summer by the Fees Office at Westminster and by the Parliamentary Commissioner for Standards, Mrs Filkin, and they had both closed the matter.

Swinney said the rumours would continue to fly and undermine me and demanded a personal statement. I did not think it merited a formal personal statement, which is a momentous event in any parliament and is done only in an exceptional set of circumstances. I firmly believed it when I told him: 'Quite simply, I do not think that what has happened over the past three or four months satisfies that criterion.'

Also, if a personal statement is made, no questions can be asked; I was prepared to go further than that and have an open debate about my record as First Minister. I challenged Swinney and Tory leader David McLetchie to pick their day and use the available parliamentary mechanisms to tackle my competency, my probity or my commitment to Scotland as First Minister. It was, however, depressing when I told McLetchie he should stop grubbing around in the gutter and there were Tory shouts of: 'You're already there.'

I assured the Opposition leaders: 'I will not run away from answering questions. I am saying: put up or shut up – pick a debate and let us respond. I remain proud of the fact that we are doing a lot of good work for the people of Scotland.'

In fairness, as party leaders they had to exploit anything which could be of political advantage. In the new political hothouse that is the Scottish Parliament, scoring points is all important and it was perhaps not surprising that they sought to link my personal difficulties with causing maximum discomfort to the Labour Party. There is not much sentiment in politics but, interestingly, I received more support, sympathy and encouragement from Opposition backbenchers than I did from some 'allies'.

There is a wider issue about the adversarial nature of the Scottish Parliament. The pack mentality in the media was matched by the pack mentality in the Parliament. Leaders should have the maturity and perspective that allows them to distinguish between right and wrong and give credit; they do not always have to pander to media demands and pressure from backbenchers to constantly be in attack mode.

When the parliamentary onslaught on me became so personal, I thought it reflected their weakness and inexperience as politicians. Over the years, in local politics and both parliaments, I have noticed that those politicians who do not have the insights, expertise or command of language tend to be cruder and more malicious.

To my chagrin and frustration, the good work we were doing was being overshadowed by the affair and the increasingly hysterical tone of the media and the Opposition. That week I had opened a new £100 million general hospital in Lanarkshire; attended a UK ministerial meeting in Cardiff; welcomed to Scotland the vice-president of China, who would soon be one of the most important people in the world; had the crunch meeting with Mr Panagopulos on the Rosyth–Zeebrugge ferry service; and made the most significant announcement about housing ever made in post-war Scotland – the transfer of Glasgow's housing stock and the erasure of its £900 million debt burden.

It is the nature of news gatherers that such achievements rarely get the full measure of publicity they deserve but because of 'Officegate', they were being virtually ignored. The media priorities were made forcibly clear to me when I went to meet some elderly people in Glasgow to reassure them about the housing transfer and I found myself in the thick of a media scrum, with Bernard Ponsonby of Scottish Television asking me questions that I thought were offensive and disgraceful.

On the evening of what had been a towsy First Minister's Questions, I took part in what proved to be a disastrous event: the BBC 1 *Question Time* programme from the Queen Margaret Drive studio in Glasgow. I have been asked why I took the risk of taking part in this nationally transmitted programme with its free-for-all format and an audience which we knew would include some vocally hostile elements. The answer is we had agreed to the appearance weeks before the problem spiralled out of control.

Although I had nothing to hide, I had mistakenly kept the whole affair away from my special advisers and tried to deal with the problem myself. In many ways, that was an inexplicable part of my behaviour, but it had been a Westminster matter and I did not think I should involve my Edinburgh team. Because I kept it so personal, my advisers were not as forceful as they were in other policy areas. They could only work with the information at their disposal.

There were occasions when I accepted advice that was wrong and dangerous, and going on *Question Time* was one such occasion. I thought it was not sensible because we would not know in advance the questions from an audience and a panel that we all knew would include aggressive supporters of other parties. My senior media adviser insisted it would look worse if we cancelled the appearance: the media would have interpreted it as running away from questions and it would have heightened the wrong impression that I had something to hide.

It was obvious that the timing could not have been worse and I was prepared for a rough time, but the whole performance proved embarrassing and desperately damaging. Most humiliating was the derision and ridicule when I was pressed by question-master David Dimbleby on how much money was involved. My reply was: 'David, I don't know what the sum involved was. There were other sub-lets that have been in the media, but that's not new. I want to make it clear that not a penny of that was for my own personal benefit. I have not benefited at all from what has happened.'

I genuinely did not know because inquiries were still being made, going back over 15 years. I was not being dishonest or evasive; I simply did not have the details and it took a considerable amount of homework to find the papers. I also had in mind that these inquiries were uncovering a muddle of other rental income resulting from what had been an honest mistake 14 years previously.

In the wake of the *Question Time* debacle and the coverage that followed that weekend, we decided to fight back with a media blitz with the aim of getting everything out into the open once and for all. For 18 hours a day, my advisers and I went through books and constituency files and I found myself poring over papers, accounts and correspondence that were mostly new to me. We did not take meal breaks and lived off takeaways and someone said later: 'It was a mess of papers and fish and chip wrappers. Three weeks' work was crammed into three days.'

On Tuesday, 6 November, in the first-floor drawing room of Bute House, I gave the media the results of our investigation and told them: 'This was a muddle – it was certainly not a fiddle. Even my political adversaries have not questioned my honesty over this issue.'

I gave a full account of the five tenants of my Glenrothes office from 1987 to 2001: Honeywell-Shield, a security company, who paid £4,000 in rent between December 1987 and August 1989; Capital solutions, an office equipment company, who paid £12,000 from October 1989 to December 1994; Fife Council Economic Unit, who paid £10,122 from May 1995 to July 1997; Thompsons, a firm of solicitors, who paid £1,000 between December 1997 and May 1998; and Digby Brown, who paid £9,000 between November 1998 and June 2001.

Documentation circulated at the media briefing showed the rent from these sub-lets went into a constituency office business account, paying for office costs like phone calls, faxes and stamps. I published the correspondence with Mrs Filkin, the Parliamentary Commissioner for Standards, and the former Tory Shadow Scottish Secretary Dominic Grieve. I also gave proof that when I agreed to pay £9,000 to the Commons Fees Office, I had paid it personally. I had written to the Fees Office asking them to clarify the confused situation over the rules governing MPs' office cost allowances between 1987 and 2001. The income from all these sub-lets totalled £36,122, including the £9,000 from the Digby Brown sub-let. Eventually, at the conclusion of all the inquiries into all the lets, including, as will shortly be explained, that of Third Age, I personally paid back a total of £38,550 to the House of Commons. Of course, I had not benefited personally from a penny of this money.

I repeated: 'Uppermost in my mind has always been the desire to provide a better service for my constituents. I take full responsibility for this affair. In hindsight, it should have been dealt with better and more quickly. But the essential point is that this was a muddle. It certainly was not a fiddle.'

On the political front, I addressed a meeting of the Parliamentary Labour Party for over half an hour and won their unanimous support. My fellow Fife MSP Marilyn Livingston, the convener of the 55-strong group reported:

> Henry gave a fully comprehensive account of the situation surrounding his office expenses. The detailed explanation satisfied everyone in the group.
>
> I've worked with Henry McLeish for many years before this, being in the neighbouring constituency, and Henry is an honest man. I think we have all made mistakes in our career and I think Henry has admitted he made a mistake and has now put the facts before us. We can see there was no personal gain at all for Henry McLeish. What he did was the best for his constituents; I am convinced of that and I am sure the people of Scotland will be.

Gordon Jackson QC, the Glasgow Govan MSP, added there was no basis for me to resign: 'I don't think anyone's ever going to pretend there was never any mistake made, but it's not a serious matter. It's grown out of all proportion.'

The unrelenting media reaction and the continuing antagonistic tone of the coverage of my explanations made it clear there would not be any closure. With less than 24 hours to what I knew would be a make-or-break debate on an Opposition 'no confidence' motion in the Scottish Parliament, my case for the defence received a shattering blow.

At a sports gala dinner in the presence of Princess Anne at the Palace of Holyroodhouse, I was weary but managed a rueful smile at the jokes of one speaker, a well-known comedian, at my expense. As a hardened politician, it was nothing I could not handle – but then I received a message which changed everything.

The next morning's papers would carry a story about a sixth office rental by the Third Age group, a local charity for the elderly. This was to have totally unfair consequences for my wife, Julie, who was a senior official in the Fife social work department, specialising in the care of older people.

Of course, I knew Third Age were in the building but I regarded them as a good cause who deserved to be supported and I attached absolutely no financial importance to their presence. In fact, investigators have described the £25 a week they contributed to office costs as 'paltry' and an 'insignificant peppercorn fee'.

Be that as it may, I knew it dealt a death-blow to my hopes of survival as First Minister. The insignificance of the amount involved did not matter; at the media conference the day before, I had been asked several times if everything had been declared. In my conviction that we had researched everything, I had declared with absolute confidence that there was nothing else. As one of my Labour colleagues commented: 'If the information about Third Age had been included in the package of disclosures, he would still be First Minister.' But it was not – and I knew with a sickening certainty what the consequences had to be.

I returned to Bute House for that long, agonising night. All of my experience in politics over 30 years had not prepared me for what had become an impossible situation. I felt sadness and anger with myself, because I knew I had contributed hugely to the mess I was in.

What made it more difficult was that I knew in my heart of hearts that I was innocent of any moral error. At that stage, inquiries had been set in motion by Parliament, the Inland Revenue and the police and, although it looked like the rest of the world did not believe or agree, I knew they would find no wrongdoing on my part. No one questioned my honesty, but at the same time the majority verdict appeared to be that I should not stay in office. I was not guilty, but I felt as if I was in prison and could not get out.

I had failed to understand or counteract the clamour from the malicious elements in Scotland. Even at that late stage, I was at a loss to comprehend the viciousness and malice of many of the attacks to which I had been subjected. It seemed to me that to some politicians and a certain section of the media, my scalp was a necessary trophy in a bigger struggle. They did not like the success that the administration and the Parliament were becoming. They wanted to damage Labour, damage the Parliament and damage politics. Their agenda needed a hook to hang on – and I was hooked.

Interestingly, Professor Lindsay Paterson of the University of Edinburgh commented at the time that the Scottish Parliament represents a threat to the power of two groups in Scotland. The first is the Conservative establishment in and around Edinburgh who have hefty support from right-wing newspapers. And the second group is a faction within the Labour Party who oppose modernisation.

Professor Paterson explained:

> This whole episode has not been about Henry McLeish and his expenses but the reluctance of these two establishments to see a truly radical body having its way.
>
> The two establishments have been systematically trying to undermine the Parliament because they feel the Parliament has been undermining them. The radical forces trying to democratise Scotland did not recognise the scale of the battle on their hands.

That may be going too far in elevating my own personal problems to symbolic status. However, there is a limit to what you can take day in and day out, when all your work is being undermined and a shadow hangs over everything you do: you are under relentless attack from the Opposition and the media.

I was disheartened by the reaction of certain colleagues, opportunism by a few members of Labour's leadership in Scotland and by the worst excesses of the other political parties. It was a bandwagon they found too good to allow to roll past them.

With notable exceptions in the Parliament, the trade unions and the general secretary Lesley Quinn, the attitude in the Scottish Labour Party was disappointing. Some colleagues believed what they were reading, others were creating mischief and reinforcing the warped propaganda by briefing the press, and the rest had their heads down.

I had been too much of a loner in politics. I got on because of what I did and I did not have a large circle of friends, nor the protection of a clique or a political 'mafia'. For some in the Labour Party, it was a predicament and for others it was an opportunity to be exploited. There was no closing of ranks and no tangible help in defence that a leader might have expected. Indeed, some who clearly saw opportunity for advancement under a new leader joined in the feeding frenzy.

A small but damaging cabal had formed within the Scottish Labour power structure. Of course, I knew who was behind every move, who was briefing what to political journalists and who was mobilising behind my back. There are no secrets in Scottish politics and 'off-the-record' character assassinations are not what they used to be.

When the party you have served or been a member of for 30-odd years does not want to know you, then it becomes difficult to carry on.

All of that was swirling around in my mind, but the overpowering consideration for me was the distress the whole business was causing to my wife and family. As a politician, I could cope with adverse publicity;

but, although completely innocent and unconnected with the dirty business of politics, they were being subjected to unfair harassment and intolerable pressures. I could not allow that to happen to those who are nearest and dearest to me.

It was an emotional as much as a logical decision, but, in reality, my options were limited. I could have made another statement in that afternoon's debate in the Scottish Parliament, but my political opponents and the media did not need facts or information to continue their onslaught – fiction is easier. I could have carried on and taken the advice of some to 'tough it out', but that was not realpolitik.

My other major motive was to protect the integrity of the office of First Minister. I could not allow it to be tainted by any stain. There could be only one decision: the principled course was to resign.

I went to St Andrew's House and told the advisers – who were equally weary – and the Permanent Secretary what I intended to do. There was no argument because they could see how determined I was and they limited themselves to giving me some good counsel about how things should be handled. It was a very emotional day, but I have a very rational mind. I did not see any way of moving forward which would have quietened the media frenzy, removed the pressure from myself and my family or done anything to undo the damage.

There were phone calls from Tony Blair and Gordon Brown, neither of whom wanted me to resign. The Prime Minister declared it was a 'tragedy' but he accepted my position when I explained my thoughts.

I phoned Julie to tell her what I had decided and then went to prepare my statement to the Scottish Parliament. I admit that I was actually grief-stricken, not so much at the loss of office, but that so much was being lost over so little.

Fortified by a lunch of bridie, chips and beans in my private office, I changed into a new suit and went to Parliament, where Tom McCabe had arranged with the Presiding Officer that First Minister's Questions would be replaced by my personal statement. There was strong support from a number of individuals, but it was lonely in the middle of the hubbub. I had to be calm and composed, exuding a confidence that was light years away from what I felt. I was smiling for self-preservation and, although I hope I behaved with dignity, it did not lessen the hell I was experiencing.

I can do no better than reproduce the statement I made to the Parliament on Thursday, 8 November 2001:

> I acknowledge again today my mistakes in the matter of constituency office sub-lets and in the way in which I handled that matter. There is no need to go over the details again. What is

important is that I take full personal responsibility. Others who worked with and for me have been criticised, but the ultimate responsibility is mine and mine alone. I recognise the mistakes that I made.

I have been surprised and dismayed over the past few weeks at how my family, friends, staff and colleagues have been brought into matters that are my responsibility alone and at how they have been made to suffer. That focus and attention has astonished them and me.

I value this Parliament. At Westminster, I was the lead minister for devolution and chaired the consultative steering group, which established the very principles by which this Parliament operates. I am proud of my role in that, but I take even greater pride in the role of my party and in what it has done for Scotland. We led on devolution, we delivered devolution and, with our colleagues in a historic coalition, we are and remain determined to make devolution work.

Scottish devolution, a Scottish Parliament, a Scottish Executive. I would be the last person to willingly or knowingly put the principles behind those new and great institutions at risk and in doing so put at risk everything that I have cherished in more than 25 years in politics, from becoming a councillor in Kirkcaldy district in 1974 to holding the highest office in Scotland over the past year. Even my harshest critics over the past few weeks have had to acknowledge that I made no personal gain from any of that.

I did not come to parliament simply as some kind of career choice. I did not enter parliament because it was some kind of family tradition. I came to parliament to work for the people I know and grew up with and to serve them. That has been my purpose since the day and the hour that I was elected. I came to parliament, and eventually to the office of First Minister, to serve my constituents and, eventually, all the people of Scotland. If I have let them down in this matter, I hope that I have served them well in many others.

It has been a privilege to do that through the work of government here in Scotland. I believe that that work over the past year has strengthened the roots of our devolved Government and secured it irreversibly in the life of our nation. It is now time for others to lead us as we take that work forward. The future of Scotland is the responsibility of every one of us here today. That is why this Parliament must now turn its energies once more to its real and pressing business: the concerns of the people of

Scotland. I want us to be allowed to do that with a minimum of distraction. That is why I am resigning. I call on Scotland to give all of us, and my successor, the fair and reasonable circumstances that we need to allow that to happen.

I am proud of what I achieved in parliament, in the Executive and as First Minister. I will continue with my duties as MSP for Fife Central, serving the people I know and grew up with. That in itself is and remains an enormous privilege for me.

It was natural that there would be Cabinet changes, but in the purge that followed, 'Team McLeish' was dismantled and talented people were replaced by less-talented individuals. Some of the leadership wanted me to become a non-person, even when I offered discreetly to provide background and continuity to things initiated during my term of office. I was seeking nothing apart from the chance to help with the bid for Euro 2008 Cup finals, but some in the new Executive simply did not want to know and I was completely rebuffed.

My constituents were appalled. In the daily streams of vitriol, they did not recognise the person they knew and who had represented them for 30 years. The people in my constituency have been extraordinarily supportive throughout and have been warm and friendly, as ever, when we meet in our daily lives. It is heartening to know they appreciate my contribution to our community and their belief is unshaken by what they have read and heard.

It has been a pleasure and a privilege to serve the people of Fife Central over so many years. An important part of my success as a constituency MP and MSP has been the tireless work of my personal assistant Gwen Newell. She started as my secretary when leader of Fife Regional Council in 1982 and spent over 20 years in the job. MPs know the real driving force in any constituency is the secretary or personal assistant who faces the public daily, deals with an astonishing range of human problems and is the link between the people and their elected representative.

Sadly, at the same time my constituency executive had been having secret meetings to undermine my position. After reflecting on my situation and all that had happened, I decided not to stand for re-election to the Parliament in May 2003.

It was a side of Labour politics I had not experienced before, having been nurtured in the comradeship of the movement. Perhaps naively, I found it hard to understand because it all seemed to have very little to do with the ideas, principles and values that attracted me into the Labour Party in the 1970s.

Months later, after a long and exhaustive police investigation, the Procurator Fiscal's office sent me a letter saying there was no case for me to answer. Julie asked why I was not elated and I replied: 'Because nothing has changed. I have always known that was the case.'

What appalled me more than anything about my difficulties was the behaviour of Fife Council in relation to my wife, Julie. The council embroiled my wife in the Third Age non-issue in the harshest possible use of power.

Third Age was a tiny project which had been running for nearly a decade with the sole aim of helping older people. A valuable service had been maintained in the face of difficulties getting volunteers to run it. It was always clear that no money had gone missing. The way Fife Council handled the matter, however, did not make this clear and indeed led to my wife being wrongly presumed guilty for something that never happened. The only reason was that she is married to me.

Julie was a senior manager in the social work department with an exemplary record and reputation. She was very popular, extremely competent and virtually ran her department. In her 25 years in social work, she had made a career of giving to others and was an expert on the care of older people.

In the wider context, what happened at that time and since has been saddening and sickening and really a scandal in itself. Inquiry after inquiry, the engagement of two retired chief executives who went over the ground time and time again – and for what? The council has still to report in public on these investigations. Council employees who were Labour supporters were targeted and, amid a catastrophic loss of morale, senior staff are being systematically removed.

My election agent, Maureen Rodger, was suspended from work as a council employee for a year, at the end of which she was reinstated. To this day, she does not understand what she was supposed to have done.

My wife was fully exonerated by the council, which was no surprise since everyone knew she had done nothing. Yet another untrue report said that Julie was suing the council for a million pounds – but anyone who knows Julie would know that is a malicious lie. She has said repeatedly, as a matter of principle, that as someone who has spent her life in public service she would never take public money that could be spent on services for others. All she has ever sought was for her name to be cleared. That has been done in full measure, but at immense personal and professional cost.

The net effect of these council-inspired intrigues has been the squandering of large sums of council money. I can remember nothing like it in my 30 years of elected office; having been a Fife councillor for 9 years and leader for 5 years, I feel ashamed for my council.

It is for others to inquire into why this fiasco resulted in so many being treated as scapegoats, causing so much damage to the lives of dedicated public workers. Serious and far-reaching questions have to be asked about the spending of so much public money to so little effect. Fife Council's behaviour may require a book of its own.

PART IV

The Future

XVI

The Politics of Hope

The politics of hope means a confident, but candid, look at the future of our country. I have described the influence of my early life and 30 years in elected office at three levels – local, UK and Scottish; first local councillor, then minister in the Blair Government and finally minister in the Scottish Executive, culminating in the post of First Minister. In view of this life of public service to country and constituency, but also as a Scot, I am not a dispassionate, disinterested observer in all of this. It is my country and I care deeply about it.

Extensive travel in Europe and the US, teaching and learning about other countries, other cultures and other forms of politics have also enabled me to assess Scotland in the modern global setting. We now live in an age where we have to rekindle that sense of internationalism that has earned us so much credit over the centuries.

This is not a blueprint, not a model; it is about ideas, issues and the inspiration we need not only in politics but throughout the economic and social fabric of our country.

We have to look at the complex, deep-seated and enduring problems which are so often overlooked and certainly understated. Solutions will take time, but what we can do now is to have a totally different way of looking at Scotland in the twenty-first century – and that means a new role within the UK and Europe, and internationally.

It is important that we apply a sense of urgency. We forget that while we are drifting into the twenty-first century the rest of the world is moving on; the things we think we will do one day, they are doing today.

Not just government, but every institution in every part of Scotland should be waking up to the challenge. We must accept that a successful and productive economy is absolutely vital if poverty and social deprivation are to be tackled seriously. We do not *need* to do anything; we do not *need* to acknowledge the problems and difficulties; we can continue as we are – but we owe ourselves more than that.

Scotland is not facing up to the accelerating pace of change in technology, communications and science. Change is not going to be easy because the pressures to conform and to remain complacent are all in place, but if we look around us, globalisation, European integration and the 'new regionalism' in Europe do provide a compelling case for us to change.

If change is not easy, we can help create the momentum. Throughout history, changes often come when countries are in crisis and receive a major shock to their systems. Germany and Japan, post-Second World War, are outstanding examples, but a more recent and more appropriate model is Finland. With the collapse of the Soviet Union in the early 1990s, the Finnish economy was badly undermined by the loss of one of its largest trading partners. Faced with this crisis, Finland embarked on a remarkable programme of social, political and economic change. As a result, a country of 5 million people on the edge of the Arctic Circle has now become one of the most productive and competitive countries in the world, with one of the best qualities of life.

In the absence of any crisis or major shock to our system, we need to look long and hard at both the problems and the potential of Scotland. There is a growing consensus about these challenges (less so about the choices that Scotland has to make) and my impressions are informed by what other people have written and said.

To better understand and effectively deal with the challenges and choices Scotland faces, they have to be part of a wider strategy – a road map to show where devolution goes from this point onwards.

At present there is no structure, shape or direction to the constitutional debate within the UK, in particular concerning the future of devolution in Scotland, Wales and Northern Ireland; the cautious and tentative steps towards the creation of regional assemblies in England; and the London assembly. These may be separate entities, but they are all part of the continuing programme of constitutional reform.

At Westminster, devolution has always been seen as a response to the demands of historic nations, cultural and political movements and the need to make the already existing and extensive administrative decentralisation more accountable. For Westminster this was the end of the journey and, as a result, the end of the debate. In fact, it should only be a start.

For Scots, the will of London still seems to prevail. Within Scottish Labour, there is no real debate; the SNP seems to have learned nothing and still talks about independence in the tired old rhetoric of the 1960s;

the Conservatives were never interested in devolution and remain ambivalent; the Liberal Democrats, the only party with a worked-out strategy, have been conspicuously silent when they could have been advancing their federalist case.

Faced with this paralysis, we need to anchor the debate on the future of devolution and embrace four important factors: devolved federalism within the UK; the 'new regionalism' of Europe; a new model of social and economic development based on Scandinavia; and developing Scotland on the world stage. These are the issues which represent the bigger picture for Scotland.

Devolved federalism makes sense for Scotland and the UK, and offers Labour a way out of its current inactivity. It is an alternative to separatism; it is shared power not devolved power; it offers symmetry and coherence – a concept that gives some meaning to the proposals for English regions; it gives a wider credibility and significance to the Scotland Act; it makes devolution less exceptional and more mainstream in European terms and in the political and constitutional debate within the UK.

The nation state of Great Britain will have to acknowledge and embrace the growing impact of globalisation, supra-nationalism, the growth and further integration of the European Union and, in turn, the increasing pressures from the regions and the devolved countries.

In fact, Westminster and Whitehall must accept that the constitutional map of the UK has only been partially redrawn and that the concept of devolved federalism represents a more mature, serious and intelligent way forward. It provides a more effective counter-argument to the sentiment and symbolism of separatism. The limited notion of devolution has, by its very nature, to move forward.

The transfer of power from the Scottish Office, a department of state in Whitehall, to the Scottish Executive, a government in Edinburgh dealing with the domestic affairs of Scotland, was a historic change. It also required considerable institutional, practical and psychological changes. While the institutions have been set up and are working in practice, the changes in attitudes and thinking have not taken place.

Devolution should also have meant a loosening of Whitehall control and the acquisition of new competence and capabilities in Scotland. Instead, we tried to adapt the civil servants and organisations we already had to deal with to different roles and larger tasks for which they were not equipped (the new Scottish Parliament is a very pertinent case in point).

There are still fundamental questions to be answered at the heart of the devolution settlement. When a national partnership is viewed as a superior devolving to an inferior, the psychology of that is not encouraging and is out of step with what is happening in the world.

We think devolution is exceptional, but it is really part of a worldwide tendency and we have to see ourselves as part of a new twenty-first-century order, especially the European pattern of 'new regionalism'.

Part of the solution is for the UK, one of the late entrants into devolution and regionalism, to make another significant constitutional shift and adopt a form of devolved federalism. It would also have to mean constitutional safeguards for power sharing within the United Kingdom and competitive economic status for each British region. This is a radical proposal, but my instincts tell me the problems of the north-east, north-west and south-west of England, as well as Scotland, Wales and Northern Ireland cannot be solved by Westminster alone.

Vernon Bogdanor, the constitutional expert and frequent commentator on the constitutional changes introduced by Tony Blair, has set out a coherent and compelling concept of devolved federalism for the future of Scotland and the UK. In his book *Devolution in the United Kingdom*, he argues that recent constitutional change has seen the UK move towards a more codified constitution and suggests that the reforms are irreversible as they will permanently alter the landscape of British politics. Despite the lack of safeguards being set out in a written constitution, he regards validation in a referendum as the next best thing.

Bogdanor also contends that devolution is introducing the federal spirit into the British state for the first time. For devolved Scotland, Northern Ireland and Wales, Westminster is no longer a supreme parliament but a quasi-federal parliament.

The Scottish Parliament may be subordinated constitutionally, but not politically, and Bogdanor defines this as the main point of political tension. This is reinforced by the fact that there are no constitutional guarantees of devolved powers.

He reinforces his thesis by outlining three characteristics of a completely devolved federalism:

1. Supremacy of the constitution
2. The distinction among bodies with limited and coordinated authority of the different powers of government
3. The authority of the courts to act as interpreters of the constitution

The Scotland Act reflects these characteristics, i.e. it has distinctive powers, it introduces a judicial element into the determination of that distribution and supersedes the supremacy of Parliament, since the UK Parliament will not in practice be able to alter its provisions within the context of a Scottish Parliament.

Bogdanor further argues that the Scottish Parliament and Northern Ireland Assembly will, in practice, become the supreme authorities for devolved affairs and that devolution is a mere delegation of power from a superior political body to an inferior one. If the Scottish Parliament is the supreme authority over domestic affairs, the relationship between London and Edinburgh will be quasi-federal.

Despite devolution to Northern Ireland, Wales and Scotland, there does not seem to be a great deal of enthusiasm for moving further and faster to establish a federally devolved United Kingdom. Some tentative steps have been taken towards establishing regional assemblies in certain parts of England but, to date, there has been no acknowledgement from Westminster that globalisation and European integration will continue to have a dramatic effect on the nation state. For the United Kingdom, the global rule book will mean more limits on the ability of the Westminster Government to intervene in the economic and social problems of any part of Britain.

Within nation states and within Europe, the idea of the competitive region is growing, so that regions like Scotland would compete for economic advantage in the UK, Europe and globally. Subsidies will have to give way to sustainability, and redistribution will have to give way to competitiveness. These changes will have profound consequences for Scotland, which we should be identifying now. The present danger is that we are not doing that.

Looking in retrospect at the early years of devolution, we have not thought through what we want to do with it – and we also regard it as something narrow, exceptional and complete. We fail to see Scotland as part of a global trend and as part of Europe's 'new regionalism'.

Throughout Europe, the new regionalism takes many forms – for example, the federal systems in Germany and Austria or the autonomous regions in Spain. What they have in common is that, while all are working closely with their national governments, they are also in Europe, building new relationships and alliances.

Michael Keating is professor of regional studies of the European Institute in Florence, Italy, and professor of Scottish politics at the University of Aberdeen. He is a prolific author and prominent academic. In his book with James Hughes, *The Regional Challenge in Central and Eastern Europe*, he outlines the changes taking place in territorial restructuring and European integration.

His core argument is simply put. He argues that twin processes are reshaping politics and government in European societies, operating from above and below: integration and the emergence of regions. At the same time, he argues the nation state is challenged by the shifting boundaries of the private and public sectors and the growth of a more autonomous civil society. As the nation state loses power to the EU and the regions, it is losing more and more of its importance, becoming 'too small for the bigger problems and too big for the smaller problems'.

Keating says there are four main factors driving this new regionalism: economic restructuring; globalisation; the transformation in the nation state; and European integration. The result of these factors is the emergence of different boundaries. The new context weakens the influence of national governments and their capacity to intervene in the economy and at the same time gives new opportunities to the regions.

We should see ourselves as others see us and understand the changes we have to make. There is a limited debate which has been narrowed down to: stay as we are or go for full independence. The level of that debate does a disservice to Scots because it is false, unimaginative and stereotypical – which, unfortunately, characterises much of our political thinking in Scotland.

It encourages adversarial politics, and the challenge for the two major parties in the Scottish Parliament is to widen the choice from 'stay as we are' devolution or separatism. There are many alternatives to these two positions.

Within the UK, there is real potential to develop federalism as part of our constitution against the exciting developments of regionalism in Europe. That would not only be a much healthier prospect for Scotland but we would also be living and learning from what is going on around us.

Devolution is seen as a (to some, grudging) concession from Westminster. The accession of the eight central and eastern European countries to the EU (the other two new members are Cyprus and Malta) this year will strengthen this 'new regionalism' and will throw up interesting ideas and lessons for us.

The Scottish National Party once tried to woo Scottish voters with the slogan 'Independence in Europe'. A better slogan for New Labour would be 'Federalism in Europe'.

There is no shame in copying success and learning from countries which have already grappled with problems and changed themselves to meet the needs of the twenty-first century. We should be looking across the North Sea towards Sweden, Denmark, Finland and Holland.

Independent writer and government adviser Charles Leadbeater in his book *Up the Down Escalator: Why the Global Pessimists are Wrong* praises the qualities of those countries:

> Although small in populations, they have highly educated workforces and effective public sectors, especially in transport and

welfare. They have also opened themselves up to international trade and exchange in commerce and culture. They are high-tech societies, with intensive usage of the Internet, they warmly welcome new technologies and consumer innovation. They have overhauled their labour market policies and as a result have high participation rates and thriving private sectors.

Yet they have not sacrificed human values, offering public support for families and effective civic mechanisms to help people cope with change. They also value consensus and practise inclusive politics – in which equality and community are valued as highly as individualism and innovation – and they all have highly advanced environmental policies.

Significantly, there is an emphasis on the political leadership, who are expected to provide the conditions for change and the determination to see it through. Leadbeater's key message is that countries have to invest in capacity for innovation.

Nowhere is this more obvious than Ireland: a remarkable success story with a transformation in their economy and society over the last decade. This success is outlined in Crotty and Schmitt's *Ireland and the Politics of Change* and *Ireland on the World Stage*.

Interestingly, they argue that the scope for economic policy is highly restricted in a small, open economy such as Ireland. These limitations are widely recognised: joining the euro limits independent monetary policy and constrains fiscal policy, and close links with Britain's labour market limits the scope for divergence on wages.

The consequence is that economic debate centres on the micro-economic issues such as the education system, job incentives, training, foreign investment and encouraging local entrepreneurship. These powers are devolved to the Scottish Parliament and tend to undermine the argument of the SNP, who forget that globalisation and European integration limit flexibility on macro-economic policy. For Ireland, the leadership role of government and other political institutions managing and responding to change are of vital importance.

It is widely known that the Irish success is based on a number of important strategies which have been pursued with consistency by successive governments. These are investment in education, positive industrial policy, promotion of foreign direct investment into Ireland and the opening up of the economy and society to the outside world. The creation of an enterprise culture is the key to long-term economic success.

One striking idea I looked at, and was preparing to replicate in Scotland, was Finland's 'Committee for the Future'. Finland, a nation of five million people, is now the global leader in the development of the knowledge society, ahead of the USA, according to the World Economic Forum. How has a country with the same population as Scotland achieved this?

The Parliament of Finland is the only governing body in the world in which preparation for the future is seen as so important that a special committee has been established to ponder the future's pressures for change.

The Finnish Council of State and its Parliament have had a continuing political dialogue on the long-term future of their nation since 1993. Setting up the committee was an acknowledgement that the world is changing from an industrial society to a knowledge society – and that the search for new knowledge needs large-scale investment in education, lifelong learning, and research and development.

It recognises that parliaments have a relatively short time-horizon, dictated by electoral cycles, and they are focused on day-to-day legislative work. Timeframes of 5–20 years are necessary for long-term evaluation and policy making.

The Committee for the Future was set up in answer to the socio-economic crisis in 1992. Finland's dependence on forestry and papermaking, and the effects of the upheavals in the former Soviet Union, its major market, were stifling the country.

Since then, Finland has developed a modern, competitive economy, adding to the traditional timber and metals industries a substantial telecommunications sector – as everyone knows, Nokia is the world's number-one mobile-phone maker. As the sector boomed, the rate of economic growth topped 6 per cent in 2000 and, even with the tough times in telecommunications since then, the country is still thriving and attracting investment. Over 2,300 foreign companies have invested in Finland and produce 16 per cent of the country's output.

The Committee for the Future reports at least once in every electoral period, including a searching examination of the Government, as well as providing parliamentary committees with statements on such matters as climate, population, energy, the information society, crisis management and globalisation. To involve ordinary citizens, it also inaugurated a Forum of the Experienced and Wise and the Forum of Young Future-Builders – which are expected to be 'unofficial, critical and creatively conversational'.

The Parliament of Finland admits:

> A fear exists that Finland will succumb to what all of Europe has been criticised for, in relation to America: writing history, looking for old and small-scale problems, and concentrating carefully on their resolution at a time when those who are succeeding are

seeking the non-existent in everything, creating new things and
trying new approaches even in the context of the old.

They could have been writing about Scotland . . .

Scotland, which has always been an internationally minded nation, does
not make enough of its worldwide contacts and the ready-made resource
of Scots in exile. We already have a global network of individual people
and offices but they are not working for Scotland as they should.

At all levels, Scotland has to internationalise its economic, learning and
cultural activities. New working relationships and alliances will
strengthen our international presence and make better use of existing
international offices and development opportunities.

This global network will complement, but not duplicate, the work of
the United Kingdom; instead, it will sell Scotland more directly abroad.
Raising our international profile should therefore comprise a complete
overhaul of our overseas outlets for Scottish Enterprise, Scottish
Development International and VisitScotland, providing more coherence,
focus and strength in overseas marketing. Worldwide, there are about 20
of these overseas outlets, but they are not working as one. A 'Scotland
United' approach would achieve a more identifiably Scottish brand.

We want to establish Scottish representation in some of our embassies.
We already have a First Secretary for Scottish affairs in the Washington
embassy and we could have similar representatives in Beijing and Tokyo
with possibly more in the future depending on where our interests lie.
This would have to be done in close consultation with the UK
government. We need to enhance the role of Scotland House in Brussels
and develop new alliances in Europe, building on the Flanders Initiative,
and strengthen our presence within the British Council and British
Tourist Authority. Further technology alliances should be created with
high-tech states in Europe, North America and the Far East, similar to
those already established with Maryland, Virginia and California. The key
to this is the involvement of our universities.

Underpinning all of this should be a comprehensive and more
professional approach to harness the Scottish diaspora – a sleeping giant
worldwide but especially in the United States, using Scots at home and
away to improve our country's prospects.

XVII

The Challenges and Choices

Scotland has been described as a state of mind – and that state of mind has been created by history, culture and even religion. We Scots do have a talent for what an Irish writer has called 'begrudgery', a resentment of individual success, an unwillingness to bestow praise and delight in the misfortunes of those who try something new, but fail.

There is a 'know your place' mentality and, for some, being competitive is a dirty word. It is confused with capitalism, and confidence is confused with arrogance. It is reinforced by a media whose influence is far-reaching but often strikes a negative chord.

This simply has to change because my experience is that any country effecting change has needed an upbeat national mood to drive it. As a loyal Scot, I would hope that our true mood is far from pessimistic, far from cynical and far from negative.

That does not mean a society without criticism; but as a society we must begin to see the glass as half-full and not half-empty. With such a change of mood, we can be more understanding of failure in business; more individual and less dependent on government; show more initiative, innovation and entrepreneurship. We need a leadership with the ability to enthuse and excite and with the urge to see Scotland playing a more significant role in the world.

The Prime Minister has said he would like to see the solidarity of Europe combined with the enterprise of America: I often feel we have too much solidarity and not enough enterprise. Too much dependency means looking for someone to blame, instead of taking responsibility for our own affairs. Scots have always been ruggedly independent and self-sufficient.

It is all very well having people come and visit us, but we also want people to live and work here. In a situation where the national mood is so negative, is it any wonder that people leave the country? There are no economic frontiers and no barriers to communication around the world in the twenty-first century. This enables people to live where they want without feeling cut off from families and friends. You can speak to someone in Beijing as quickly as you can speak to someone in Birmingham, and improved transport links make the world a smaller place. We should never forget that Scots have a choice where to live and work.

The tragedy is that those who are leaving are the individuals with the spirit of enterprise that we need. If the mood is not more encouraging, it will be hard to attract them back and we will not attract nationals of other countries with a similar spirit of enterprise. It is harder to reverse the population loss in a nation where the mood is often sombre and pessimistic.

Our failure to think through what we do with devolution is a major worry. Setting up the Scottish Parliament and getting people elected to it were both important. However, although we had campaigned for it for 100 years, since we actually achieved it there have been no big ideas really and no coherent thinking about what should lie beyond the practical achievement and the bricks and mortar.

Further, we have to recognise it is not a stable settlement. While the first four years have been largely successful, there are no constitutional safeguards surrounding devolution. In these early years, we have been fortunate that strong personalities in government at Westminster and the politics of Labour and likeminded politicians in control in London and Edinburgh have created the ideal conditions for the birth and nurturing of the Scottish Parliament and Executive, but this may not always be the case:

- Although the Parliament was established on the back of a referendum, it only really exists because of an Act of the Westminster Parliament. While it is unthinkable that the Scotland Act could be repealed, there are possibilities that the balance could be altered in the future. Any change in government in London or Edinburgh, or both, would have ominous consequences.
- The basis of the financial settlement, the Barnett formula and the block grant, have already been the subject of criticism. In Gordon Brown, we have a Chancellor of the Exchequer who sees no need for a reassessment – but, in the long term, it could happen. Again, there are no guarantees.
- The powers and capabilities of the Scottish Parliament are enshrined, but that, too, could change. We will want to increase the powers in the

future but centrist, anti-devolution politicians could take the opposite view.

There is a need for proper safeguards for the settlement and we need to see a United Kingdom debate, with Britain taking regionalism and change within the Union more seriously. In fact, we need to be moving towards some form of devolved federalism. This is not on the Westminster agenda but it should be on Scotland's, and we should take the lead in promoting that debate in the United Kingdom.

The nation state that is the UK will change, and the question is whether we will try to shape the future in our own interests or allow things to take an unplanned course. We should stop thinking and using the term 'devolution' and be thinking instead about 'new regionalism'. Different countries with different problems at different times have found constitutional settlements where they share power (such as the German *Länder* and their central government) – not a parliament passing power down to what they would regard as an inferior body. We need to share power.

When we consider the performance of other countries (and there is an abundance of comparative statistics and information by which we can measure progress), the hard truth for Scotland is that on growth, productivity, competitiveness, research and development, science skills and the rate of business formation, we lag well behind the best in the world. On these measurements, the UK as a whole is doing better than Scotland.

These things did not happen yesterday but are the product of long-term changes in the economy; the massive transformation of our economy in the twentieth century. Very complex factors are at work which are not amenable to quick solutions but have to be worked on over a long period. Ireland, for instance, has transformed itself by being focused and disciplined over the last dozen years.

One factor that is never given enough attention is the economic activity rate. Scotland has a low workforce participation rate and a higher number of people who are economically inactive and not contributing to the growth of the economy. What that essentially means is that there are still far too many people who, for a variety of reasons, do not work when they could work. As a result, they are the recipients of welfare but are not aiding the economy.

We keep talking about these issues but we are not doing a great deal about them. It often feels as if these issues are so big and so difficult to deal with that we continue to be in denial.

Recent disclosures suggest we have a serious population problem on our hands: Scotland's population is due to fall below five million by 2009 for the first time since 1946. The falling birth rate combined with an ageing population are tell-tale signs of more significant factors that we have to understand and act upon.

In Europe in 1965, the birth rate was 2.7 children per woman, which was well above the 2.1 rate needed to maintain the population size – but by 1995 it had fallen dramatically to 1.5.

The forecasts suggest that by 2050 the average age in America will be 36.2 and in Europe it will be 52.7 (currently, there is near-parity at 35.5 in the US and 37.7 in Europe). At the same time as the American population will be getting younger, the working-age population in Europe is set to fall by 40 million or 18 per cent by 2050.

While the trends show that the USA will be thriving, in Europe the Italians and Spanish are going to be the worst affected. The UK population is going to be stable but Scotland's population will fall.

These reduced birth rates and falling population figures are an old-world phenomenon; the USA has higher fertility and rising rates of immigration. At present, the European Union population is some 90 million greater than the US, but by 2050 America could have 40–60 million more people than today's 15 EU member states. In 50 years' time, Europe's population could be down to 300 million and falling; the American population would be over 550 million and rising – i.e. there would be twice as many Americans as there are now.

Among our neighbours and competitors, the Irish have been most successful in recognising and tackling these trends. They are stemming outward migration; attracting back to their homeland Irish nationals, including young people who have gone abroad for experience (what is known as the 'homing pigeon' phenomenon); and they are attracting nationals from other countries. Consequently, the Irish economy is expanding with the right mix of high-tech jobs and good opportunities, and Ireland's status in Europe and the world has risen dramatically.

In every respect, the opposite is true of Scotland. We have a declining and ageing population; our workforce is likely to shrink in size; the talented and skilled young people are leaving; and we are not attracting foreign nationals. We should be asking ourselves: when we boast so proudly about this great country of ours, why do so many valuable people want to leave and so few want to come?

The economic and social consequences of the combined shrinking population and rising life expectancy are alarming for Scotland. The present figure in Europe of 35 people of pensionable age for every 100 of the working population will rise to 75 in 2050. That is, the dependency ratio of older people (65+) to those of working age (15–64) will double. Understandably, much of the debate is about pensions, but there are other far-reaching implications.

With a shrinking working-age population and the serious dilution of talent and skills in the workforce that remains, the consequences could be quite devastating for growth. The low activity rates and the worsening ratio of workers to those dependent on the state will undermine our economy and require significant expenditure on the support of the ageing population.

As a matter of urgency, we should be looking for economic and fiscal solutions to bring about an off-setting rise in workforce participation rates and productivity. That will require a more effective application of new technology and retaining more and better-trained people in the workforce. Attracting skilled workers from abroad will have to become a priority.

Those Scots of working age who do not work must be encouraged or guided into jobs. We cannot afford to have the depressing situation where a worker is thrown on the scrap heap at 45. That has never been appropriate and, if it had been, this would be the time for change because we need these people in our workforce.

More controversially, we will need older workers to stay in work longer. While the debate is increasingly about whether people will have to work on because we cannot afford to give them a decent pension, another reason may be that it would be for the good of the economy. We may need older people to stay on in their jobs until they are 70 to replace the young people who are leaving the country – or are not being born.

Experiencing all of this, Scotland should be acting *now* to create a smarter workforce, more technology, higher productivity and a better ratio of economically active Scots to those who are dependent. Remember, our performance in all of these is below par even before the population decline accelerates.

Scotland has seen an astonishing transformation of its employment and industrial structure over the last 100 years. Early in the last century, when 50 per cent of the ships that sailed around the world were made in Glasgow, our steel, coal and heavy engineering were dominant. After these were decimated in the 1960s and 1970s, there was the move into electronics with mixed results. Now our economy has all the modern hallmarks – financial services, tourism, a sophisticated food and drinks industry, information technology, electronics, communications e-business, creative industries, oil and learning-based activity. In Scotland, we have to acknowledge that the only certainty is change. We can be sentimental and nostalgic about the bygone days of 'real' jobs, but that kind of work has largely disappeared and will never return.

In certain traditional industries, we can add value and concentrate on the quality end of the market, as our textile industry is doing. However, if we are far-sighted, we will have to prepare for the fact that the bulk of low-skill, low-wage manufacturing jobs will go to China, Asia, central and eastern Europe and eventually Africa.

There has to be a recognition that the structure and location of industry, employment patterns and the nature of work will change with new technology, the e-revolution, the Internet and the development of 'human capital' in a future society. All of that means that learning becomes the pre-eminent issue for Scotland.

An interesting side issue is the gender mix of the workforce. We are about to reach the point where more women will be working than men and the implications for family and society will be formidable.

As the twenty-first century begins to unfold, Scotland still tolerates too many social evils that are simply unacceptable. They range from 'slopping out' in prison (which does not happen in the rest of the UK) to teenage pregnancies, drugs and a still-violent culture.

No matter where you are in the world, there are similar problems to be faced and every country has a very complex and challenging social agenda. What is depressing about Scotland is that on far too many of these key issues, our ranking within the UK and Europe, and sometimes globally, is so high in the league of shame. This is borne out by the reams of statistics from the UN, EU, OECD, World Bank and organisations such as the Rowntree Foundation in Britain. We should not be placed where we are in the league tables for women in prison and teenage pregnancies, for domestic violence, violent crime, general intolerance, bigotry and sectarianism, knife culture, alcoholism, solvent abuse and drugs.

There is a too-easy acceptance of what should be unacceptable and a tendency to allow shameful aspects of our national life to drift. Standards are sacrificed and antisocial behaviour, youth crime, the 'macho' culture, graffiti and litter, and the veneer of chewing gum on every pavement, are all too easily tolerated.

Some old people live in a state of fear and alarm when they are entitled to expect peace and respect: their last years are made miserable. Women are subjected to violence, abuse and discrimination on a scale that is still unacceptable. Minority communities and asylum seekers are still harassed and made unwelcome.

As a former Minister for Prisons, I hark back to one source of shame that should have been ended long ago: why, in this astonishing and sophisticated technological age, do we still accept the Victorian humiliation of 'slopping out' in prisons? Let us not mince our words, it means prisoners peeing in pots.

Where are our standards? In a civilised, tolerant and liberal-minded society there should be rights and responsibilities; but above all there should be civilised standards.

The failure of successive governments to modernise and, even more disappointingly, the failure of organisations to reform themselves is a major issue in Scotland. A good example is local government, the subject of heated debate in Parliament over the last two or three decades. This sector spends vast sums of public money, is the biggest employer in Scotland but in important respects has not changed very much over the last 30 years.

Again, it is a question of lack of focus and modernisation. One problem of devolution is that we are too close to constituencies of interest, who do not want change if it directly affects them and the amount of money they can spend. We have to have the courage to take on these vested interests. Unions and councillors have a job to do, but we have to bring our institutions into the twenty-first century.

We should accept that the need for more finance and investment must mean the involvement of both the public and private sectors. At the end of the day, people are worried about the quality of their services; instead of blurring the source of the finance, we should be breaking down the barriers between the two. Perhaps we do have to acknowledge that councils and other organisations need not necessarily deliver services themselves. The alternatives are for them to become enablers and to develop more non-profit organisations in Scotland – a better mix of provision.

Generally, within the civil service there is scope for acquiring new competencies and capacities to deal with new policy issues that did not exist 10 or 15 years ago. If they do not, the Holyrood building fiasco and, more recently, disclosures about 'key weaknesses' and discrepancies in the Scottish Parliament's own annual accounts are examples of the institutional failures that will continue to happen.

There is no reason why our Scottish civil service should not eventually be devolved, instead of continuing to be a branch of Whitehall. Under devolved federalism or an updated constitutional set-up, we may see our civil servants employed by the Scottish Executive and not by the UK government.

Under devolution, we could build up capacity and competence and bring about a change in the psyche, all of which are difficult to achieve from Whitehall. The Permanent Secretary, who is head of the Scottish civil service, attends the weekly meeting of Whitehall department heads under the head of the UK civil service. Logically, there must come a point where loyalties and aspirations are in conflict. A step away from Whitehall would build on devolution in a logical way.

We have often heard criticism from the private sector and business community about how we are not embracing e-business, e-learning or e-commerce. All of that exploded in the mid-1990s, but in government we still do not have the capacity and competence to promote these areas. Why do we not harness the skills of the private sector? We cannot expect civil servants to have the expertise, but it requires leadership to go outside the public sector.

It also has to be said that we have far too many economic development agencies in tourism and enterprise: 14 area tourist boards, 22 local enterprise companies, 32 local councils with their own agencies and a myriad of private and quasi-public bodies. There are not 32 different economic climates, 32 different causes of unemployment and 32 different types of workforce in Scotland, so there cannot be any justification for so many different agencies. We have an over-complicated, expensive and bureaucratic system that is not found in other countries, and the effect is to blur the national focus and make change difficult.

If the economy is to be crucial to our future, our agencies must be up to it. Scottish Enterprise is much criticised but, as our national economic agency, it deserves more consideration by the politicians. There are many at Scottish Enterprise who would want to see us re-create a powerful national agency similar to the Scottish Development Agency, as is the case in other countries. Scottish Enterprise should be smaller, more dynamic, more creative and more focused, without being the umbrella for so many smaller bodies and the administrator of Westminster policies on unemployment in Scotland.

As one whose 30 years in elected office began with 13 years as a councillor, I know local government's strong points and its shortcomings as well as its unrealised potential. The reform and modernisation of Scottish local government should remain an important priority.

Local government makes an enormous contribution to our quality of life; provides services from cradle to grave; employs nearly quarter of a million people; and spends more than £6 billion per year. Local government finance should be the subject of an early review. The small amount of money raised at local level, the lack of accountability and the often unfairness of the council tax, suggest there has to be better, fairer and more efficient ways of financing our local councils.

The introduction of proportional representation for local government, while praiseworthy, will not automatically improve the quality of policy-making nor enhance the status of councils. Councils need more freedom to try new solutions – like cabinet-style leadership and not only elected mayors but also appointed departmental heads on fixed-term contracts and performance-linked pay.

One of the things still to be realised from devolution is that it was supposed to create new politics and new systems of representing the interests of the people. That was underpinned by the intention of removing ourselves from the adversarial politics of Westminster. It is obvious very little of that has happened so far, although it is still early days. What I think we need to do is create the conditions in which these changes can take place.

We are right to have proportional representation, which is a fairer electoral system delivering a truer reflection of the will of the voters, but the list system is not working in Scotland's best interests. We accept that we will now have coalition governments and the Labour–Lib Dem partners have done well. But it must also be right that those elected to the Scottish Parliament have some sense of a constituency base and some sense of direct responsibility.

One obvious option would be the single transferable vote with every MSP elected, not with a proportion of them nominated by party as at present. There needs to be a clear link between what people vote for and what is delivered, and the gap between expectation and delivery must be narrowed.

We have to try to renew interest in the eyes of the voting public. This is not a particularly Scottish problem; in countries all over the world, participation in elections is declining and in some of them turn-outs are exceptionally low. If nothing is done, interest in single-issue politics will continue to increase, especially among young people. Worst of all, an astonishing number of people have never voted in their lives and are lost to the democratic process before they are 18.

We must look at new ways of getting people to vote. Apart from stimulating interest and creating a desire to vote, with all the effective communication systems we now have, we should have more attractive ways of voting. We may want to look at reducing the voting age, although that may be a frightening prospect for some, particularly because young people tend to care deeply about single issues. Electronic voting systems are long overdue; if you can spend hundreds of pounds and operate your personal finances and bank accounts via the Internet with confidence, it should be possible to develop a secure voting system.

These challenges are formidable and affect every aspect of life in Scotland. Some may argue that they are not, in themselves, important enough to force us to make new choices with a sense of urgency. Some will acknowledge change is needed but will be modest in their expectations. But I hope there will be those who share my view that they lie at the very heart of what kind of country we want Scotland to be.

They require radical, immediate and honest examination and the right leadership so we can start to shape our future. We are fortunate in Scotland that we do have areas where real choices can be made and where we can start to release the potential of our assets and the talents of our people.

This is where devolution should come into its own. Within the Executive and Parliament we do control significant levers of change, but they are not being used to good effect.

When we consider that the knowledge society will be the key to the future, we must also acknowledge human capital and learning are the ways to achieve it. Compared with other countries, Scotland is in a good starting position.

From nursery provision right through to the higher levels of the academic world, Scotland's record of achievement stands up to examination with many of the best. It is a remarkable achievement that, while 39 per cent of young people in England attend university, the figure in Scotland is 50 per cent. We should look at what we can do to build on that and make ourselves the learning capital of the world. This is ambitious but it is not unrealistic.

This education-for-all philosophy is captured by J. François Richard in his book *High Noon – 20 Global Issues, 20 Years to Solve Them*. He describes education as central to the construction of a genuinely democratic society where individuals have the power to reflect, make choices and steer towards a better life. Education is the key to building a sense of global citizenship and a sense of shared values. Learning is a powerful instrument for reducing poverty and inequality and laying the basis for sustainable growth; it also creates tolerance, understanding and cohesion in communities. In a world economy which is so knowledge-intensive, education is vital.

We only have to look back through history, especially to the Enlightenment in the eighteenth century, to see how Scotland can lead the world in thinking and learning. Was that just a once-and-never-to-be-repeated happening? Was it only the coalescing of factors and a flowering of genius at one moment in time? Or was it something intrinsic to our Scottish nature that we can repeat? I prefer to think it was the latter.

We have world-class universities, world-class research facilities and, although regarded by some as the 'Cinderella service', our further education colleges are among the best in Europe. In the spirit of 'a mind is a terrible thing to waste', we now have a learning-for-life approach so that from cradle to grave our people have access to learning, whether formal or informal. We can genuinely look to the future with optimism and hope because of the learning platform we have built.

The priority of education for the knowledge society is especially important to us, because education is one of the substantial devolved powers of the Scottish Parliament. In particular, our universities need more funds as we build on excellence, enhance our research, modernise our infrastructure, increase pay, widen access and compete on the world stage.

On this front, there can be no excuses. We can set the priorities. We can provide the investment. We already have the people.

Linked to 'human capital' is the quality of our people. When we consider the changes that have taken place in Scottish society and Scottish industry, we can see that we do have a very adaptable workforce. Rooted in the culture of the coal mining, steel, shipbuilding and heavy engineering industries, they have a strong work ethic. Although most of these industries have all but disappeared, we have been flexible enough to attract major electronics companies and now we are moving into new technologies and services.

In our learning-for-life culture, everyone should be able to access skills and training and it should no longer happen that people are thrown on the scrap heap in their 40s and 50s. Apart from the human anguish caused, this is an unacceptable waste of talent and energy in what should be one of the most productive periods of life. Older workers will now have to become a key part of the national asset – and not just in giving advice in do-it-yourself stores.

Another deficiency that casts a long shadow over Scottish society is that so many people are functionally illiterate or innumerate, or both. Some estimates suggest that as many as one in six of our population (perhaps 800,000 Scots) cannot read, write or add with any degree of proficiency. These estimates may be on the high side but it is still a bewildering state of backwardness at the start of the twenty-first century: a terrible problem for the individual but an appalling waste for society and the economy.

No young person should leave school after 12 or 13 years of formal education and be unable to communicate effectively, read, write or add, unless they have a special educational need that prevents them from doing so.

Scotland is not unique in this, but we have the chance to do something about it. Tomorrow's Scotland will be about higher levels of technology and academic excellence, but it will also be about making sure every Scot has basic skills, enjoys their life and makes a greater contribution to society and the economy.

As well as our thinking, Scotland's physical infrastructure needs modernising and we need to develop rapidly our electronic infrastructure. Let us use the analogy of the nineteenth and early twentieth centuries, when the roads and railways were built and spread across our land to open up transport opportunities for industry. The modern-day equivalent is the information superhighway where the diffusion of technology, Internet penetration and the spread of e-business into every corner of Scotland will open up and support our country for the twenty-first century. We should have the same pioneering spirit which requires courage and a better partnership between the public and private sectors.

This can be achieved by closer government links with business, building up trust and confidence – and actually listening to what the leaders of business and industry have to say about their needs and what they and we can do for Scotland.

This will also require a more open and innovative approach to public and private spending, with more public value partnerships. The source of the investment is less important than the quality of the outcome for the people of Scotland. Or, to coin a phrase: 'What matters is what works.'

Science and technology are the driving forces in determining the future of nations in the knowledge society. They are transforming the world economy, the structure of society and our ways of living.

Innovation is the key and, as Charles Leadbeater says, it has a number of ingredients. Innovation calls for a capacity to develop new ways of doing things. It needs variety and diversity and thrives in systems, cultures, organisations and societies that are open and transparent. Markets are central to innovation and cultural activities are vital to promote learning and creativity in the knowledge economy.

One of the principal roles of political leadership will be to make sure these ingredients are in place, creating the conditions for original thinking, experimentation, risk-taking and invention: the building blocks of an enterprise culture.

We have in Scotland modern sectors that are in demand internationally and are growth industries – financial services, information and communications technology, biotechnology, tourism, food and drinks, oil, creative industries and learning. They are not the traditional industries but they are global in application and they have a future. All of them can obviously do more for the country. We must build on our strength.

In tourism, we have truly world-class assets but not yet a world-class industry. Despite the setbacks in international travel, tourism still contributes nearly £3 billion worth of income and has an even greater future. Although Scotland is not a low-cost destination, people are prepared to spend more to come here.

The creative industries – art, architecture, advertising, computer games, crafts, design, fashion, film, music, new media, publishing, radio and TV – support 100,000 jobs and earn £5 billion a year for the Scottish economy. Through the generation and exploitation of intellectual property, they have massive prospects for wealth and job creation. When we carried out a survey for the National Cultural Strategy, we were alerted to the fact that they are set to grow significantly faster than the Scottish economy as a whole. The predicted 'massive growth' in the global infrastructure for rapid distribution of information and creative content would mean that there are literally no limits to the potential.

Scottish companies have already carved out a niche in some of these global industries – in everything from modern and extremely sophisticated cartoon comics, computer games and popular TV programmes to high fashion and culture – yet they are under-appreciated. With the right encouragement, they will continue to find new applications of technology that will generate still more cultural forms and new businesses such as web and digital arts and video games.

The sheer volume of the global markets and the size of the competing corporations may seem a significant threat to the small Scottish players. The reverse is true: by concentrating on becoming niche players, using information technology to break down the barriers between industries and exploiting the Internet, digital audio-visuals and broadband, small companies can be global players.

Scotland has one of the most attractive environments in the world, with a coastline and climatic conditions that create the potential for developing new forms of energy like wind and wave power. We are committed to a target of 20 per cent of our needs being supplied by renewable energy: it is to be an important objective for us, but we can do more.

Our clean environment, a productive energy base and new forms of generation, the skills in our universities, one of the finest wilderness areas in Europe and magnificent assets all coincide with the worldwide push for renewable sustainable energy. We can be at the forefront of developing the sophisticated new technology for which there will be a global market. We should learn the lesson of the oil industry: companies that grew from the exploration, discovery and exploitation of the North Sea fields are now exporting their skills, services and technology. As exploration around our shores dramatically decreases and the reserves are becoming depleted, these companies continue to prosper in developing deep-sea oilfields all round the world.

By moving into renewable forms of energy, we will also show our concern for the rest of the world and help developing countries (which also happen to be potentially huge markets) to meet their fast-growing energy demands responsibly.

From experience in other countries, I believe the quality of our cities can be a basis for building local economies and success in the information age.

We now have five cities in Scotland, each with its own unique history and character, and they can be the drivers of growth, change, innovation and business creation in Scotland. With better and closer links between city government, central government and the private sector, they should be allowed more freedom to develop for the good of Scotland as a whole.

They should be competing in financial services, information technology and learning markets; Glasgow and Edinburgh should have closer contacts and twin with each other for tourism; our cities should be places in which young people can find the lifestyle and environment that will attract them back to Scotland. Our cities are special places and we have still to tap into their potential to drive our nation forward.

Some of this is happening, but we can still do much more. Scotland as a competitive region needs cities seeking competitive economic advantage.

Devolution gives us the chance to go beyond the United Kingdom and build new relationships, not only with small countries and regions of Europe but also regions and states in the US. We will be helped in this by our nation's credentials, the huge Scottish diaspora and the affection in which Scotland is held worldwide.

Something that is not tangible, but is vitally important for us, is the history of Scots in the world. Far too often, we remember the bad things about our history, looking inward on our historic grievances – wars fought and lost, especially to the English – but it has a more positive value. Much more significant is that, of all the 'old world' nations, we Scots have a history of outward-looking internationalism which chimes in with the modern world-view.

I have often been struck by the very positive view of Scotland held by people around the world. Often it is an old-fashioned image built around our traditional attractions of tourism – the world's most famous drink and the home of golf – with little awareness of how much we have changed and modernised in recent years. Generally, however, Scots are held in warm regard and no matter where you go in the world there will be a recognition of Scotland's worth – probably disproportionate to our size.

History has made the impact for us and creates a very positive sentiment. Arthur Hermann's book *How the Scots Invented the Modern World* encapsulates the contribution Scots have made since the Enlightenment in such fields as science, technology, philosophy and literature. Particularly in the days of Empire, Scots became administrators and teachers on a global scale and many countries still want to learn from us.

An outstanding Scottish cultural asset that is miserably under-used is Robert Burns: our failure to promote our national bard is inexplicable. 'Auld Lang Syne' is an international anthem, Burns Suppers are held around the world and he is honoured in every country, not only by the far-flung Scottish diaspora – yet the support we give to Burns organisations and their associated tourism is meagre. The same could be said of Sir Walter Scott, Robert Louis Stevenson, James Hogg, J.M. Barrie, Sir Arthur Conan Doyle, John Buchan and our other literary figures, as well as the Scottish Enlightenment. I used to joke with the Irish consul-general that we in Scotland had cultural assets they could only dream about. I also said that about our golf courses, but they do much more with less. This is not about nostalgia or cultural snobbery – it is about Scotland's future prosperity.

Different parts of the world, including Europe and the US, are excited by devolution, have a positive view of its development and have a much greater appreciation of its historical and constitutional significance. There is more interest in our devolution in Denver, Colorado, than in Dundee.

Too often, what emanates from within Scotland is cynicism, negativity and a blame culture. The way we see ourselves and our future is not mirrored in the international perception of Scotland. It gives a whole new meaning to 'Others wad some Pow'r the giftie gie us, To see oursels as others see us?'

We always find reasons why we have not done as well as we should and seek to find someone to blame. We should take ownership of our own future within the United Kingdom, within Europe, within the international context. That important sense of national identity and pride must be translated into something that motivates and drives what we do in the future.

We can no longer afford to be armchair patriots. I would like every Scot to be pulling on the jersey with the Lion Rampant. I represented Scotland on the football field, but throughout my life I have felt I was playing for Scotland. We should all feel the same.

XVIII

Manifestos for the Twenty-first Century

The Labour Party

Labour in Scotland, successful for so long and in so many ways, is now in danger of losing out. This may seem an unduly dire prediction in view of the party's traditional hold on large swathes of Scotland, its seemingly impregnable majorities in the heavily populated areas of local government, the size of its representation at Westminster and its dominant position as the largest party in the Scottish Parliament. However, Scottish Labour could lose its grip unless it corrects its failures – to modernise its thinking, to grasp the dramatic implications of the European and global changes that are already well advanced and to develop a coherent debate about where devolution goes from here.

Labour needs a distinctive concept of devolution, one that will consolidate the early success since 1999 and develop new ideas for the future. This will not be easy because breaking free from the existing attitudes and prejudices will be fraught with political difficulty north and south of the border.

Westminster, whilst embracing devolution to varying degrees, has no real appetite for fresh thinking and to a large extent is dragging its feet on the development of regionalism in the UK. Those Scottish MPs who have always been reluctant to acknowledge the new order of devolution, sections of the Scottish media and opposition parties will be less than accommodating if Labour moves the debate onto new ground.

Paradoxically, the devolution of power to Scotland and its own parliament after nearly 300 years was mirrored by a decline in the power and authority of Labour's own internal organisation in Scotland. Despite all the dialogue that takes place in the Scottish Labour Party executive, most of the funding and the appointment and payment of staff is by UK

Labour. If the party had more autonomy in Scotland, it would be forced to shake itself up.

Membership is falling, young people are not being attracted in the same numbers and there is a continuing decline in the number of people voting in elections. All of the political parties have failed to understand and manage these changes in our society – but it is for Labour, as the dominant party, to give a lead.

There does not seem to be the same sense of purpose and direction either among the Scottish leadership or rank-and-file. My own constituency party is like a poorly attended social club and perhaps, as MP and MSP over many years, I have to take my share of the responsibility.

The party in Scotland has no sense of self outside its interests in local government, the Scottish Parliament or the European Parliament. It has been a successful election machine (which has also been fortunate in having a very poor and inefficient Opposition) but as the future of politics in Scotland changes, so will the nature of the challenge.

There is a tension that has to be resolved. Do we need a strong Labour Party central apparatus? If we do, what is its role? What are the new relationships with the UK and its constituent parts, other than being a vetting procedure and an election machine? There is no radical thinking being done about Scotland and Scotland's place in the world at the centre of the Labour Party and, worse, nor is it being done in Scotland.

The Scottish Labour Party does not have the same national authority it once did. It is fighting elections and acting as broker between factions but has lost its role as a positive force for thinking and action. Between elections, I do not read headlines saying 'The Scottish Labour Party executive say . . . ' or 'The Scottish Labour Party executive's new policy . . . ' No one is being dragged into John Smith House and having strips torn off them for damaging and disloyal comments about the Scottish Parliament and the Scottish Executive leadership.

I disagree with individual members and those in the trade unions who are disenchanted with New Labour, who feel they are not being listened to and complain Labour governments have not been radical enough. I disagree strongly with those who talk of severing their links with the Labour Party and involving themselves with the Scottish Socialist Party or the Scottish Nationalists.

While some of these complaints have to be recognised, they really miss the point. New Labour in Westminster and Holyrood has delivered for Scotland in a way that no other party could. These other parties are not credible and cannot be regarded as alternative governments.

However, my concern is for the future, and Labour has to take the lead in the debate about where devolution goes from here. Otherwise, it risks being out-manoeuvred as both the Scottish National Party and the Liberal Democrats seize the opportunities being offered by a changing world and, even worse, fuelling the disenchantment of the Scottish people.

For the good of itself and of Scotland, the Scottish Labour Party must become more autonomous, more vibrant and more future-thinking.

The Scottish National Party

The SNP is tired, dispirited and old fashioned; it lacks any sense of conviction about its basic policy of 'all or nothing' Nationalism. It may still be party doctrine, but few really believe in it and its MSPs are merely going through the motions.

As the world becomes more interdependent, interconnected and international, separatism is a stale and increasingly unrealistic policy – for the simple reason that it bucks all the trends of globalisation, European integration, 'new regionalism' and the decline of the nation state. When frontiers are disappearing, ancient national prejudices are being erased and new relationships are being forged, the creation of new borders and harping on about historic grievances becomes redundant and plainly ridiculous.

The SNP's performance has been the most disappointing of all the political parties since the 1999 election and the creation of the Scottish Parliament.

For many Scots, the SNP has provided no more than an opportunity to protest. That may have worked to its advantage in the past, but with PR and the list system enabling the election of more single-issue candidates and out-and-out protest parties, the Nationalists will continue to lose ground.

The SNP has had great difficulty in adjusting to the new political landscape in devolved Scotland and has no certainty about its tactics and its ultimate direction. It is split from top to bottom by the rift between the forces of fundamentalism and pragmatism.

More dramatic and worrying for the SNP, it has simply failed to understand or adjust to a rapidly changing world of globalisation and European integration. Inexplicably, it ignores what should be the opportunities presented to them by the 'new regionalism' in which parties and regions more nationalistic than the SNP are participating and modernising their thinking.

At the heart of its failure is its inability to learn from Europe, especially the experience of the autonomous regions of Spain, and update its approach to constitutional and political change in the UK. Instead of benefiting from devolution, the SNP has missed the opportunity to achieve its aspirations.

The SNP is currently letting Scotland down. Sadly, its only response to every argument in the Scottish Parliament is to demand more money or powers, or both. In doing so, Nationalists have been blind to the potential weaknesses of the constitutional settlement and have impaired the quality of the debate on the future of Scotland.

Their contribution to the future of Scotland is meagre. Their constant refrain is 'we need more powers, we need fiscal autonomy [whatever that means]. Westminster is always to blame.' The rest is shrouded in sentiment and nostalgia.

Instead of a more open mind about where constitutional change will eventually take Scotland, they have purged some of their most effective MSPs, who take a more constructive view.

The resignation of Alex Salmond as leader of the party had an impact because there was (and still is) doubt about his motives. It was clear to me he left Edinburgh with a purpose and he has now said he is going to resign from Westminster at the next election to return to the Scottish Parliament. Alex is a very effective, shrewd operator and an exceptionally good advocate for the brand of narrow-minded nationalism for which the SNP has come to stand. Donald Dewar respected Alex Salmond but did not like the sharp invective to which he was subjected and which made it very difficult for him to make an argument. Salmond's style is cocky, divisive and very adversarial, the kind of person and politician Donald just did not like.

Salmond's 'sabbatical' at Westminster has given the new party leader, John Swinney, some space to change the party and attempt to make it more acceptable. But there is no doubt in my mind that Alex Salmond can re-take the leadership any time he wants and move the party in the direction he wants.

Salmond's departure did change the dynamic in the Scottish Parliament by reducing the effectiveness of the Opposition. John Swinney has many decent qualities but lacks Salmond's incisiveness, abrasiveness and arrogance.

However, their message is basically the same: if you are not a Nationalist, you are not a real Scot. Along with the majority of genuine Scots, I resent that smug and self-righteous view of Scottishness and will always oppose it. This is deeply insulting to Scots of all parties because no one in this country can claim a monopoly on patriotism.

Because of what it claims to represent, the SNP should be more concerned with Scotland's role on the world stage and the performance of the Scottish economy in the global market. Why persist with separatism and independence when other nations are benefiting from interdependence? Why persevere with outdated demands to be a nation state when the ability of nation states to intervene in economic and social spheres is becoming increasingly limited? What does 'nationalism' mean when communities have no borders and economies have no boundaries; when historic nations are measured by what they do, not where they are or whom they blame?

Narrow-minded, unimaginative and old-fashioned nationalism is fading from the political spectrum. If intelligent commentators can see all of this, why can't the SNP's leadership?

The Liberal Democrats

The Liberal Democrats have probably gained more from devolution than any other party: their electoral support has been steady and consistent; thanks to coalition, they have achieved their dream of power and a place at the heart of government in Scotland. A new sense of realism now tempers their actions, policies and ideas – although it does not curb their more undisciplined and fractious members.

As a federalist party, devolution has been a significant step forward in realising their aspirations for the whole of the UK. A system of PR they have consistently supported is now in place for the Scottish Parliament and is likely to be adopted for local government elections.

Jim Wallace has led his party with some skill in the problematic early years of devolution. Behind the scenes, the Liberal Democrats have strengthened their position in the Executive and increased their influence in the Parliament.

It is now time for the Liberal Democrats to be talking up and forcibly advocating devolved federalism. If Labour can't move on and the SNP fails to learn from Europe, then the Lib Dems are well placed between the two extremes to make a case for federalism. This would be consistent with their own historic commitment and with the enthusiasm for the 'new regionalism' in Europe, which represents a coherent, albeit long-term, solution for the UK. It would also give a harder edge to the debate in Scotland.

The Tories

The Scottish Parliament, with PR and the list system, threw a political lifeline to the Scottish Tories – one they did not deserve, in view of their often-hysterical opposition to devolution and their attempts to prevent the Parliament ever being born.

They might have been expected to learn some kind of lesson from their humiliation in the 1997 Westminster election. The party that, within living memory, had boasted the biggest number of Scottish MPs was wiped out and Scotland became a Tory-free area in parliamentary terms. Yet they continue to belittle and begrudge the very institution that has saved them from extinction.

There is little sign that they even bother to think about the future of Scotland and the development of devolution. Their ambivalent attitude to devolution, their uneasiness at the kind of radical reforms required in the UK and their ineffectiveness in winning the hearts and minds of the Scottish people all combine to defeat any attempt to reshape their identity or modernise their thinking.

The Scottish Tories are still thirled to Westminster and a leadership that wants to turn back the clock, just when they desperately need new ideas and a more distinctive sense of Scottishness. They should only look back for one reason: to realise that there was a time when they had the majority of Scottish MPs and that was because Scotland knew what they stood for.

The lesson for their current leadership in Edinburgh is to cease being obstructive and derisive – and perhaps surprise everyone by producing some positive policies for Scotland.

The Scottish Socialists

The so-called Scottish Socialist Party has developed from a personality cult into a loose coalition of like-minded discontents in the Scottish Parliament. The truth is that it represents no more than a distraction – but a dangerous and dishonest one.

Encompassing a ragbag of remnants – from hard-line revolutionary parties, Trotskyism, the Militant Tendency and the failed attempt to destroy Labour in the 1980s – a large section of the Scottish Socialist leadership is rooted in the extremist politics of the past. Their manifesto is an improbable mixture of fantasy, Utopianism, exaggeration and envy.

It provides a refuge for the disillusioned, particularly those who are disenchanted with the SNP and activists from the furthest fringes of the hard left. Because of proportional representation and an undeniable flair for grabbing headlines, they now have a place in the public life of Scotland. Because of the news hunger of those sections of the media keen to highlight the more eccentric elements of the Scottish Parliament, their effectiveness and importance are exaggerated. It remains to be seen how long they will maintain their place in the spotlight of publicity.

The SSP's stunts, antics and adolescent behaviour are seen by some as brightening up a dull Parliament. However, their real effect is to damage its work and its public image.

The sad truth is that they are an embarrassment to Scotland and perpetuate the damaging myth that Scotland still provides a breeding ground for the looniest of lunatic-fringe parties – and, worse, takes them seriously enough to give them places in the Parliament. The SSP may masquerade under the guise of socialism, an honourable and historic movement, but a vote for the SSP is a vote against any attempt to create a sensible or credible future for Scotland.

Epilogue

I began this book at the end – the long and lonely night when I decided to resign as First Minister. But, of course, it was not the end.

There was a positive side to my trials and tribulations: there is a life outside politics and there are other ways of serving both country and people.

As someone in his early 50s, I had always thought of that life outside politics and the opportunities I could have to use my experience and the lessons I have learned. I expected to give myself a few more years, but wanted to get out to have another career.

What I am doing now is very real and fulfilling: travel, thinking, teaching, lecturing and advising. The step I took on 8 November 2001 may not have been as big or as drastic as people thought.

My 30 years of elected office have been eventful, rewarding and memorable. They have taken me to high office and places I could never have dreamed of, and I have met some of the most influential personalities of our time. Above all, there is satisfaction in trying to serve the interests of your own people, whether they are the friends and neighbours among whom you have grown up, the Fife Central constituency or fellow-Scots.

Those years have also given me insights, ideas and a vision of a new Scotland, a better Scotland, a Scotland with a proud place in the world and the twenty-first century – the kind of Scotland we all want to live in. I will continue to work for my Scotland.

Index